I0821043

Praise for *The Repentance of YHWH*

Sonya Shetty Cronin has written a daring, rich, suggestive interpretation of the Gospel of Mark that is thick with subtext and suggestive citation. We have nothing like her book, as she experiments with new modes of interpretation. She finds, everywhere in Mark, in every episode and word, allusion to a rich inventory of Old Testament texts. She shows us how Mark declared the end of Israel's exile, but then so much more. On offer in Mark, as she shows, is good news for Gentiles as for Jews. This new opening for Gentiles requires that God repent of exclusiveness for Jews. Her book, in its long lingering over texts, invites us to see afresh. We see in her writing, as in Mark's Gospel, an effort to clarify how radically new the way of Jesus really is. The book invites close attentiveness to a mass of citation and allusion that she fuses together as a great, fresh disclosure.

—Walter Brueggemann,
Columbia Theological Seminary

"YHWH repents." This shocking thesis serves as the through-line of this remarkable study of Mark's Gospel. Cronin masterfully unearths the cavernous underground of Mark's creative reading and sifting of his Old Testament tradition (in Greek *and* in Hebrew), revealing intertextuality to be not simply a garnish on a messianic biography but rather the very means by which Mark paints a new genre: gospel. Joining the growing number of those who find in Mark's Gospel a divine Christology, *The Repentance of YHWH* subverts expectations in depicting Mark's Jesus to be YHWH reconciling his own past dealings with Israel and Gentiles by establishing a gospel truly for all nations. No longer the stumbling novice bested by his literary successors Matthew and Luke, Mark shines anew under Cronin's sympathetic scholarly eye.

Read this book and watch your appreciation for Mark and his Gospel deepen with every page.

—Roberto J. De La Noval, assistant professor of theology,
Mount St. Mary's University

The Repentance of YHWH: Mark's Gospel of Universal Inclusion is a remarkable fusion of poetic artistry and narrative storytelling. Sonya Shetty Cronin elegantly guides readers through the ebb and flow of Mark's Gospel, drawn from the stories and themes of the scriptures of ancient Israel and reinterpreted by the gospel writer to create a new, complex narrative that understands Jesus's mission and YHWH's mission as one and the same—universal inclusion and salvation for everyone. Cronin's work is a marvelous resource for scholars, preachers, and other readers, inviting them to contemplate YHWH's redemptive plan for humanity through an innovative perspective that unmasks the mystery, promulgating a new message that is good news for us all.

—Terry Ann Smith, associate dean of Institutional Assessment
and associate professor of biblical studies,
New Brunswick Theological Seminary

Erudite, poetic, and refreshingly inclusive, this book offers an inspired reading of intersecting biblical narratives. Moving gracefully between the Hebrew Bible and the New Testament, it revisits, contests, and suggests alternatives to common dichotomies: Gentiles and Jews, the chosen and the rejected, the saved and the doomed, the future and the past. An ingeniously intertextual and truly polyphonic achievement.

—Gilad Elbom, Oregon State University, author of
Kabbalah as Literature: The Revolution of Interpretation
and *Textual Rivalries: Jesus, Midrash, and Kabbalah*

With poetic prose, Sonya Cronin aims to show how the good news about Jesus in Mark's Gospel limns a portrait of YHWH and his salvation that is at once new and yet thoroughly steeped in the biblical stories that depict YHWH and his dealings with his people. Mark's Jesus, she is arguing, fully and gloriously displays the character of YHWH. Cronin weaves together the results of her labors in the biblical texts to produce a biblical theology of YHWH in Mark's Gospel that spotlights the indefatigable desire of the Maker of heaven and earth for renewed and restored relationship with his creatures.

—David M. Moffitt, professor of New Testament and early Christianity, University of St. Andrews

THE REPENTANCE OF YHWH

THE REPENTANCE OF YHWH

MARK'S GOSPEL OF UNIVERSAL INCLUSION

SONYA SHETTY CRONIN

FORTRESS PRESS
Minneapolis

THE REPENTANCE OF YHWH
Mark's Gospel of Universal Inclusion

30 29 28 27 26 25 1 2 3 4 5 6 7 8 9

Library of Congress Control Number: 2025930216 (print)

Cover design: Hannah Katanic

Print ISBN: 979-8-8898-3475-5
eBook ISBN: 979-8-8898-3476-2

To Carey C. Newman,
editor and friend,
for teaching me how to write

CONTENTS

ACKNOWLEDGMENTS

Some projects are all-consuming. You tuck away in your closet for some years, nose to the grind, and when you emerge, the world has changed. But there have been many to peek their head in the closet, inquire as to progress, and remind that the world outside, still on its axis, turns.

Thank you first to my family, Brian—support his middle name—Jeremy and Paige, Hannah, and most definitely not least, Micah Elendil—Elf friend and Star Lover. To Marie and to my dad, Subbayya Shetty, who wanted me to be a doctor as all Indian immigrant parents do but found himself able to be content with an underwater basket weaver, so long as I became expert.

For their encouragement and the cheering on, Joey Gans, Bill and Trish Lyons, John and Lisa Blackwell, Bill Bryant, Roopa Das, Ellen Murphy, Martha Schwartz, Kathleen Paul, Sean Cronin, Kevin Cronin and Jackie Wendorf, Amy Cronin, Fr. John and Ashley Wallace, Marla and Justin Capes, Fr. John Cayer, Fr. Richard Schamber, Fr. Chris Winkeljohn, and Bishop Bill Wack.

To the Gideon family, Trent and Iesha Wynn, Blair Woolverton and Waldo Craven, John Hurtabise, and Dean Kate Moorehead Carroll.

To Roberto de la Noval and Fr. Dustin Feddon, who engaged me in my Markan dialogue, thought creatively, and were patient enough to read my early drafts. To Jason Staples, who answered the phone on any whim, whose brilliance could match any obscure and random question I had, and whose response—the pause and then the "oh my god," was the litmus that told me when I was really on to something. Jason has endured the day-in, day-out of all the years of this project.

In my early struggles, trying to find the book's voice, I was gifted with *The Book of All Books* by Roberto Calasso. Between RC and J. R. R. Tolkien, my literary heroes were set. This book would not have been without them plotting the road before. Tolkien, long ago, opened up the world of Faerie. My citizenship is there, and I will wander until I find home in its gardens.

To Sharon Gordon-Girvin, who gave me my first fairy tales and opened this whole world that became my life.

To Jenn at Schilo's in San Antonio, who reminds that serendipity happens and the sparks of friendship can ignite in mere minutes with simple smiles, kindness, conversation, and hot coffee.

To Joseph House—JoJo, Pre, Andra, Arthur, Jeff, Gabriel, Qwan, Michael, Lamaar, Rachel—who teach about grace, forgiveness, and acceptance.

To everyone at Baldovino Firenze, my people in Florence. Massimo and Lara Bocchetti, Adriano, Marta, Claudio, Luca, Franco, and every other person there who makes the restaurant home.

Thank you to David Moffitt and his invitation to share my work at the University of St. Andrews, to Florida State University for remaining my home institution, and to the Religion Department and International Programs for making this research possible. Thanks especially to Jon Bridges and Susan Stetson, who make everything run smoothly, all while being kind.

I am grateful to Richard Hays, in whose writing I found a scholarly kinship that I had not known before, and for his shout-out to the extraordinary kindness of his editor, Carey Newman, who I would not have found without that mention.

It is to Carey this book is dedicated, for insisting that academics be better poets. For giving the lost and the small a seat at the table (he has done this for countless many)—those of meager backgrounds lacking connections, women, people of color, and all the overlaps. And for his book *Mango Tree*. *Mango Tree* dares the potential author to run off the cliff, challenging and demonstrating how not to be boring. I hope I have managed both.

PREFACE

The Gospel of Mark began with misunderstanding—nearly two thousand years of misunderstanding. It seems fitting, as if Mark knew how it was to go. He embedded misunderstanding into the fiber of his story. The disciples, those in the know, misunderstood Jesus at every turn. With them at a loss, it was a fool's errand to think anyone else really ever had a chance. Then the irony. Irony on all levels. Meta-irony. The irony that as Mark was writing about Jesus being misunderstood, Mark's very story about Jesus would also be misunderstood. Rather than clear up the misunderstanding, Mark leaned in, hard. He did so with good reason. Some things simply cannot be told; they must be shown, and so rather than try to explain, Mark shows . . . those with eyes to see.

The misunderstanding, understandable. At first glance, Mark seems to have written a story about the life of Jesus, but the story is odd, and trying to fit that story into some sort of classification and therefore ascertain the aim and purpose of his book has proved an elusive task from the beginning. Through the ages, attempts at generic classification have been frustrating. The eventual pairing of Mark with his particular symbol, the winged lion gave hint—a mythic animal, not present in our temporal reality.

When Ezekiel first saw the vision of the flaming chariot, his words read like a man who had grabbed his writing gear and quickly began to scribble as fast as he could lest he miss the moment: "I saw a creature and it was like . . . " In that first chapter, Ezekiel uses "like" no less than twenty times. Those describing Mark similarly stumble: "Mark is like . . . "

But whereas Ezekiel knew what he was seeing came from another realm, those reading Mark have missed that important distinction. Mark is neither genre-conforming nor genre-mixing. He has created something completely new, a new genre, utterly foreign. Mark announces a glorious invasion, the transformation of life; he describes the imposition of another world upon ours, the ushering in of the kingdom of God. It is not metaphorical; it is metaphysical. The winged lion that represents him is not a mutant, created through imagination and pieced together from species of this world, but it is a magnificent creature from that other realm. And so Mark joins the community of world builders.

The nagging intuition was always that the shadows on the wall were something more, but when Mark tears open the sky, that other world floods through. Everything changes in an instant. The demons, always suspected, can now be heard out loud, vocal, testifying to the son of the god of Israel, and thus to an order of the cosmos and Jesus' prominent position in it. Mark's Gospel reveals the world of YHWH (always already there but just out of reach) through the meeting of Jesus' life with stories from the tradition. These stories, though, are not merely utilitarian, objects to which Mark simply tethers episodes of Jesus' life to make intellectual or theological claims, or even a simple proof text of fulfillment. No, the stories of old are organic; they live inside of Mark. They are one with Mark's being, Mark's ethos, Mark's way of thinking. Mark paints from memory; there are no numbers; and he blurs colors, images, and scenes.

The Repentance of YHWH assumes the reader has been exposed to earlier volumes of the story—the story of Israel, but likely without full awareness of Mark's saturation in it. The tie between Mark and the Old Testament (Greek and Hebrew) has never been doubted, the foundations clear. But that Mark's Gospel not only lives, thinks, and breathes in the Old Testament universe but speaks in the shorthand dialect of Scripture so adeptly that a mere one-word allusion can summon an entire substratum of its history has not been so widely claimed. Moreover, in

Mark's story, there is no old, no new. There is now, where old and new fuse into a world of hope, of redemption, of love, of longing met, of a middle between heaven and earth.

Mark takes us to a world without time, where Noah's ark was just yesterday, where the god of Israel's independent conversations with Moses and Elijah were only just overheard. It is a world where manna still falls and Job still makes his claims. It is a world with pulsating power and moody extremes, where the god of Israel can spend his temper, bound down the mountain, and destroy everyone, knowing he has both the ability and arguably the intention to resurrect them again. In the end, he gathers them all to himself—nobody, not a one, excluded. This is the world that Mark reveals and why genre always fails to classify. The misunderstanding was thinking that Mark had mapped the life of Jesus when, instead, Mark has mapped the world that Jesus comes from. Mark has mapped the kingdom of God.

And so *The Repentance of YHWH* is also something new. *The Repentance of YHWH* is not an attempt to recover the historical Jesus by looking through Mark's textual window, even if the things the historical Jesus said and did could have inspired such a gospel. Nor is it a book on Christian origins, mining Mark for information about what the earliest followers of Jesus believed about Jesus, even though it inadvertently does make claims about such. *Repentance* is not an exercise to prove early high Christology, though it does make that claim as well, all while giving a richer profile about how Mark imagines Jesus as YHWH's messiah.

The Repentance of YHWH is not a book about Mark's narrative architecture, though it does throw light on Mark's literary techniques as it explores the underlying story that informs his Gospel. It does not simply examine the way Mark uses the Old Testament (Greek and Hebrew) through citation (explicit footnote to a specific text), allusion (implicit nod to a specific text), or echo (implicit nod to a passage). Instead, *The Repentance of YHWH* tracks the way Mark mixes multiple stories simultaneously and constantly. It has taken its cues from

Mark—showing rather than telling, highlighting the currents of movement, and demonstrating how Mark melds Old with New to open up a new world. In the end, *The Repentance of YHWH* exposes the narrative fusion throughout Mark's Gospel to reveal that, for Mark at least, the story of Jesus and his followers is really, still, the story of YHWH and YHWH's Israel.

This fusion is detectable through Mark's purposeful utilization of language. Certain words, phrases, odd constructions, extraneous details, even misinformation operate like seams, opening up the world underneath Mark's surface story. It is as if Mark is a master craftsman who has built a house. If one does not understand that under the house is a maze of hidden passageways, another world, accessible only through secret doors and detectable only through seams in the tile, one will trip over these seams and berate Mark for his incompetence—there is a long history of this in Markan scholarship. But if one detects the seam and decides it deliberate rather than ineptness on the part of the craftsman, then will that person gain access to the tunnels of history below. The strange noises, mysterious wafting scents, and unique structure of the house will now make full sense. The house exposed to have been built not only on a simple foundation but atop an ancient site—indeed a bustling, fully operational underground city, functioning like an iceberg, with only a fraction of the total structure visible at the surface.

The seams, verbal cues, are placed deliberately to evoke Old Testament passages. They mix together as Mark sometimes strings many scriptural passages in one sentence or story. Searching for simple Greek overlap is not enough to find related passages as Mark is adept at and uses both Hebrew and Greek Old Testament texts (whichever suits best his purpose), thus explaining why some of these connections have been missed until now. As such, all translations in this book are mine. *The Repentance of YHWH* spotlights these words and phrases, the Markan seams, by means of *italics*. It is the only time *italics* are used in the prose, and it is used both to note Mark's use of a particular word or phrase and then its corresponding spot in the summoned Old Testament passage.

The Repentance of YHWH reads the Gospel of Mark as understanding itself to be the latest installment in a long, complex, multivolume story, complete with atmosphere, setting, genealogies, ancient friends and foes, and all the other facets normal and natural to such epic tales. But make no mistake, *Repentance* does not suggest that the genre of Mark is fiction. Rather, the claim is that Mark believes himself to have written the next "chapter" of a carefully crafted, true, mythological history. The full tale, one that Mark sees his contribution as bringing up to date, follows family and generations over the course of millennia. It opines on good and evil, navigates through the grandest kingdoms and quietest hidden rooms, recounts the hopes and regrets of characters and company large and small, and involves every aspect of creation including the heavens and the divine who created it all.

Many modern scholars have long agreed that Mark was the first of the four Gospels written—I am in their camp. As such, one of the principles guiding this study has simply been to ask the question "why?" with fresh eyes. Why the Jordan? Why a baptism? Why John the Baptist, the encounter with Satan in the wilderness, or the finding of fisherman disciples? Even if one were to assume that every word of Mark is historical, with no narrative crafting, Mark could have told his story of Jesus any number of ways, picking other scenes, settings, organization, and minor characters to feature. And so "why" governs the day.

Being the shortest, most economical, and fast-paced of the canonical Gospels, why would Mark waste time on seemingly irrelevant details, such as the age of the twelve-year-old girl compounded with the twelve years that the bleeding woman suffered? "Five thousand men," in particular, fed at one miraculous feeding in the wilderness, and "about four thousand" fed at another. My assumption throughout is that none of these details is accidental but serve as breadcrumbs, clues that Mark deliberately left for those curious enough to dig further. Such presupposition naturally presumes even more—namely, that Mark was not a clumsy writer. He was not incapable of keeping track of his details or his information. He was not sloppy or ignorant of leaders, politics, place locations, or other relevant details, but he was instead so insightful, careful, and exacting choosing every word with distinct purpose. If Mark's information seems erroneous to the knowledgeable historian (e.g., Mark's wrongly naming Abiathar as high priest instead of Ahimelech [2:26] or the nonexistent town of Dalmanutha), we can be sure Mark knew. Moreover, Mark was counting on such discovery to unlock more, like someone deliberately giving the wrong date, place, or narrative details regarding a private but mutually shared event so as to trigger alertness from their recipient and signal to something valuable encoded in the misinformation.

No book on the Gospels is complete without a real and proper emphasized disclaimer regarding anti-Judaism. That Christian texts have been used to persecute Jews and Jewish tradition throughout the centuries is well-documented. While Mark does not find his primary antagonizers in οἱ Ἰουδαῖοι, "the Jews," the religious authorities with whom Jesus is in conflict are Jewish leaders: the Pharisees, Sadducees, scribes, and Herodians. Mark's Jesus, however, is not post-Jewish but thoroughly Jewish, as are the disciples. *Repentance* oftentimes narrates the conflict between Jesus and religious leaders in Mark's tone, from Mark's perspective. The debates between Jesus and these religious groups are often marked with hostility, and I do not interrupt the prose with disclaimers. The disclaimer is here and sporadically in the notes. Anti-Jewish attitudes, especially fostered by biblical text, are morally reprehensible and completely unacceptable. Moreover, it is my contention that Mark himself was not anti-Jewish, or even anti-Pharisee, anti-scribe, anti-Herodian, or anti-Sadducee in the sense that he wanted these groups gone or harmed in any way. Mark thought their theology and practice needed revision, though arguably no more than Jesus' own disciples and thus the Church of his day. Mark's aim is universal inclusion, not simply the swapping of an in-group for an out-group.

The god of Israel has a proper name throughout the biblical text. Often written as LORD, and reflecting the Hebrew יהוה, the transliteration YHWH is used throughout this work. It remains unvocalized as a point of respect. Jewish tradition pronounces this name "Adonai" (Lord), which is how I would encourage readers to vocalize it when reading this book. Another necessary explanation is this book's use of the term "Old Testament." The term "Old Testament" is wrought with implication. "Old, outdated, superseded by the New and better testament," is what some consciously or unconsciously have understood the term to mean. Hebrew Bible would be a preferable choice, except that Mark does not rely solely on Hebrew or LXX/Greek but uses each at will, thus making "Old Testament," the common ground for simple discussion, used here without any negative intent.

Finally, the difference between "Exile" and "exile" is an important distinction throughout this work. Exile, capital "E," is a specific reference to the Exile that Israel and Judah suffered under Assyria and Babylon. It is a historical event—though even this "event" is the conflation of multiple events, as even during the time of Assyria and Babylon, there were many phases to Israel and Judah's exile, thus multiple exiles. It is THE Exile.[1] But exile, lowercase "e," references the general state of exile, both physical and proximate, pertaining to land and home in general, but also the existential concept of exile. Joseph, son of Jacob, was exiled, but did not live through the Exile. David, lived in exile, but lived long before the Exile. Israel and Judah, lived through the Exile, but also suffered exile. Much of this book hinges upon these two terms, in particular, that while the Exile seems to be the biggest problem at hand, it is actually exile, all exile, in all forms, including and especially the power of death, that Mark's Jesus has come to address. Part of the irony at play is that despite the capital letter, salvation from exile, is far more powerful than simply redemption from Exile.

I have grown to love Mark's Gospel and the mission of YHWH he describes. Mark's understanding of Jesus' mission as a continuation of

YHWH's mission to the world, and one of inclusion, solves not all but many of the problems associated with "God so loved the world," combined with the practice of many Christians to exclude at will. This project began with the desire to know, without whitewashing, why Jesus would rudely call a desperate mother a "dog." What I found is more than I ever expected—Mark's god desires that all come and that none are excluded. I hope you find this fresh breeze, blowing once again in the cool of the day, as refreshing as I have.

Six years of my life I have spent completely immersed in this particular work. The final period, bittersweet, is made sweeter in that it comes in the most appropriate place in the world, in the company of winged lions all around, watching, witnessing. I am grateful for their company and comradery.

Sonya S. Cronin
June 22, 2024
Piazza at Basilica di San Marco
Venice, Italy

CHAPTER 1

A Savior Comes

The Exile Is Over

The Gospel of Mark picks up where the Old Testament leaves off—the winding down of the Exile with an end seemingly in sight. But that end never quite comes about. The texts all seem to agree that YHWH would burst into Israel's history as in the days of old and personally reinherit his people back to their homeland. But it never happened, and his promised messiah never arrived. Mark's opening, heralding the good news of Jesus the Messiah, is in part the declaration of Exile's end. But more than that, Mark is saying that the return was no return at all, certainly not in the way that satisfied promises and hopes; that a deeper, more fundamental, more sinister exilic captivity still persists; and that Jesus has come to end that exile and effect the return of all returns.

The Jordan

Inheritance. "Land, people, and their god"—the fulfillment of it did not begin in Egypt, though the grandness of the Exodus makes it seem so. It began at the Jordan. Promises realized, sovereignty theirs, the Jordan is where Israel finally came into their inheritance. It is also where they were disinherited: The place where the last great prophet of Israel was seen and where the last kings crossed as they were dragged out of their homeland, ushering in, both literally and symbolically, the beginning of the Exile. This setting bursts with meaning. The Exile ends at the same place where it all began, with prophet, YHWH, and messianic king.

Mark 1:1–8

Exodus 23:20; Isaiah 40:3; Malachi 3

The Gospel of Mark opens with memory. Mark conjures the long ago of Israel's past by purposely setting the opening of the gospel at the Jordan River. A character in its own right, the Jordan evokes YHWH's remembrance, hope, transition, freedom, and a future.[1] For Israel, the Jordan is symbolic of home. It is generations and genealogy. It is the past, present, and future. It is the domestic seal on the soul of a people. It is the turn onto the familiar path laden with history, complexity, and identity. It is haven. To cross the border of the Jordan is to cross into "god's country"—the homestead of Israel, a land just as chosen as its people. It would be easy to assume that the god of Israel was provincial, but that is not so. The god of Israel lays claim to the god of the universe, the maker of all creation. YHWH's preference for this locale does not speak of YHWH's limitation, but its importance.

It was at the Jordan that Jacob crossed with nothing more than a staff in hand as he fled from his brother Esau, returning home twenty years later with two camps and a limp that signified blessing. It was at the Jordan that Moses would hand the baton of leadership over to Joshua, ushering in a new era of divine guidance. It was at the Jordan that Israel left the life of slavery behind, crossing over from forty years in the wilderness to the land of promise, to their home. It was at the Jordan that twelve stones representing the twelve tribes were placed as a memorial at the bottom of the river, the very spot where the priests' feet had stood with the ark as the waters were held still, reminding Israel of where they were going, and where they had been.

It was at the Jordan that, generations later, King David and his weary family were refreshed as they fled Jerusalem and the insurrection of Absalom, David's embittered son. It was at the Jordan that the people of Judah welcomed him back home again when they returned safely after Absalom's death. It was at the Jordan that Bathsheba's son, King Solomon, had the sacred vessels cast in its clay for the LORD's temple he was building in Jerusalem. And it was at the Jordan that Elijah was taken up by a whirlwind, and Elisha saw the chariots of fire and the heavenly horsemen of Israel.

The Jordan serves not just as a border between home and abroad but as a meeting place between heaven and earth. A locus of activity on all planes, the Jordan acts as a watchman to nearly all of Israel's coming and going—the good and the bad. It was witness to the desolation of the land. It was there for the conquering of the last king, and the divine departure of that prophet exemplar not just from Israel but from the world. It saw a new and devastating exodus, of the people exiled into slavery instead of rescued from it. And now, the Jordan stands guard once again, its long memory washing over, baptizing all that will be said in Mark's Gospel.

"The *beginning* of the *good news* of Jesus *Christ*, the *son* of god."[2] Words heralding new announcement while simultaneously steeped in tradition. A perceived seamless continuation of the biblical saga, breaking the long years of YHWH's seeming silence. What comes forth now is different than anything seen before. It will disrupt. It will reflect, reframe, and reform the past.

The suffering and hurting long for good news, for an end to their pain, to be remembered once again. Israel and Judah's circumstance resulting from their own actions all the more devastating. Healing bound up in forgiveness, the remediation of their sins, and punishment declared satisfied. Hope dependent on their god, no longer absent but present in their midst again. Isaiah offers such words of assurance after long years of devastation: "Go up to a high mountain, oh, proclaimer of *good news* (εὐαγγελιζόμενος), Zion. Lift up your strength with might. Oh, proclaimer of *good news*, Jerusalem. Lift up, do not fear, say to the cities of Judah, 'Behold your god.' Behold the Lord YHWH with strength he comes, and his arm with authority. . . . Like a shepherd he will shepherd his sheep. And in his arms he will gather the lambs. And he will comfort, having them in his womb."[3]

Isaiah calls for the mountains themselves to announce good news. Zion and Jerusalem, YHWH's earthly seat, witness to YHWH's return. They herald comfort and rescue rather than punishment, signaling a change in the wind.

Bolstering against the looming threats of surrounding powers, the psalmist had long ago taken confidence in YHWH as the protector of Israel and its king, bantering with knowing wit as one of YHWH's inner circle: "Why are the nations restless and the peoples plot in vain? . . . Against YHWH and against his *anointed* (Gk: his Christ / Hb: his messiah). . . . The one sitting in heaven laughs; the Lord mocks them . . . 'I have set my *king* upon Zion, my holy mountain. . . . You are my *son*, today I have begotten you. Ask of me and I will set the nations as your hereditary property.'"[4]

Such carefree assurance has been gone for generations. There is no king, and YHWH has abandoned. Those nations that plotted, they, have been the ones to mock and deride. They have taken Israel's hereditary property. Though expectancy laces every conversation on every street corner, it has also long forsaken these parts, the psalmist's words now bitter on the tongue.

But talk of good news rekindles anticipation, and the Jordan setting resurrects corporate experience, raising once again the possibility of a hope beyond hope—the long-awaited king has arrived: "I will raise up your offspring after you who shall come from your body . . . I will establish the throne of his kingdom forever. I will be a father to him and *he shall be a son to me*."[5] YHWH's promise to David had been a lifeline for the whole nation,[6] sustaining them in their darkest days, but it never came to pass. The dream faltered, an impossibility save the meddling of the divine.

Yet this is the claim—that heaven intervenes in the affairs of Israel once again, that their god has not forgotten them. YHWH will gather the outcasts into community and bring the exiles home. At the Jordan, one can almost hear the voice of the prophet ring out from communal memory as he strikes the river with his mantle and says, "Where is YHWH, the god of Elijah?"[7] The god of Israel responds. YHWH is here. YHWH is here, once again, in the good news about Jesus the Christ, the king. YHWH is here in the words of the prophets that bolster the announcement, the announcement that the whole of the people have been longing for: The Exile is finally over.

As it is written in Isaiah the prophet,[8]

> Behold, I send my messenger before you,
> who will prepare your way,
> the voice of one crying in the wilderness:
> "Prepare the way of the Lord,
> make his paths straight."[9]

It is not just the king that signals; there is a cast of characters who must coalesce to mark the moment, each one adding a different flavor to fulfillment and their necessary weight to gravitas. After deliverance from oppression in Egypt, YHWH had assured the children of Israel he would not leave them alone: "*Behold, I myself am sending a messenger before you* to guard you on *the way*, and to bring you to the place which I have *prepared*."[10] Weary from years of slavery, they would not have to navigate their way to the land of promise without an escort, a protector. Centuries later, this time tyrannized by Assyria and Babylon, YHWH's care and concern do not change. Neither Israel nor Judah will return to promise unaccompanied. A messenger will once again show the way.

Both Isaiah and Malachi caught glimpse of this messenger; their individual prophecies mingle together with the memory of the Exodus guide to form a distinct portrait: "The *voice of one crying in the wilderness: 'Prepare the way of YHWH, make his paths straight'*" Compassion overflowing for the hurting, Isaiah's vision follows soothing words. "Comfort, comfort my people," YHWH implores for those who have suffered in exile. "Speak tenderly to Jerusalem, and cry to her that she has served her term, that her penalty is paid, that she has received from

YHWH's hand double for all her sins," that the time of punishment is over.[11] Isaiah's messenger, however, does not guide the children of Israel to their land of promise; he readies the road for YHWH. Just as in the days of old, keeping his promise to Moses, it is YHWH himself who will lead his people home; YHWH has been with them in their exile all along.[12]

Malachi's messenger, too, *prepares the way* for YHWH—who comes swiftly for judgment. The messenger has been sent ahead to ready the hearts of the people as the god of Israel has always preferred mercy over judgment: "I, YHWH do not change, therefore you, O children of Jacob, have not perished." The messenger, until now, has remained mysterious, unidentified, veiled. Malachi, however, cannot keep a secret. "Behold," he says for YHWH, "I am sending the prophet Elijah," and so hope is bundled with excitement, laden with enigma, and awaiting the supernatural.[13]

It is no mystery, then, who John is. Appearing out of nowhere like the prophet of old, John comes wearing camel's hair, that notable leather belt, and donning the same kind of untamed look as one fed by the ravens far from civilization. He calls out in the wilderness, proclaiming a baptism of repentance, turning the table on the devourer with every *locust* he eats, rebuking that which had added insult to injury by smiting the homeland of those displaced from it.[14] Elijah, too, had wandered the wild and then compelled the people to come back to their god when they had followed after the Baals. And like the children of Israel drawn to Mount Carmel to reconcile with their god, "all the country of Judea and all the Jerusalemites were going out [to John] and were being baptized by him in the Jordan river, confessing their sins."[15]

Called together, at this moment, through time, through generation, through promise, despite hopes dashed, land scoured, and the eleventh hour come and gone, here at the Jordan they all come—the king from the line of David, Elijah the prophet, and the people who had been hauled off to slavery. Now the Jordan witnesses again—the restoration of the land, the return of the king, the mediation of the prophet, the redemption of the people, the voice of their god, the beginning of the end of Israel's exile. Good news indeed.[16]

Baptism at the Jordan

As with the first Joshua, leading Israel to claim its inheritance, heaven is watching, waiting, and once again involves itself. The events now mirror the events of old: the end of exile, the (re)inheritance of Israel, the reunification of land and people, and the breaking of YHWH's silence as the voice from heaven calls out from the sky. YHWH is finally gathering his people.

Mark 1:9–20

2 Kings 5; Joshua 3; Genesis 6–9, 12, 22, 33

It is fitting that Jesus' ministry would be inaugurated here. Coming from Galilee, Jesus participates in the same ritual of repentance as the people from Jerusalem and Judea. He is *baptized* in the Jordan. He is one of them, not just one with the people to whom he will preach, heal, and minister; but he is one of the Israelites of old. Jesus' baptism at the hands of Elijah, in the Jordan, summons memory from the reservoir of biblical tradition.[17] Scene after scene from Israel's communal religious history rises to the surface as Jesus plunges under the water. All the memory, all the experience, floods in an instant—wave after wave, exile and return, recalled all at once, layered, distinct, visceral; it is the past that frames the future.

The Aramean commander, a hero in his hometown for his valor in battle—yet for all his favor and accolades, money and renown, he cannot find his way free of illness, leprosy. Contagion separates him. Borrowing the faith of a child, tales of a god who can heal bring him to Israel. There the king has lost his own faith and tears his clothes at receiving the letter preceding this foreign dignitary's arrival. "Am I a god?" says this king of Israel, fearful, incensed, and perplexed that this man comes to him for healing. But the voice of the prophet rings out again. "Let him come to me," Elisha says boldly, "so that he may learn that there is indeed a prophet [and a god] in Israel."[18]

At the prophet's instruction, and with the coercion of his companions, this mighty commander humiliates himself and deigns to dip into this inferior stream. The gift is free. There are no conditions, even for this gentile who holds captive in his home a daughter of Israel as he simultaneously begs help from Israel's god. *He dips* (*baptizes*/ἐβαπτίσατο) himself into *the Jordan* seven times, and he is healed, no longer unclean. His skin reverts to that of a youth, clean; he is restored.[19]

Naaman's story foreshadows what the role of Israel would be as they find themselves scattered among the nations. Through the word of a little Israelite girl, serving as a slave in a foreign land, Naaman, her master, finds salvation with the god of Israel. She is a light in his darkness. She is a witness to the power of her god, Israel's god, and this god's willingness to save those of other nations. Naaman is not judged for holding her captive. Instead, he finds remedy and restoration by her innocent enthusiasm over her god and her prophet. She is a model, transforming herself from prisoner to emissary.[20] She exudes a genuine hope that her master would be cured, and her selfless generosity leads to this gentile's salvation.

For Naaman, the Jordan River is a nexus of transitions. It is the transition from leprous to healed, from unclean to clean, from doubting to believing, from pride to humility, from outcast to included. It is the transition from Aram to Israel as he follows the thread of hope. The god of Israel would make fluid that border by healing this gentile and winning him as a believer. No longer is this river beneath him. He takes the very earth that bears it home, because Naaman the Aramean has discovered that there is a god in Israel. This god has met him in the flowing waters of the Jordan and has brought him back into full community.[21]

Freedom, promise, and hope loom large as a weary people, delivered from slavery, stand at these banks, longing for a future. It has been forty years since the last waters parted for them at the Red Sea, defining them, giving them identity. They are a peculiar people, and they have a god who saves and redeems with "the outstretched arm." But YHWH is not an easy god, and this moment, on the edge of the land of promise, is vital. It is a sign. Will YHWH come through for them once again, despite their failures? Does the covenant hold, especially for the new generation? Does this god, the god from their memory, remember them? Does YHWH still care for his people, Israel?

No longer Naaman, a new commander enters the picture, Joshua (Jesus/Ἰησοῦς). He tells them, "When you see the ark of the covenant of YHWH your god, and the priests of the Levites carrying it, then you shall set out from your place and you will go after it. . . . Sanctify yourselves; for tomorrow YHWH will do wonders among you."[22]

Anticipation builds. They wait. Their future lies before them, one of promise, of newness, of hope.

This seasoned commander of Israel, however, is not new to this. He has been this way before. He was there, at the Red Sea, the first time YHWH parted the waters for them. He remembers slavery. He was with Moses on the presence-filled mountain with thunder, lightning, and the quaking earth. He was there to hear the sounds of revelry ascending up the mountain when the Israelites failed in faith and practice and created an idol, a lifeless golden calf in place of their mighty and living god. Joshua experienced as well the anger of their god as Moses stood between his wrath and the people. Joshua witnessed all their failures, the grumbling over Egyptian onions and garlic, the serpents in the wilderness, but most notably their failure in doubting YHWH even after the miraculous parting of that great Red Sea. They could not muster the faith to believe that the god of their ancestors—who remembered them, heard their cry, and saved them from slavery in Egypt—was able to defeat the giants, the inhabitants of Canaan. It cost them forty years in the desert and the lives of an entire generation. It was exile; they were outcasts to the world, roaming the wilderness with the wild animals, with no country to call their own. Yet they were not alone; their god was with them.

Joshua saw grace as well—manna rain from heaven, tablets of the law given a second time after the first set destroyed, a new generation of Israel grow and become strong in the desert, where nothing grows. He lived providence in the everyday. The evidence of it is palpable here as he looks at this people, who for all accounts and purposes should be dead, but they are alive, and free, and on the edge of promise: "Behold, approach and hear the words of the YHWH your god. . . . In this you shall know that the living god is in your midst. . . . When the soles of the feet of the priests bearing the ark (κιβωτὸν) of YHWH, the Lord of all the earth, rest in the waters of the Jordan, the waters of the Jordan flowing from above shall be cut off; they shall stand a single dam."[23]

This god, Joshua claims, is living, active, potent, present, and not just particular to Israel but Lord of all the earth. As the people set out from their tents, they watch, and they wait: "So when those who bore the ark had come to *the Jordan*, and the feet of the priests bearing the ark (κιβωτὸν) *were dipped* (*baptized*/ἐβάφησαν) in the edge of the water, the waters flowing from above stood still."[24] In that moment, ordinary turned to miracle, anticipation met, confidence bolstered once again; there is indeed a god in Israel, and he cares for his people.

The priests remain with the ark at the bottom of the riverbed, empty, while all the people of Israel cross. As this new generation passes this way, each person present would be seared with this memory, of the underside of the water, where their god proved his love for them, the same way he did for the generation before. Crossing the river on dry ground, nobody—no man, woman, adult, or child—would be able to forget. They had met their god, individually and communally, as they crossed into promise on dry ground. The relationship was renewed. They were indeed YHWH's people. It is not just memory that is formed; it is living memory, as alive and flowing as the river itself, the living memory of YHWH's presence showing up in desolate times.

As Jesus emerges from the same ancestral waters, the heavens are torn open,[25] and Spirit in the form of a dove comes to rest upon him. A voice from heaven proclaims, "You are my *son*, the *beloved* (ἀγαπητός); with you *I am well pleased* (εὐδόκησα)."[26] At the foot of Mount Moriah, an old man walks with his young son, young enough to be his grandson, the son of his old age, a promise. He does not know where he walks; this god will point the way. The recollection of a similar journey on similar command must be in his mind: "Go from your country and your kindred and your father's house to the land that I will show you."[27] Abraham did not know where he was going then either, but he found himself walking into blessing and into covenant with this god. A nomad, a stranger, he was called from afar, chosen to follow a god whom he had not known before.

YHWH promised him land, descendants, and a future, calling him to forsake his family inheritance and claim this unknown god as his inheritance instead. The child, Isaac, arriving late in the hour, was born not of the will of the man, but of the will of YHWH. All the hope and promise are wrapped up in this child, but the god who gave him, now calls for him to be given back: "Go, take your *son, the beloved* (ἀγαπητόν) . . . and offer him as a burnt offering." At the moment of the sacrifice, of crisis, this god intervenes, and a ram is substituted in the child's place. The promise lives on. "Because you have done this . . . in your offspring, all the nations of the earth shall be blessed,"[28] the fate of the whole world resting on the faith of this one man. YHWH's good news is not just for Israel, but it goes beyond to the entire earth. Through Abraham, YHWH would reach out to all the other peoples, bringing them into community with him from wherever they have found themselves. Peering forward, the god of Israel will give his son to secure this blessing for the nations.

It does not take long, however, for the blessing of "chosenness" to highlight an opposite, "the unchosen." Instead of Abraham being chosen so that all the nations of the earth could be blessed, his grandchildren Jacob and Esau highlight the dichotomy. These two were bound together from conception. Already, from the womb, Jacob was "chosen," destined to rule over his twin, Esau. With his own shrewdness, he preyed on his brother's boorish nature and took from Esau his birthright. With his mother's coercion, he managed to deceive his father and steal the blessing of the firstborn, Esau's both by right and fatherly affection. Jacob's offenses were so odious that he had to flee lest Esau murder him. It was Jacob, the chosen, who spent years of his life in exile away from his land and immediate family. As he deceived, so he was deceived, first by his uncle and later by his sons.[29] Chosenness did not inoculate him from reaping consequence from his actions.

But when he finally returns and meets his brother Esau on the road home, there in the Jordan Valley, he finds that Esau's anger has abated, and Esau, the "unchosen," has been prosperous enough that he needs none of the gifts or caravans that Jacob has sent ahead. Instead, the chosen is reconciled with the unchosen; twins, brothers, a dyad, each incomplete without the other, the pair is finally together again, weeping over the reunion. Despite Esau's prosperity over the years, Jacob insists on him keeping the gifts because, he says, "I have seen your face, as one who sees the face of god[30] and you will be *well pleased* (εὐδοκήσεις) with me."[31] Esau the unchosen is the face of god to Jacob the chosen. The hostility that was is no more, and Jacob's god shows up in the face of the person least expected.[32]

The father in heaven speaks the words, "*I am well pleased* (εὐδόκησα)"[33] over Jesus at his baptism, the words spoken the moment that the exiled comes home and is welcomed by the one who drove him into exile in the first place. It is Israel and their god—Israel that was sent into exile among the nations by the very god they rejected, the one they did not choose. Israel's god appears here in the role of Esau, the unchosen welcoming the chosen, confirming the words of Jacob that god is indeed *well pleased* with Jesus, the one who stands in the Jordan in Jacob/Israel's place.

The details of YHWH's good news and the servant who will enact it unfold soon after the announcement of the messenger—freedom for the captive, sight for the blind, justice and light for the gentiles. Isaiah pronounces the end of the Exile, but YHWH's rescue is not just for Israel; it is for the whole world. YHWH delivers from exile, not just Exile:

> Behold, my servant, I will uphold him; my chosen, in whom my soul is *well pleased*. I have put my spirit on him. He will bring forth judgment to the nations/ gentiles. . . . He will not grow dim or crush until he establishes justice/judgment in the earth. The coastlands wait for his law . . . I will strengthen your hand and keep you, I will give you as a covenant for the people, a light to the nations/gentiles, to open the eyes of the blind, and to bring out from the prisons the prisoners, and from the house of bondage, those who sit in darkness.[34]
>
> Isa 42:1, 4, 6–7

The primeval deluge. The other ark (κιβωτὸν) that saves.[35] Rather than an entire people, preserved as the priests stand with the ark of the covenant in the Jordan, this ark will carry only Noah's family to safety as the rain pounds for *forty days* and consumes the earth in flood. The entire rest of the world will perish. They are the damned, the lost, the unchosen, all the flesh that corrupted itself upon the earth. Nothing is saved, only what makes it on the ark—one human family and the *wild animals* (θηρίων), the representatives of every animal family that will repopulate the earth. As the heavens tear open in this story, it is not a dove bringing a message of peace here; it is judgment. All creation is destroyed, submerged under the waters of destruction until it dies.

The thematic waves of the Noah story crash onto Jesus' baptism. The entire flood story of old begins with the sentiment of regret. YHWH regretted, repented of making humankind "because every inclination of the thoughts of their hearts was only evil."[36] His solution to the problem of evil people was to "blot them out from the earth"[37]—complete annihilation. Only Noah and the bit of creation saved as a remnant on the ark would survive.

But hope remains. Even here in this primordial desolation "God remembered . . . the ark." The god of Israel remembers. YHWH has never forgotten his people, and there is good news. The kingdom of god has come: "Never again." "Never again will all flesh be cut off by a flood; Never again will there be a flood to destroy the earth."[38] YHWH does not simply canvas the sky with a rainbow at Jesus' baptism, reminding of the Noachite covenant and the promise that YHWH would not flood the world again. Rather, what flutters onto the scene is the powerful symbol that marked the end of judgment and ushered in an era of newness and life. The Spirit, in the form of Noah's dove, now breaks through the heavens at the moment the rains of judgment would be expected and offers peace instead.[39]

John serves as both witness and facilitator: "He [Elijah] will turn the hearts of parents to their children and the hearts of children to their parents, so that I [YHWH] will not come and strike the land with a curse."[40] As Jesus stands there at the Jordan, having just come out of the waters of baptism in the presence of Elijah (John), the heart of the Father in heaven is turned toward his son. The words "You are my son, the beloved; with you I am well pleased"[41] are the confirmation of this. It is not a rainbow that will catch YHWH's eye and stay the judgment. It is Jesus, the son.

Jesus' baptism does more than just evoke communal memory; it raises it like a banner announcing that YHWH is still in the business of reconciling, the chosen with the unchosen, and the entire family of creation with himself. The dove settles on Jesus, marking him and ushering him into the wild. There he will encounter Satan and be tested like Job. There he will be fed by the angels like Elijah. There he will dwell with the wild animals (θηρίων) for forty days like Noah.[42] There he remains until the metaphorical flood passes, and then he walks the shore of Galilee and recruits fishermen.[43]

Amos describes in vengeful detail the use of fish hooks to haul away as prisoners the wealthy women of Samaria to faraway places. Jeremiah, too, speaks of YHWH's recruitment of fishermen to enact judgment. The Chaldeans, expert fishermen, had turned their eyes away from fish and became *fishers of men*, drawing them out with their hooks and carting Judah off to exile.[44] Their fishing, the rod of YHWH's judgment. But they went too far. Jesus marks the end of that domination, employing the captors' own trade to accomplish the reverse, salvation instead of punishment, gathering to himself those *people who had no ruler*. But Jesus is not content to save just those devastated by the judgment of exile in Babylon. His memory ventures as far back as the ark; the flood had *made people like the fish in the sea*.[45] The dove heralds once again. Jesus' *fishers of men* will save the damned from the deluge, all the unchosen that ever were, marking not only the end of the Babylonian Exile but all exile, the exile of humanity from their god.[46]

"The beginning (Αρχὴ) of the good news." It recalls a similar proclamation, "The *beginning* (ἀρχῆ) of the creation of all things," where god created everything, and all of it was good.[47] Its recollection here is not just about words and parallel; it is about scope and reach. The "good news" is as wide and encompassing as the "everything" that YHWH created. It is for all creation. Like Naaman the gentile, and the children of Israel standing at the banks of the Jordan, desperate for a future and exhausted from wilderness wandering, and like the individual and collective nations that YHWH will gather through Abraham, the god of Israel wants to save "all"—from exile, from judgment, from destruction, even from death. YHWH wants to bring his people home.

Reinheriting the Disinherited

Loss of land, loss of sovereignty, and what seemed to be a breach in the relationship with their god—this is what the Exile imposed. The end of the Exile is the reversal of all these things. The land and people, torn apart, are now reunited and reconciled. The king has returned. And it is YHWH, Israel's god, present, who accomplishes this for them once again.

Mark 6:53–56

Joshua 1:3, 6; Isaiah 8:23–9:1; Zechariah 8:11–23

Home. Throughout history, the god of Israel was known to show up at will, stepping out of eternity into the present, strolling about with his own over talk of inheritance, over talk of home. YHWH walked with Adam in the cool of the day at the time of the evening breeze, even calling out to Adam when he seemed to run late. He established Adam as master of the Garden, where Adam remained until the moment he was cast away from it. YHWH brought Abram outside, had him gaze into the expanse of the night sky. "Look up to the stars," he told him. "Count them if you are able . . . so shall your descendants be . . . I brought you up out of Ur of the Chaldeans to give you this land."[48] This land would be their home. And yet those descendants were destined to leave the land before they ever came into it—slaves on foreign soil for four hundred years, a precursor to inheritance.

On the other side of that bondage, YHWH mapped another walk. "Every place the sole of your feet will tread," YHWH tells Joshua, "I have given to you . . . you shall bring this people into the inheritance of the land that I swore to their fathers to give them."[49] Joshua and the Israelites crossed the Jordan, claiming the earth their god promised them with every step they took and every people they defeated. Descendants and land, the two things promised to Abram finally knit together. Disinheritance would happen the same way, Assyria and then Babylon driving them out again, their feet dragging the ground, clinging to home while being torn from it. Like tides, coming in and going out—inheritance and disinheritance, judgment and restoration, exile and return.

The ebb and flow continue. "The *time is fulfilled*," Jesus proclaims as John is arrested and the ministry changes hands, sorrow mingled with good news once again. "The kingdom of god *has come near.* His very words provide the bookend to Ezekiel's proclamation, one of the many prophetic warnings heralding the beginning of the Exile. "The *time* has come . . . *the day has come near,*" YHWH had said to Ezekiel, a day of doom, punishment, judgment for sin. "An end, the end has come upon the four corners of the earth." The punishment was not just for Israel, but all the lands would suffer. Tobit, however, had predicted the judgment's end, that when "*the times* of the age *were fulfilled,*" YHWH "would again have mercy on [the inhabitants of the land of Israel] and return them back to the land . . . then all the nations in the whole earth would turn back to him."[50]

That far-off future that Tobit glimpsed has now come about. Jesus' pronouncement is for all, and like the god of old, he walks among his people once again.[51]

"And having crossed through on the ground, [Jesus and his disciples] came to Gennesaret and anchored."[52] Gennesaret, also known as Chinneroth, rests in Naphtali's territory.[53] Naphtali, first to go into exile, first to be carried off by Assyria and never seen again.[54] Before its dispersion, it had nineteen towns with their villages—and then, with swift devastation, it was all gone. People and land were separated so thoroughly that a reunion could only be possible through wild imagination and radical hope. Isaiah saw promise in their future despite their tragedy, despite being the first to disinherit: "For there is no gloom for those who were in anguish in the former times. He cursed the land of Zebulon and the land of Naphtali, but at last he will *make glorious the way of the sea*, Galilee of the gentiles. The people who are walking in darkness have seen a great light, those dwelling in the land of deep darkness, a light has shined upon them"[55]

Long ago, during the initial conquest, inheritance for tribes of Israel had been chosen by lots and given in the form of *towns*, *villages*, and the surrounding *fields.*[56] Arriving by boat from across the Galilee, this new Joshua embarks on a similar task as the old: "When they got out of the boat, immediately [people] were recognizing him. And they ran about that whole region and began to bring those having sicknesses on mats wherever they heard that he was. And wherever he entered, to *villages*, or to *cities*, or to *fields*, they placed the sick in the marketplaces."[57]

With every step he takes, Jesus reinherits the disinherited. The promises that the god of Israel made long ago unfurl in new ways. Their potency continues, evidence of their binding power. Isaiah's hope mixes with Zechariah's; the god of Israel keeps his word and never forgets: "And now I will not treat the remnant of this people as in the former days, says YHWH of hosts. For [there will be] a sowing of peace, the vine will give its fruit, and the land will give its produce, and the heavens will give their dew, and I will cause the remnant of this people, to *inherit*, all these things. And as you have been a curse among the nations, house of Judah and house of Israel, thus I will save you and you will be a blessing. Do not fear, strengthen your hands."[58]

The very mention of the house of Israel is hope beyond hope. Even as Zechariah prophesies, there is no Israel; only Judah remains. Yet his vision for the future specifically includes Israel as separate from Judah. Those *ten* lost tribes will inherit in this land again: "Thus says YHWH of Hosts. Peoples shall yet come, the dwellers of many cities. The dwellers of one city will go to another saying, let us surely go to *be sick* (לְחַלּוֹת) before YHWH and to seek YHWH of Hosts, I myself also will go. . . . Thus says YHWH of Hosts, in those days *ten* men from every tongue of the nations *shall take hold of the fringe* of a Jewish man saying let us go with you all for we have heard that god is with you."[59]

Ten men. *Ten* tribes scattered to the nations. *The sick* lying on their mats in the marketplace, "begging him in order that they might *grasp the fringe* of his garment, and as many as touched it were saved."[60] It is not just YHWH they cling to; the fringes represent YHWH's commandments, the very law against which Israel hardened their heart, causing them to be scattered among the nations.[61] Zechariah's sick, scattered, now return, grasping the Torah they once abandoned. Israel's god has promised that they will inherit again; Jesus fulfills those promises now.[62]

Ten men. Ten tribes. Sons of Jacob. Israel, YHWH's firstborn: "Out of Egypt [and long years of slavery] I called my son."[63] Boys, all boys. But YHWH has daughters too.

Redeeming YHWH's Daughters

The scriptural tradition has often treated Israel as YHWH's son. But long have Israel and Judah also been characterized as YHWH's two daughters—YHWH's two rebellious daughters. They were punished harshly; their actions against god and neighbor resulted in exile. But YHWH has not abandoned them. Jesus' healing of the two representative daughters of Israel and Judah enacts the restoration of YHWH's two daughters back to their land and to their god, marking the end of the Exile.

Mark 5:21–43

Numbers 32:1–27; 1 Kings 16:21–28; 2 Kings 21:1–18

Jairus (*Jair*), the synagogue leader, waits anxiously for Jesus to disembark from his ship. In another world, it would be Jesus waiting in the throngs for something he needed from Jairus, a religious minister by trade. Prominent and pious, Jairus is helpless to help his child. Desperate, he falls at Jesus' feet: "My little daughter is at her end, come and lay your hands on her so that she might be saved and live."[64]

Twelve spies from twelve tribes spent forty days scoping out the land promised them by YHWH. Only two returned bolstered. The other *ten* wilted: "The land has giants . . . and we are like grasshoppers." Fainthearted and fearful, they crumbled when their moment to inspire and stand strong arrived. Only Joshua and Caleb remained confident—the Nephilim irrelevant with YHWH on their side. Unable to convince the others, these two alone would come into their inheritance. As for those faithless spies and the congregation of Israel that rallied to them, "their dead bodies would fall in the wilderness."[65]

Forty years passed; that generation gone, Israel found themselves on the brink of the land again. The tribes of Reuben and Gad, herders, asked not to cross over but rather to stay on the east side of the Jordan—its rolling hills and pastures ideal for their flocks and cattle. Moses' reaction was swift: "Will you hinder the hearts of the children of Israel from crossing over to the land which YHWH gave to them? Your fathers did this."[66] But this was not a repeat of the past. These along with the half tribe of Manasseh would fight for their brothers across the Jordan, only inherit on this side.

The sons of Machir, son of Manasseh, went to *Gilead* and captured it, dispossessing the Amorites who lived there. Gilead was known for its healing balm—rare, effective, regarded, traded. A heap of rocks stood watch on Gilead, guarding over promises made there long years prior. It was the spot where Jacob and Laban had made a covenant upon Jacob's return to his homeland after his many years of exile away.[67] Moses gave Gilead to Machir as inheritance, making official for posterity what had already occurred on the ground. *Jair*, another son of Manasseh, took the villages of Gilead, renaming them after himself. From the very beginning of Israel's coming into the land, Jair was one with claim to the healing balm of Gilead.[68]

Gilead would pass down from generation to generation, even through the days of King Solomon.[69] But sometime after, in the skirmishes with Aram, Gilead was lost, though no less important; Elijah the prophet hailed from Gilead. It was King Ahab who lamented to King Jehoshaphat of Judah, "Do you know that Ramoth Gilead belongs to us, and we are silent rather than take it from the hand of the king of Aram?" But YHWH had not willed it. When the prophet Micaiah was summoned to weigh in on Ahab's plan to take it back, he exposed the heavenly council's plan to entice Ahab to fall at Ramoth Gilead. Rather than win back Gilead and its medicinal balm, King Ahab died in the battle over it, unable to recover Jair's inheritance and unwilling to heed the prophet's warning. Gilead, that prime commodity, was among the first of Israel to be captured by the Assyrians, its people carried away into exile.[70]

Without hesitation, Jesus departs with Jairus; the day's agenda can wait. But that crowd—it swells, it follows, it conceals another *daughter* of Israel in its midst. She wants to be hidden, to be swept up by it, inconspicuous. An incurable ailment consumes her; a blood flow renders her unclean.[71] Separate. Stigmatized. She has spent all she had, suffering under many *physicians*, *twelve years* looking for a cure, the same age as Jairus' daughter.[72] *Twelve years*, twelve tribes, another father, and his two daughters: Israel and Judah. The god of Israel cares for his girls too.

King Omri reigned over the northern kingdom of Israel for *twelve years*. He caused her both to sin and to suffer under his idolatrous reign. He formed a dynasty and established Samaria, a city on a hill, as the capital of Israel in the north. The house of Omri would encompass Ahab, make alliances with Phoenicia, welcome the notorious Jezebel as Ahab's queen, and embrace her gods along with her. The house of Omri would be synonymous with oppression, idolatry, and Baal worship. To serve the Baals constitutes adultery. Israel had been unfaithful to her god.[73]

This woman with the flow of blood symbolizes faithless Israel, even if she herself has not been faithless. Her afflictions mirror her counterpart; she stands, the embodiment of YHWH's elder daughter. Jeremiah explains, "YHWH our God *has given us bitter waters to drink*, because we have sinned against the LORD. We hope for peace, but find no good, for a time of healing, but behold terror [instead]." Speaking for YHWH, he continues, "For they are all adulterers . . . from evil to evil they go out and they do not know me, says YHWH. . . . Behold, here I am, feeding the people with bitter food, and *causing them to drink bitter water*."[74]

Ancient Israelite law had a solution for the jealous husband who suspects his wife of adultery. Sotah.[75] He would bring her before the priest to be tested:

> The priest will set her before YHWH. He shall take holy water in an earthen vessel and mix into it dust from the floor of the tabernacle, along with the words of a curse that he has written out and washed into the water.[76] The priest will make her *drink these waters of bitterness* that carry the curse and will compel her to swear the oath as she drinks. "If no man has lain with you, if you have not turned aside to *uncleanliness* . . . be immune to these *waters of bitterness that curse*. But, if you have gone astray and made yourself unclean with some man other than your husband . . . then YHWH make you a curse among your people when YHWH makes your loins drop and your *womb discharge*."
>
> Num 5:16–22

This Sotah ritual would determine her guilt or innocence before all. Her integrity would preserve her from the judging waters of bitterness if innocent. If guilty of adultery, the bitter waters will have their way in her body, and her guilt will curse her with the uncleanliness of her unfaithfulness.

Adulterous Israel needs a savior. She has been a victim as much as anything else. For the *twelve years* he reigned, King Omri led her astray. The worthless physicians and idolatrous prophets took all she had and, still, no healing. YHWH himself laments for her: "My joy has gone up and away; sorrow is upon me; my heart is sick . . . over the *wound* of the *daughter* of my people am I wounded. . . . Is there no *balm in Gilead*? Is there no *physician* there? Why then has the *health of the daughter* of my people not been restored? . . . Is YHWH not in Zion; Is her King not in her?"[77]

Centuries after its first utterance, Jeremiah's longing finally meets its cure. YHWH is now in Zion; her king is in her. He does not need to take back Gilead; he is Gilead—the embodiment of its healing balm. What Jair and Israel have lost is being restored. The Exile is over. Jesus, their physician, stands just a short distance from this daughter of Israel issuing blood.[78]

His *cloak*. If only she can touch Jesus' cloak. Elijah's *cloak* fell as he was taken up to heaven in the whirlwind, passing on both his prophetic power and the literal mantle of authority to Elisha. Elijah's cloak split the Jordan.[79] Here the cloak carries power once again. But as with Elijah and Elisha, the power resides in the man; the cloak simply conducts it. After twelve years of suffering, the touch of his *cloak* indeed heals her. She can feel the flow of blood stop immediately; so constant was its oppression that in an instant she *knows* it is over.[80]

Fear replaces relief. It is not the first time a woman has taken without permission and found herself knowing and afraid; and once again, despite the crowd, there is nowhere to hide because Jesus knows too. He felt his power leave, though he does not yet know to whom. He searches the crowd. "Who touched my garments?" he asks, though he could have just as easily asked, "Where are you?" The disciples, incredulous, respond, "In this crowd you ask who touched you?"[81] But this moment is between Jesus and the woman, between Israel and her god. Nobody else matters.

She approaches in *fear and trembling* (φοβηθεῖσα καὶ τρέμουσα), no longer hiding. She falls before him, like Jairus, only as a woman already cured, having grasped for herself.[82] She confesses the entire truth. "*Daughter*, your faith has saved you. Go in peace and be whole, free from your suffering."[83] She is healed; she is saved—she is Israel, no longer running after other gods or incompetent physicians but now running to her god and finding that he has no desire to punish her but to restore her and make her well. She has nothing to fear. Eve, bold, alone, repentant, unchastised, healed, restored. One woman, rescued—Israel back from Exile.[84]

Delay here causes tragedy elsewhere. Messengers from Jairus' home bring word: "Your daughter is dead. Why trouble the teacher any further?" Hope spent, there is nothing left to do; it is over. "But overhearing . . . Jesus says to the synagogue leader, '*Do not fear; only believe.*'" "*Do not fear.*" Joshua and Caleb had said those same words to the congregation of Israel when all they saw were giants and grasshoppers.[85] Their inheritance before them, they doubted, and they all died. But death is already upon Jairus. He has little to lose and everything to gain. He need only believe. Jairus' inheritance, Gilead, healing, balm, stands before him. This king will not fail him; heaven is on his side.

Commotion is in full swing at the house. The *weepers and wailers* have arrived; the *mourning* over this child has officially begun. Jeremiah speaks again: "Thus says YHWH of hosts: 'Consider, and *call for the mourning women* to come . . . let them hasten and raise a *wailing* over us, that tears may run down our eyes and let our eyelids flow with water. . . . For *death has come* up to our windows . . . *cutting off the children* from the streets.'"[86]

This young girl's situation weaves with the woman flowing blood, two halves of a whole. The woman was Israel having suffered under Omri for *twelve years*. This *twelve-year-old* girl is Judah, suffering under Manasseh, the child king who was only *twelve years* old when he sat on Judah's throne.

"Manasseh did what was evil in the sight of YHWH, leading Judah to do even more evil than those nations that YHWH destroyed before the people of Israel." Manasseh caused so much collective damage that even the good kings who followed, purposely making amends, were unable to atone for his accrued sin: "The LORD did not turn from his great burning anger, his anger which was kindled against Judah, because of all the provocations with which Manasseh had provoked him."[87]

Like Israel before, Judah was led astray by her king: "At the command of YHWH, this [exile and punishment] came upon Judah to remove them from before his face, on the account of the sins of Manasseh, and all that he did." Jeremiah's indictment of Judah corresponds to Israel's: "Why does the land perish and fall into ruins like a wilderness, so that no one passes through? Because of their forsaking my law which I gave before their faces, and they did not obey my voice or walk in it but walked after the stubbornness of their own hearts and after the Baals, as their fathers taught them."[88]

Jeremiah had called for the mourners as a sign of what was to come, but that time is now past. Judah has long suffered. Jesus has had enough of the weeping wailers. He has not come to let this child die but to bring her to life, to health. "Why do you make a commotion and weep?" Jesus asks them. "The child is not dead, but sleeping."[89] Jesus takes her by the hand and says to her, "Little girl, rise up." The uncleanness of death yields to the power in his hands. He heals her and brings her back. This is the god of Israel's plan for his daughter Judah as well: life, restoration from Exile, from exile, from death—and a future. Jesus orders that this little girl be fed, not with bitter food, the punishment for Israel and Judah in Jeremiah, but with nourishment.[90]

> *Here I am, bringing up to her health and healing, and I will heal them* and reveal to them abundant peace and truth. I will restore the fortunes of Judah and the fortunes of Israel, and I will rebuild them as they were at first. I will cleanse them from all the guilt of their sin against me, and I will forgive all the guilt of their sin and rebellion against me. And this city shall be to me a name of joy, a praise and a glory *before all the nations* of the earth who shall hear of all the good that I do for them. And they will *fear and tremble* over all the good and over all the peace I will do for her [the city].
>
> Jer 33:6–9

The histories of YHWH's two daughters were always intertwined. Two rebellious sisters, they both vexed and melted the heart of their oft-frustrated father. It is only fitting that their restoration, marked by the rescue of these two individual yet representative daughters, happens together as well. The sins of the nation forgiven and their punishment declared over through healing. The depths of the netherworld relinquishing its claim with no hint of resistance. Death and wasteland, those dreaded places that opened their ravenous mouths to consume those who died in exile, not beyond the bounds of YHWH's dominance or care.

But the restoration of Judah and Israel is not just about healing for the daughters of the god of Israel and their redemption from Exile, though it is indeed both those things. Their restoration a testament, a witness, for all the nations to see. These gentile nations watch with *fear and trembling*,[91] just like the woman healed from her afflictive flow of blood.[92] They also long for the good that the god of Israel, the god of the universe, offers. The healing of Israel and Judah anticipates the healing of all the nations. Their restoration is hope for Jew and gentile alike. Just as Tobit predicted, the god of Israel has come to rescue from exile not only his girls but the entire world.[93]

CHAPTER 2

YHWH's Man

The Man YHWH

YHWH once walked with humankind in the cool of the day. During the time of Moses, YHWH's thundering and majestic, tangible presence, dwelt with his people, visible in their every day. The promise was that YHWH would return to personally shepherd Israel once again. Hope tied as well to YHWH's messiah, his righteous and anointed king. But from the beginning, YHWH was supposed to be Israel's sovereign. The simplest solution scandalous: YHWH becomes a man, his own messiah, to walk with his people once again and reign as their king.

The King and His Prophet

Elijah (John the Baptist) is back at the Jordan, and he is not the only one back from times past. Ahab and Jezebel have returned as well. But just when it seems that the echoes and allusions are cut and dried, it is not so. John the Baptist is killed, rewriting history and changing the old, familiar pairings. John's situation is interdependent with the others in his story, casting light on Jesus' mission and identity.

Mark 6:14–27

Judges 11:1–31; Esther 1, 2, 5, 7; 1 Kings 18–19

From the moment of his baptism, Jesus is drenched with power. Power pulses through his being. It hangs on him like a mantle. It flows from his garments. Sovereignty is his birthright; the very majesty of heaven rests upon him. Demons obey. Sickness leaves. He teaches as one who knows. Jesus exudes authority, and when the light hits just right, he is recognizable as the man with royal claims to other realms.

"The Gospel of Jesus *Christ*"—christos/messiah was announced from the beginning.[1] But there have been many anointed: Aaron the priest, his sons, Saul, David, Solomon, Elisha, and others, even Cyrus the gentile.[2] The uniqueness of this anointed one, ***the anointed***, begins as mystery.[3]

The barrier to the netherworld gives way when Jesus calls Jairus' daughter back. No hesitance, no resistance, no pushback; death relinquishes its claim without a fight. Not since Elijah and Elisha has there been such. But even theirs are wanting in comparison. Elijah raised the widow's son from Zarephath, and Elisha, the Shunammite's.[4] Each walked into the rooms where the lifeless bodies lay, closed the door behind them, and raised these boys from the dead. Resurrection was not easy, though; there was strain, desperation, effort. There was stretching out, body to body, eyes to eyes, mouth to mouth, breath to breath, sneezing, and calling out to God. None of that here; this miracle mighty because of its ease. The mourners laugh, they mock, but they are not fools. They know death when they see it. What they don't know is Jesus. They don't know that Jesus is far greater than the prophets of old. Sheol knows exactly who he is and, thus, "she is not dead, only sleeping."[5]

Fame of Jesus spreads. Even Herod, the local "king," hears the news. "Who is this Jesus?" Rumors abound. "It is John the baptizer raised from the dead." "It is Elijah." "It is a prophet, one of the prophets of old." Herod, guilty Herod, powerful Herod, perhaps even hopeful Herod, sides with resurrection. "John, the one I beheaded, this one has been raised."[6]

John's purpose had been to "prepare the way of the Lord."[7] He stood guard as a watchman at the Jordan, waiting, one baptizer sent to recognize another. He readied Israel with his preaching of repentance and baptism and then identified Jesus as one greater than himself. His arrest just after the pinnacle of Jesus' baptism was both surprising and not.

Herod had been married to a princess, the daughter of Aretas of Arabia. Years of married life had passed when Herod traveled through Rome, stayed with his brother Herod Philip, and there fell for Philip's wife.[8] Divorce was a simple matter. Some whispered quietly, "It is not appropriate," "It is not right." But it was John the Baptist who boldly spoke out, "It is not lawful! For you to take Herodias, your brother's wife, as your own."[9]

For every king of Israel, YHWH would send his prophet to guide. Loud, invasive, disruptive, speaking truth. Despite the irritation, the infuriation, the gall, the prophet reminded the king that he was not alone. The god of Israel was still there. The prophet was a light in the darkness, the very faithfulness of YHWH. Most especially in their rebellion, in their evil, in their power-fueled depravity, the god of Israel did not leave the kings without a moral compass; the prophet was his voice.

"Have you found me, my enemy?" Ahab would say to Elijah. Relational, a pairing, symbiotic. "I have found you because you have sold yourself to do what is evil in the eyes of YHWH," Elijah would say back.[10] Herod, too, had sold himself to do evil, and John his Elijah. Eventually Herod put John in prison. A confluence of motivations. No doubt Herod enjoyed having John close, controlled, publicly silenced, and at his personal disposal for conversation. Imprisonment was certainly appeasement of Herodias as well. Her grudge against John for condemning her marriage at least as large as John's grudge against the unlawfulness of it. She could not kill John because Herod protected him.

Herod's birthday. All the powerful of Herod's kingdom would come, *a banquet, for courtiers and officers, all the leaders of Galilee.* Herodias' *daughter* would *dance.* So pleasing, so emotive, so compelling, so charged was her performance that Herod was moved beyond himself. *Vowing* a vow, solemnly swearing, Herod promised her whatever she wished, *up to half his kingdom.*[11]

Quickly she steals away to the other room where the women have their own separate banquet. Mother would know what to ask for. The opportunity presented more than Herodias could ever have dared hope. A stinging birthday rebuke for Herod. This young *dancing daughter* returns to him parroting her mother's answer, "The head of John the Baptist." Of her own accord, she adds, "Immediately, on a platter."[12]

Long before the kings, the judges ruled Israel. These heroes fought off local threats and armies not yet vanquished from the time of Joshua and the initial conquest. Jephthah, son of Gilead, judged Israel for six years. The son of a prostitute, he had been driven out of his father's house by his half-brothers lest he inherit with them. Jephthah was mighty in battle, a situational necessity. As irony would have it, those very combat skills would turn his ostracized life around. The Ammonites attacked, and his brothers came begging: "If you defend us, if you fight for us, you can rule over us." Blood is blood; better Jephthah the outcast than bondage to foreigners. Honor. Acceptance. The eating of words. The haughty humbled—Jephthah now judge over them all.[13]

Jephthah's rule began with promise. Measured. Thoughtful. He tried to avoid war with Ammon. When diplomatic attempts failed, the Spirit of YHWH came upon him—a sign of chosenness, a good omen for a hopeful outcome. Yet, as he drew nearer and nearer to the battle with so much at stake, he *vowed a vow* to the LORD. A tragic vow. An unnecessary vow. A vow that should never have been made, and if made, made with caution, caveats, and exceptions: "If you will surely give the sons of Ammon into my hand, whatever comes out the doors of my house to greet me when I return in peace . . . will be for YHWH and I will offer it as an offering."[14] Like Herod, he was as rash as his vow. He didn't understand his moment or his god. He didn't know the battle was his because YHWH is YHWH, and not because of any vain promises that Jephthah himself could make.

The battle was indeed victorious. The god of Israel came through, and Jephthah became a hero for all time.[15] Twenty cities dominated, the Ammonites subdued. Glory, victory, everything Jephthah could have wanted. Elation all the way home. But the shadow of his trade looms. Evil crouches. It is not animal sounds that burst through the door as he arrives home in Mizpah; joyful tambourine fills the air. Jephthah's beautiful *dancing daughter* is the first to greet him as he returns, his only child. Brightness turns to gloom. The wind he sowed is now a whirlwind. He rends his clothes. "You have brought me to my knees! You have become my ruin! I have opened my mouth to the LORD, and I am not able to return it." *The vow.* The vow has come home and wreaks its havoc. Some years later, a better man than Jephthah would also make a rash vow. But he would dismiss it, prioritizing the innocent lives of Abigail's household rather than his own prideful piety.[16] After giving his daughter two months to mourn with her friends, Jephthah "did to her according to the vow which he vowed," and this time, no voice from heaven stayed his hand.[17] Like Herod, he would allow the foolish utterance of his mouth to bind him, shedding blood he desperately didn't want to shed.

Hadassah, Esther, a Jewish orphan girl renamed after a beautiful gentile goddess, long after the kings of Israel and Judah have come and gone. Israel had been scattered among the nations and Judah, too, captive in a foreign land. Esther was the cousin and adopted daughter of Mordecai, son of *Jairus*.[18] The other daughter of Jairus represented Judah—not dead, only sleeping. Esther, granddaughter of Jairus, is Judah as well, vulnerable in exile, not dead, but sleeping in a faraway place. Like her namesake, Ishtar, she, too, will return.

King Ahasuerus *threw a banquet for all his officials, ministers, nobles, governors, and armies.* After seven days of feasting and drinking, the king summoned his queen, the gorgeous Vashti, to enamor his guests with her regal and beauty. She denied him, humiliating him in front of his audience. Inflamed by her public refusal, the king put Vashti away, rejecting her defiance. The search for a new queen takes time. But finally, the perfect girl is found.[19]

Esther, the newly chosen queen, delights, endears, and shines with beauty, eliciting the favor of all who meet her. But unknown to her husband the king, Esther is a Jew. Soon she finds herself in a dangerous quandary. A plot against her people brews, hatched by the king's evil advisor Haman. To speak out is to risk her life. To be silent, complicit in their destruction. The words of her adopted father, Mordecai, ring out: "Perhaps you have come to this position for such a time as this."[20]

Esther calls her people to pray, to fast, to implore their god, the god of Israel, for favor and safety. Then she approaches the king unsummoned—a death sentence if his mood is unfavorable. As soon as his eyes rest on her, the king is instantly moved to compassion. Death commuted; his favor is hers. "What is it Queen Esther? And what is your request? *Up to half of my kingdom* I will give it to you." Another beautiful girl melting the heart of a king, stirring generosity in the flicker of a moment. Esther's request also ends with the death of an enemy. "Save my life, and the lives of my people . . . from this wicked Haman," she implores. Though not quite *beheaded*, evil Haman is hanged on his own gallows, the Jews saved by this gentile king.[21]

Herod is deeply grieved at the scandalous request.[22] Weak. He's weak. Weak if he keeps the oath, weak if he renounces it. If he keeps it, Herodias has won, successfully using her daughter to manipulate Herod to do what he had adamantly refused time and again. If he renounces the oath, all the dignitaries will know that Herod does not keep his word. Herod is caught in a predicament of his own making and the perception of his own weakness.

Herod could have displayed strength. He could have taken a cue from Ahasuerus, leaned into royal swagger, called Herodias out, and exposed her in front of the crowd: "Your mother will not have her way over mine; you have asked for something in the forbidden half of my kingdom." Instead, trapped in his own powerlessness, unable to do what is right, Herod sends a soldier of the guard to bring John's head. Just like that, the war between Herodias and John is over. John is dead. Herodias has killed him using Herod's pitiable hands.[23] Like Ahab, Herod is controlled by his wicked wife, and like Jephthah, a loved one is lost over a rash vow.[24]

It was not the spineless Ahab who would threaten the prophet's life when he put to death the 850 prophets of Baal and Asherah at the Wadi Kishon. "May the gods do to me and more if I don't make your life like the life of one of them by this time tomorrow." Jezebel's threats were not empty; she was well known as a prophet killer. Elijah was rightfully terrified and fled, despite his own mighty power. The god of Israel, however, would intervene, protecting Elijah from her fury. Jezebel did not have the last say with this prophet. He was swept up to heaven rather than be slain by her.[25]

As the situation in Israel continued to decline before finally succumbing to Assyrian domination, King Ben-Hadad of Aram laid siege to Samaria, causing a bitter famine in the city; the king of Israel helpless to do anything about it. Frustrated with the god of Israel over their suffering, the king decided to take it out on the prophet of YHWH, Elisha. Echoing Jezebel's promise of death regarding Elijah, the king of Israel would similarly say, "*May god do to me and more* if the *head* of Elisha son of Shaphat stands on his shoulders today."[26] Beheading. Calmly awaiting both the king's messenger and the king himself, Elisha was able to speak words of comfort and hope, announcing the end of the famine by the very next day.[27]

Herod and Herodias—the new Ahab and Jezebel, with John their Elijah. At baptism, Elijah was sent to prepare the way for YHWH. It is curious, though, the first Elijah was never caught by Jezebel and Elisha never beheaded. The death of John the Baptist at the hands of Herod is shocking and unexpected. This Jezebel (Herodias) should never have been able to kill Elijah (John). That she could means something is afoot. John seemed to be the prophet to Herod, but it was always a ruse.

John was indeed the prophet, and he was indeed here for the king. But Herod was never a king.[28] John's death exposes the bait and switch, the smoke and mirrors, the distraction. John was never here for Herod.

Beginning to end, John's ministry was always about Jesus—the last prophet, heralding for the kingdom of god and the king of god's kingdom.[29] It would be a gentile without sight who would have vision to articulate just the what the messiah would mean for the kingship of Israel.

The Blind Man Sees Walking Trees

Sometimes those with eyes to see cannot see. Jesus has come to heal, even this. The spiraling history of Israel and Judah is on full display through the evocation of this blind man and his walking trees. A sober account of Israel and Judah's less-than-ideal monarchies directly addresses the naive notion of Israel's glorious past. But YHWH himself has come to solve the problem for which their solution was always deficient—a simple king was never their answer. YHWH was always to be their sovereign.

Mark 8:22–26

Tobit 1–5, 11; Judges 6, 8:22–9:21; Isaiah 7; Jeremiah 5

An old acquaintance occupies the disciples' thoughts as they dock at Bethsaida, hometown of Philip, Andrew, and Peter. "They bring to [Jesus] a blind man," someone from their past, before they left everything to follow, "and they urge [Jesus] to touch him."[30] There is excitement in the anticipation. Once upon a time, such affliction was simply a tragedy. They sat in Job's dust with him, lamented, and together got through life. But now the disciples are acquainted with miracle. They have pull with one who has power to heal: "Taking the hand of the blind man, [Jesus] led him out of the village, and *having spit* in his eyes, *he placed his hands on him*."[31]

Tobit was an Israelite from the tribe of Naphtali, among the first to be dispossessed by the brutal Assyrians when they came in and razed the northern kingdom of Israel.[32] The Assyrians relocated Tobit to their capital city of Nineveh when they dispersed the population all over the region but far from home.[33] Tobit, blameless like Job, "walked in the ways of truth and righteousness all the days of his life." Even before his deportation, Tobit was not one of the ones who deserted the house of David and Jerusalem, sacrificing to the calf that King Jeroboam set up in Dan, though the rest of Naphtali did. He instead made the prescribed pilgrimage back to Jerusalem for all the festivals, taking the first fruits of his crops; supporting the priests; going over and above; providing for the widows, orphans, and those in Jerusalem; tithing not just a tenth of his livelihood but three tenths. He alone kept from eating the food of the gentiles when he was carried off into exile, remaining faithful to dietary restrictions from the Law of Moses. Tobit gave food to the hungry, clothed the naked, and even buried the dead, putting himself, his family, and his property at risk, all while captive in a foreign land. Tobit suffers in exile but not for his own sins.[34]

It came about one Pentecost that Tobit interrupted the festival meal to go and collect the body of one murdered. Offering kindness and hospitality even to the deceased, he laid the dead man in one of his own rooms until he was able to tend to him, then washed himself clean and ate his meal in sorrow. After burying the victim, he washed again,[35] slept outside in the courtyard under a ledge visited by sparrows, and in all his sadness, Tobit the righteous, Tobit the innocent, suffered with the rest of Israel for her many sins.[36]

Tobit's misfortunes, however, were only just beginning. Like Job's, they became disturbingly personal. The bird droppings were dripping as he slept under that ledge, right into his eyes, causing him to lose his vision.[37] For four years, Tobit was afflicted with blindness, with no hope in sight. Finally, Tobit prayed for death, and believing that god would answer his prayer, he began to get his affairs in order. He sent his son Tobias to Media to collect his inheritance, which had been left in trust with another relative.[38]

Unbeknown to them all, the angel Raphael ("god heals") was dispatched from heaven to restore Tobit the moment his prayer for death was received.[39] It was Raphael, impersonating a relative, who accompanied Tobias as he went to Media.[40] And when Tobias returned home safely, he came with his inheritance, a new wife, and the means to heal his father—the gallbladder of a fish, the knowledge of which came through the angel Raphael.[41] At Raphael's instructions, and with that gallbladder in his hands, Tobias *blew* (ἐνεφύσησεν)[42] *it into his* father's *eyes. He took hold of him* (ἐπελάβετο), saying, "Courage, Father!"... and with both his hands he peeled away the white film from the corners of his eyes, *clearing the way for uninhibited sight*:[43] "After *spitting in his eyes and laying his hands upon him*, Jesus continued asking him, 'Do you see anything?' The man looked up and said, 'I see *people like trees*; I perceive them *walking around*.' Then again, Jesus *placed his hands upon his eyes;* he opened his eyes wide and was restored, and *he saw everything clearly*."[44]

During the time of the judges, "the children of Israel did evil in the eyes of YHWH and YHWH gave them into the hand of Midian for seven years." The Midianites, Amalekites, and the sons of the East would come and take what they had not planted, leaving no vegetation nor any sheep, oxen, or donkey for Israel—like locusts who devour.[45]

So desperate was their situation that Gideon concealed himself in a winepress, threshing his wheat in secret so that the Midianites would not see and steal. It was in this moment of utter humiliation that the angel of YHWH came and settled himself under the local shade tree, appearing to Gideon with enthusiastic greetings: "YHWH is with you mighty one of valor! Go, in this your might and save Israel from the hand of Midian. Have I not sent you?"[46]

Gideon placed all the items of an offering on a rock as instructed by the angel of God, who then touched the broth-drenched meat and bread with the tip of his staff, causing fire to burst forth from the rock and consume it all.[47] The angel of YHWH departed, walking off into disappearance from before Gideon's eyes,[48] confirming at that moment exactly who he was.[49] Gideon tore down the altar of Baal and replaced it with an altar to YHWH, drawing Israel back to her god. Then at YHWH's command and with a mere three hundred men, Gideon went to battle and defeated Midian.[50]

Moses and Joshua were spokesmen for YHWH throughout the time of the Exodus and the conquest of Canaan, in those early days when Israel's national identity was being formed—distinctively leaders but not monarchs. YHWH was the sovereign of Israel. And as Samuel would confirm, to ask for a king was to reject YHWH.[51] Yet with the lack of leadership and the cycle of oppression that repeated itself every few decades during the time of the judges, the desire for an earthly king began to entice Israel.[52]

"Rule over us," the men of Israel offered to Gideon, "You and also your son, and also your grandson." A dynasty, the Gideon dynasty. Gideon, however, refused, "Neither I nor my son will rule over you. YHWH will rule over you," marking for the tradition once again, the ideal course of action for Israel.[53] YHWH should be their king; it was never a passing fad or an old idea to be replaced with the new. YHWH should always be Israel's king.

At Gideon's death, however, the children of Israel relapsed and "prostituted themselves after the Baals again."[54] They did not remember what YHWH had done for them; neither did they act in loyalty to Gideon. Gideon had made explicitly clear his wishes regarding his family ruling over Israel—"not me nor my sons, but only God." Yet when the son of one of Gideon's many concubines, ironically named Abimelech ("my father the king"), grew up and defied his father's wishes, the lords of Shechem, relatives through his mother's side, did not hesitate to take advantage of such proximity to power.

In contrast to his father, Gideon, who humbly stood before the angel of YHWH, acknowledging his weakness and denying rights and claims to power, Abimelech instead conspired, connived, and without any involvement from YHWH, set himself up as the king of Israel.[55] Gideon had prepared an offering and meticulously arranged it on a rock before the angel of YHWH, who accepted the offering and consumed it by fire. Abimelech found a similar rock and rather used it as a chopping block, where he treacherously slaughtered seventy sons of Gideon, murdering his own brothers with swift efficiency. In all of this, the lords of Shechem were not scandalized. In fact, they took Abimelech to the oak tree and made him king. In their twofold abandonment of the god of Israel, they went after the Baals and picked a scoundrel guilty of fratricide seventy times over to be their king, selling their own integrity for influence and power.[56]

As it happened, though, *Jotham*, one of Gideon's sons, escaped. When he heard the news that Abimelech had been made king, he stood on the top of Mount Gerazim, which looked over Shechem, and he called out to them with a parable involving *walking trees*:

> The *trees*, determined, *went walking about* (הָלוֹךְ הָלְכוּ) to anoint over themselves a king.[57] And they said to the olive tree, "Be king over us." And the olive tree said to them, "Shall I cease [from producing] the fat which through me gods and men are honored, and go to wander (לָנוּעַ) over the trees?" Then the trees said to the fig tree, "You go and reign over us." But the fig tree said to them, "Shall I cease from my sweetness and my good fruit and go to wander (לָנוּעַ) over the trees?" Then the trees said to the vine, "You go and reign over us." Then the vine said to them, shall I cease from my new wine which causes the gods and men to rejoice and go to wander (לָנוּעַ) over the trees? So then all the trees said to the bramble, "You go be king over us." And the bramble said to the trees, "If in truth you are anointing me to be king over you, come and take refuge in my shadow, but if not, let fire come out from the bramble and devour the cedars of Lebanon.[58]
>
> Judg 9:8–15

The young Jotham went further, indicting the lords of Shechem, calling them to account, lumping them together as culpable with

Abimelech: "My father fought for you, and his life he put in front of you to deliver you from the hand of Midian . . . but you have slayed his sons, seventy men on a stone." He called for their actions to bring corresponding judgment upon them: "If you have behaved in truth and perfection . . . then rejoice in Abimelech and he in you. But if not, *then let fire go out* from Abimelech *and consume* the leaders of Shechem . . . and let fire come out from the lords of Shechem and consume Abimelech." He then wisely fled for his life.[59]

"*The trees*, determined, *went walking about*," Jotham's parable began. These walking trees, itching with idleness, invite trouble with their idea for a king. They do not actually need a king. Life and production, society and the world are carrying on just fine, as is evidenced by the fruitfulness of the olive tree, the fig tree, and the vine. Who governs the trees but YHWH? Yet the trees persist; with their offer to rule rejected by the upstanding, they then stoop to the bramble. The bramble produces nothing, is good for nothing, and offers them nothing of worth, as little shade is given by a thorn bush on the ground. Instead, it binds these trees in a covenantal agreement, threatening them with destruction if they violate the terms. And still these foolish trees attach themselves and their future to this worthless briar, a bully—the parallel to the lords of Shechem and Abimelech fully transparent. Thugs, the lot of them, they will destroy each other with their fiery treachery rather than trust YHWH to be their king and keep good faith with those who proved themselves loyal.[60] The fire will burn, either to consume the offering rightfully made before YHWH, or those who refused to offer it.

Centuries after Jotham's parable, Isaiah is called by YHWH to go meet King Ahaz, the son of another *Jotham* of Judah. The situation is grave. The Assyrian attack upon the northern kingdom of Israel imminent—the very assault that would take Tobit and his fellow Naphtalites as prisoners into foreign lands. Israel, desperate, asks Judah, their brothers to the south, for help against the onslaught. Judah, however, refuses. As a result, King Rezin of Aram (Syria) and King Pekah of

Israel (Ephraim) join forces to mount an offensive on Jerusalem (the Syro-Ephraimite War) to replace Judah's king with a puppet king and take the resources he was unwilling to give. When the house of David heard of this alliance, the heart of Ahaz and the heart of his people shook (וַיָּנַע) as *trees* of the forest *walk to and fro* (נוֹעַ),[61] with nowhere to go, before the wind.

Fear. Fear consumes the people of Judah and its king. During the time of the judges, Israel longed for a king, hoping for someone to defend, conquer, and intimidate on the international scene.[62] They feared then too. Yet many kings later, here in the face of major foreign assault, it is not the human king who can rescue but only YHWH. YHWH was always to be Israel's king, though, once again, Judah would rather run to men to save them. YHWH sends Isaiah to urge Ahaz to trust: "Say to him, 'Be watchful and quiet, do not fear and let not your heart be faint.'"[63] YHWH assures him that the plot against him by Israel and Aram will not come to pass. Ahaz, however, does not trust in YHWH, but instead makes an alliance with Assyria,[64] the bramble of this generation. Very little is given in return for Judah yielding their territory to Assyria; they traded one set of bullies for another. Instead, Judah became culpable in the destruction of their brothers, like the lords of Shechem before.[65]

No longer Isaiah, now it is Jeremiah. No longer Israel, Aram, or Assyria, now the oncoming destructive power is Babylon. Here, however, it is YHWH himself who will consume:

> "For the house of Israel and the house of Judah have acted utterly treacherous with me," declares YHWH. "False they have been regarding YHWH and have said 'He will not [do anything], evil will not come upon us . . . '" "For this," thus says YHWH god of Hosts, "Because of your speaking this word, Behold, I am giving my words in your mouth as a *fire*, and this *people the trees*, and *it will consume them*. Behold I am bringing upon you a nation from afar, O house of Israel," declares YHWH . . . "And

> they will eat your harvest and your bread; they will eat your sons and your daughters; they will eat your flocks and your herds; they will eat your vines and your fig trees. . . . But even in those days, I will not make you an end. . . . According to the way you have forsaken me and served foreign gods in your land, so you will serve strangers in a land that is not your own."
>
> Jer 5:11–12, 14–15, 17–19

Centuries beyond the time of the judges, and the cycle that began there continues. When Midian had menaced, it was because Israel had done what was evil in the sight of YHWH, and YHWH had given them over to their oppressor, fulfilling the curses in Deuteronomy for breach of covenant.[66] Now the powers are bigger, the scope is larger, the betrayals are more practiced, but it is still the same. Babylon is coming. Like Assyria, Babylon, too, will take the children en masse. And as before, YHWH himself takes ownership of the fire that will consume.[67]

The blind man before Jesus is the seer, bringing to light key moments from Israel's past: the earliest temptation to replace Israel's god with a human monarch; Judah's alliance with Assyria, which contributed to Israel's exile; and then fall of Judah to Babylon. In every instance, the people like trees walking around in fear, in danger of burning before a consuming fire, each time rejecting YHWH as their sovereign.[68] The evoking of this particular history warns of its next occurrence. Bound to repeat, a new generation of foolish trees always emerges to anoint the bramble, but it was always YHWH himself that was to be their king.

Herod is no better than his predecessors—the declining kings of the past who reigned in both Israel and Judah. They rejected YHWH's law, shed innocent blood, and murdered the prophets of their god. Those kings failed and fell, along with the monarchies themselves. Herod demonstrates that nothing has changed. The earthly kings are still corrupt. They still kill the prophets. They are still violators of the law. They cannot control their own evil, much less throw off the dominion of

Rome. The gentile King Ahasuerus did a better job protecting the Jews than most of their own kings. For those longing for the good old days, hoping that the messiah will bring back the kingship from the past, it is a fool's hope. From the time before the kings, after the kings, and right in the middle of the kingship, before even the northern kingdom of Israel was scattered, none of it, none of it was glorious. Echoes from the past dispel such notions for the future; the messianic hope must be something different, something greater, something new.[69]

John's identity as *prophet* confirmed Jesus' identity as *king*. It had seemed that John was just here for baptism, the sign that was to come, Elijah at the Jordan, who would then hand the baton of ministry to Jesus. But John was here for Jesus all the way to the end, preparing the way for him all the way to death: "When his [John's] disciples heard of it, they came and took his body and laid it in a tomb."[70] John's mission is complete. Jesus has walked in step behind John, picking up where he left off, preaching and ministering. Now John has died, and he still points the way forward for Jesus. The messiah whom Israel has longed for is here, the hope of both the judges and the exiles. But his mission and identity still remain a mystery. A king, yes, a miracle-working king. But he is more.

He Passes Them By

Divine presence—power so powerful that for the sake of the prophet, it passed them by: "No one can see my face and live."[71] Moses, Elijah, the greats, saw just a hint of YHWH here on earth. Now Jesus, too, passes his own by, but things have changed. They can see this one, YHWH's man, and live.

Mark 6:45–52

Job 4, 9; Exodus 33:22; 1 Kings 19:11–12

God hovered over the face of the waters at creation, bringing order to their chaos. Waters above separated from waters below, land separated from sea, this god in complete control. In Noah's time, Yhwh released the waters once again, allowing them to consume his creation, destroying all life that had corrupted itself and more, using the floodwaters to cleanse the earth before drawing them back and containing them once again. With Moses, Joshua, Elijah, and Elisha, the god of Israel showed his dominance over Egypt's Nile, the Red Sea, and Canaan's Jordan River. This god still flexes his muscles over the waters.[72]

Jesus was asleep in the boat when his disciples woke him, panicked over the wicked storm: "Don't you care that we are perishing?" "Peace, be still," Jesus commands, and the sea calms. Simple words but not mere—like the god of Israel at creation, his words have power. "Who is this, that the winds and waves obey?"[73] these disciples puzzle, but Jonah's mariners knew.[74]

Signs and wonders accompany the passage of time. Jesus sends his disciples away on a boat to find rest while he goes to the mountain to pray. No sublime moment like Moses or Elijah on Sinai. It is not the divine that will pass him as he covers himself. Jesus is the notable presence on this mountain. The god of Israel had kept a "*night of watching*" over the Israelites as they found themselves just out of Egypt but not quite through the sea. Jesus, too, keeps *watch through the night* over his disciples, similarly hovering in the in-between. "When evening came, the boat was in the middle of the sea, and he alone was on the land," watching, waiting.[75]

Another storm blows hard across water. Last time, Jesus was asleep in the stern, needing, it seemed, to be awoken. Now it seems the disciples are alone—Jonah's gentile mariners once again, who "rowed hard . . . under a sea that grew more and more stormy *against* them." The disciples, too, are tormented under a *wind that is against* them.[76] They do not realize they are still within Jesus' sight; his attention never left them. He leaves his post on the mountain to save his people—the pattern long ago set by the god of Israel.

"He came to them walking on the sea on the *fourth watch* of the night." When the children of Israel went to cross over the Red Sea, YHWH caused that east wind to blow over the sea all night long, and the children of Israel crossed over on dry ground. But it was at the *morning watch* that YHWH looked down on the Egyptian encampment in the pillar of fire and cloud and confused the Egyptian camp.[77]

The mighty deliverance from slavery to freedom is not all that marks the exodus escape. The invisible takes form, that which was hinted to in the beyond now perceptible within the sensible realm. The children of Israel became accustomed to the cloud on the mountain, the pillar of fire, the glowing face of Moses.[78] The tangible presence of this god recorded in the history of Israel makes an indelible mark on the psyche of a people; the supernatural, the divine, has become accessible to those this god has claimed.

Jesus strolls, feet atop the waves, *walking around upon the sea* (περιπατῶν ἐπὶ τῆς θαλάσσης), like one from the myths of old.[79] He heralds the most mystical aspects of Job's divine, also "*walking around upon the sea* (περιπατῶν . . . ἐπὶ θαλάσσης) as if upon the dry ground," "wearing out the mountain, making the mountain obsolete (παλαιῶν)."[80] Job's epiphany is mysterious, inscrutable, stealth: "Look if he goes beyond me, I do not see, if *he passes me by* (ἐὰν παρέλθῃ με) I do not know."[81] Jesus, too, had intended to pass his disciples by.[82] The god of Israel passes by (παρέλθῃ/παρελεύσεται) those he favors, but in the past, he has not stopped to stay with them.[83]

"They thought that [Jesus] was a phantom and they cried out, for they all saw him and were *terrified/shaking*."[84] Eliphaz the Timnite recalls a night terror, a phantom of such, that comes in the dark of the night: "A word came stealing to me, and my ear took the *whisper* of it. In disquieting thoughts from the visions of the night, when deep sleep falls upon men.[85] *Shivering* came upon me and great *trembling* caused my bones *to shake*. A *spirit passed* before my face, the hair of my flesh bristled. It stands but *I do not recognize* its appearance, a form is before my eyes."[86]

"The whole mountain *trembled* greatly," shivering in the presence of its god at Sinai.[87] Centuries later, YHWH passed by Elijah on that same mountain: "A wind, great and strong, was tearing through the mountains and breaking the rocks . . . and after the wind an earthquake."[88] With Elijah, however, YHWH was notably neither in the wind nor the earthquake; instead YHWH *whispered* after with the "still small voice." It is the disciples now, not the mountain, who, like Eliphaz, shake in visceral fear when the phantom-like Jesus approaches them from the water.

Presence has moved from the mountain and meets them on the sea. Jesus does not pass by his disciples like he intended, as did YHWH with Moses, Elijah, and Job.[89] The disciples' upset elicits his compassion, and Jesus hops on the boat with them instead, calming them as YHWH did for Elijah.[90] "Take heart (θαρσεῖτε)," Jesus consoles. "Do not be afraid." The same words Moses had for the frightened Israelites as they prepared to pass over the Red Sea (θαρσεῖτε). "I am (ἐγώ εἰμι)," Jesus says, the words revealing divine presence and identity.[91] The long-awaited messiah is not just a king, nor even a miracle-working king. Israel's long history witnesses to who he is. He is the god of Israel himself, come to be their sovereign, the way it was always intended to be.[92] The disciples are able to see this god and live.[93]

Messiahs and More

They see the signs, and it makes them wonder. Even Peter wondered. The messiah, however, is not what they expect and not who they expect. Rather than win in battle against the gentiles, the messiah will go to his death. Not only does YHWH allow for this, but YHWH embodies this.

Mark 8:27–9:8

Job 1–2, 42; Zechariah 3–4, 14; Leviticus 16, 24

It was a time when messiahs and hopes for messiahs abounded, and yet "messiah" was not one of the rumors floating around regarding Jesus.[94] "Who do you say that I am?" Jesus asked his disciples. It is Peter who answers without hesitation, marking him forevermore—"You are the Christos," the one we have been waiting for. Peter, the first to get it, the first willing to proclaim it. Jesus "orders them sternly not to tell."[95]

"Then he began to teach them that it is necessary for the Son of Man to suffer much and to be rejected by the elders, and the chief priests, and the scribes and to be killed, and after three days to rise. He said this all plainly."[96] The Pharisees and Herodians had begun the plot to destroy Jesus after he healed the man with the withered hand on the Sabbath.[97] The elders, those lords of Shechem, will reject YHWH as king, as they always have. But this time YHWH is a man, and they will kill him.[98]

"And Peter taking him aside, began to rebuke him. But turning back and looking at his disciples, [Jesus] rebuked Peter and said, 'Get behind me Satan,[99] for you are not thinking of the things of God but the things of humans.'"[100] Satan. For forty days, Jesus endured the temptation of Satan. But long before Jesus, Satan had tested Job—another righteous one who suffers not for guilt but for innocence, not for sin but for lack of it.

"YHWH said to Satan, 'Have you set your heart upon my servant Job? There is none like him on the earth, a man blameless and upright, fearing God and turning away from evil.'"[101] The experiment began with God himself proclaiming Job's blamelessness and Satan testing both Job and God—Job's loyalty with affliction and God's willingness to let the innocent suffer.

Job's friends come from afar to console him in his suffering, and for seven days they sit in silence.[102] Soon, however, they start in with their theorizing. Somehow, someway, there must be some sin, some just cause to account for Job's suffering, evenif it is simply that all mankind is wanting, incomplete, not whole (blameless) before their maker. Positing every form of theological argument, they argue aggressively that YHWH does not permit the righteous to suffer. Job, however, maintains his innocence, going as far as to implicate god in his unjust suffering.[103]

In the end, it was not to Job, however, whom YHWH turned his anger on but Job's friends. YHWH was not looking for blind defense, for patronizing pandering, but for sober honesty, for friendship: "You have not spoken what is right about me like my servant Job." YHWH restored the fortunes of Job and gave him twice what he had before.[104] But the suffering was suffered. Job the innocent suffered for YHWH, and YHWH let him.

As Peter finally recognizes who Jesus is and understands it in all its greatness, he doesn't understand what it means. He doesn't understand that the innocent will suffer, not just for the guilty but for the god of Israel. Satan had said, "Does Job fear god for nothing?"[105] Peter's rebuke hints to the same question: "Do you fear god for nothing? You are the messiah, the anointed one, the miracle worker, surely, you of all people will not suffer." Job's friends claim the righteous do not suffer. Satan claims the righteous will not stay righteous if they suffer. Jesus rejects them all: "Get behind me Satan." Both in the wilderness temptation and here in the first proclamation of Jesus as messiah, Jesus knows he will suffer as a righteous—for the unrighteous, for YHWH, and as YHWH. Satan would tempt him again not to suffer, through one of his closest friends and through that friend's long-awaited, rightful identification of who he is. But this is why Jesus came—to suffer.

"YHWH rebuke you Satan; YHWH who has *chosen Jerusalem* rebuke you!" In Zechariah's vision, it was accusations launched against the high priest Joshua (Jesus) that prompted YHWH's rebuke of Satan: "Is this one not a brand being torn out from the fire?"[106] In Jeremiah, it was God himself who was going to burn the trees—his treacherous (בָּגְדוּ) people, with the words of fire he was putting in the prophet's mouth.[107] Not just saving the innocent (Job, Tobit), YHWH now pulls Joshua out of the fire that began in Jeremiah—rescuing the guilty from the very punishment that YHWH prescribed. God takes away Joshua's guilt and exchanges his filthy rags for white festal apparel (וִיהוֹשֻׁעַ).[108] Moreover, YHWH declares that this Joshua (Jesus) and his companions, leaders of Judah and

Jerusalem, would be a sign of things to come, of redemption and restoration.[109]

Zechariah, however, turns his focus to another—"the branch." This branch is the servant of YHWH, not the bramble that offers nothing.[110] Jeremiah had seen this righteous branch raised for David, and this branch would reign as king.[111] Joshua and his friends, the Jewish leaders of Judah, are once again the lords of Shechem, the newest generation. Instead of being destroyed by the fire, they are redeemed from it. Coming full circle from Judges, it is no longer bramble they seek through treacherous alliances, but finally, they wait, and like Gideon, they submit to the angel of YHWH who prepares for them the rightful ruler, sent by YHWH.[112] When the land is redeemed, they will invite one another to come under their vine and their fig tree, the trees and vines from Jotham's parable once more functioning as they should.[113]

As Jesus freely talks about his looming suffering and death, Zechariah's promise of the branch mingles with the experience of Job and Tobit. The guilt of the land would be removed in a single day, with that branch, but the tradition always knew that redemption comes with the suffering of the innocent.[114] Joshua and the land's cleansing from guilt is a sign of what's to come. They have been cleansed and pulled from the fire, from that nasty cycle of sin by YHWH's grace, and not because they themselves are deserving or clean. In their place, YHWH himself will suffer where Joshua did not.

But there is more. It was in private that Peter proclaimed Jesus the Christ.[115] In public, however, rather than boasting of victory and battles to be won, Jesus' words confuse: "He *called the crowd* with his disciples and said to them (προσκαλεσάμενος τὸν ὄχλον . . . εἶπεν αὐτοῖς), if anyone wishes to follow after me (ὀπίσω μου ἀκολουθεῖν), let them deny themselves and . . ."[116]

"Take up their *sword.*"

Or so they expect.

At any moment, Jesus the Messiah will beckon them to "take up arms" and throw off the enemies of Israel who have too long subjected them. It is what they have been waiting for. War, the language is that of war, and they are poised and ready to join Jesus when he calls. But Jesus turns it on its head. His fight will not end in earthly victory but in humiliating death, one devoid of glory and valor in battle. Moreover, the heavenly army that warred on behalf of Israel during the time of the first Joshua would not intervene this time; they would simply stand by and watch.[117]

"If anyone wishes to follow after me, let him deny himself." It is Elisha turning away from his old life and never looking back, the disciples walking away from their boats and following Jesus to fish for men. But that is not all. The disciples must now also deny the triumphant future they had imagined. "Let them take up their . . . *cross*"—not their sword, not arms, not violence, not war. The messiah didn't come to go to war with Rome or any of the gentile nations. He came to die.[118]

It is the seventh month of the year, and the Feast of Trumpets has just passed, all the horns blown resounding in recent memory. Sacrifice after sacrifice made, the smoke of their offering rising to the heavens, beckoning God—one of the prescribed feasts that marks Israelite worship. Nine days go by, and now the somber, sober reality of what it means for sinful human beings to live with a holy god marks the calendar—Yom Kippur. There are no spectators; every member of the community participates: "You shall *deny yourself* (*afflict your souls*/ענה) . . . the citizen, the alien . . . for on this day he will make amends for you, and before the face of YHWH you will be clean . . . it is a Sabbath of complete rest for you and you will *deny yourself*; it is a statute forever."[119] The priest has his role to play, but each individual denies themselves, taking their part in the process of being made clean as a people before YHWH. Individual, communal, and priest-led, the people follow his lead: "The priest who is *anointed (messiah/Christ)* and consecrated as priest in *his father's place*, shall make atonement . . . for the sanctuary . . . for the tent of meeting . . . for the altar . . . and for the priests . . . and all the people of the assembly. This shall be an eternal statute for you all, to make atonement for the people of Israel once a year for all their sins."[120]

Not just the long-anticipated warrior king, but the consecrated and anointed priest who stands before YHWH and entreats him to cover all Israel's sins—Jesus is both. But rather than lead Israel into a victorious battle against the foreign nations, Jesus will suffer at all their hands—with the leaders of Israel in league with the gentiles. And rather than make an offering on behalf of himself and his people, Jesus the high priest of Yom Kippur will give himself as the offering. An innocent like Job and Tobit, he will go further than both. He will go to his death for his people.

"Let him take up his . . . cross." The god of Israel hasn't changed his ways. Just as with Yom Kippur, each one is to afflict themselves, deny themselves individually, and share in the communal practice of atonement. It is not simply an invitation; it is a demand: "For every soul who is not afflicted (ענה) in their bones (בְּעֶצֶם) this day, will be cut off/destroyed (וְנִכְרְתָה) from its people"[121]; "If any one wishes to save his soul, he will lose it, if one wishes to lose his life for my sake and the sake of the gospel, he will save it."[122] God has drawn near, his kingdom has come, the messiah is among us. This is good news. But it is no easier than it was before; it still costs one's soul to be part of God's community.

"What will it profit a man to gain the whole world, and to forfeit his own soul?"[123] Hints of another conversation slip through—Jesus' defense against Satan, against temptation. "Again, the devil took him to an exceedingly high mountain, and showed him all the kingdoms of this world and their glory. 'All these I will give to you if you fall down and worship me.'"[124]

Satan's proposal is the most seductive of seductions, giving voice to the secret whispers of one's own heart. Satan offers an out. Jesus does not have to afflict himself. He can abandon his purpose, his reason for coming. He, too, can avoid the cross. Moreover, Jesus can gain power, the whole world, all the gentile nations, by shifting affiliation and affection. Worship the devil and be free of YHWH's harsh demands. The choice available to his followers is available to Jesus as well—he, too, can lose his soul, his love of YHWH and neighbor. Jesus, however, resists the devil. "Get behind me Satan,"[125] the exact words he says to Peter (ὕπαγε, σατανᾶ), betraying the dangerous temptation wrapped up in Peter's rebuke: "You don't have to die."

"What can a person give as an exchange for their soul?"[126] After the first time Satan enticed YHWH to allow Job to suffer the loss of loved ones and possessions, he comes back for a second round. "Skin for skin," Satan tells YHWH. "Everything a man has he will give for the benefit of his life/soul."[127] Satan bets that Job will curse YHWH rather than suffer the affliction of his body; perhaps Jesus will do the same. But Satan is wrong on both counts. Jesus knows the cost of one's soul, and he is prepared to give it. Each person must give his life to save his soul. This is the way of YHWH. Satan offers to give one's life back, but he deceives. In truth, he offers nothing but emptiness, a soulless life, for there is no life without one's friends, one's home, one's community, one's god. "Turn your worship from YHWH, who beckons you to suffer, and save yourself." But it will cost their very soul; after all, it takes soul to give one's life for their friend, most especially if that friend is YHWH.

Israel at Sinai. They had just experienced YHWH's mighty miracles delivering them from Egypt. Now, however, with those who oppressed and enslaved them defeated, it is just YHWH and his people, and this god is frightening: "When the people saw the thunder, the lightning, and the sound of the trumpet, and the mountain smoking, *the people trembled* and stood at a distance and they said to Moses, 'You speak with us, and we will listen, but let not God speak with us lest we die'";[128] "Then YHWH replied to me, 'They are right in which they have spoken. I will raise up a prophet for them from among their brothers like you, I will put *my words* in his mouth, and he will speak to them all which I command. And it will be that the man who does not listen to *my words* which he will speak in my name, I will require of him'."[129]

Despite the death of Moses, and the promise for another like him to follow, no such prophet was immediately evident: "And not since has there arisen a prophet in Israel like Moses who knew YHWH *face to face*."[130] It would take centuries.

It was not just covenant that YHWH had offered them—"you will be my people and I will be your god"—but friendship. The same thing offered to Moses was available for the whole of the people: "Thus YHWH spoke to Moses face to face as a man would speak to his friend."[131] It was the people of Israel who winced at the overwhelming and powerful presence of YHWH, turning from before his face, not YHWH who banished them. They asked for a mediator, attempting to save their lives, lest they die from his presence. YHWH told Moses that they were in fact correct; their lives were indeed in danger. Yom Kippur was in part about being safe, appeasing the divine, making sacrifice for their sin, and imploring him to have compassion on their fragility, their human frailty, and not destroy them. The people afflicted themselves and tiptoed around the god of Israel lest his presence break out and consume them. Only the priest could approach closely and, even then, only once a year and only after being cleansed himself. Job, however, never shrank back from the presence of YHWH but even in all his affliction, demanded his day with his god, his friend, face to face. This is what Jesus offers, not just reconciliation but a way back to friendship.

Jesus does not sanction keeping a safe distance from YHWH; he encourages the daring, the reckless, taking one's life in their hands. He knows the way back to YHWH's presence. The kingdom of god has come; once again, YHWH draws near to his people. Jesus understands fully what the children of Israel also grasped at the foot of that mountain, the function of Yom Kippur; humankind risks death to stand in YHWH's presence. And so Jesus invites his followers to come and die. Better to be close to YHWH than far away. Better to lose the world and gain your soul, your friend, your god. Better to come in his presence and be consumed than to be parted from him ever again. It is a love story. Jesus takes his followers back to that moment at Sinai and gives them the opportunity to change their minds. He takes them back to the decision made before the awesome and frightening presence of YHWH, back to the temple when the Yom Kippur sacrifices are made, and tells his followers, "Let your life be sacrifice; save your soul."

The cost for Jesus and his followers is not just life and limb, though. It is reputation and relationship. "They will be embarrassed. They will see you cursed. They will mock you and your words. You will lose your followers and friends." Jesus' ultimatum reveals, his words a response to both Satan and Peter: "Those who are ashamed of me and my words."[132] He knows the crowds will reject him. They want a messiah to defeat Rome, not be crucified by her. He knows Peter will turn away as well.[133] Peter doesn't want to die, nor does he want Jesus to die.

But "six days later . . . "

Six days after Yom Kippur, the trio of fall festivals that began with Rosh Hashana melts into Sukkot, the Feast of Tabernacles (booths). Rosh Hashana, the overture, begins the fall liturgical season with proclamation and celebration, with blasting trumpets that tear open the realm of the ordinary and beckon the influx of the sacred. The days then simmer into the communal and individual affliction of Yom Kippur—humanity's part in the somber duet sung with the divine to accomplish atonement. Then ascending again from the valley low, Sukkot completes as the powerful festival finale. Though seemingly folksy, simple, hometown, and communal, Sukkot digs deep, into the very soil, and celebrates harvest, prosperity, and the distinct flavors of the homeland. The autumnal counterpart to Passover, Sukkot celebrates the other side of deliverance from Egypt, where Israel dwelt with their god in booths under the starry sky.

For Peter and many of his countrymen, the memory of such grand deliverance and freedom raises a certain angst, bringing to stinging awareness that they are not free. Soil and harvest are not truly theirs, and future's hope hangs by a thread. Like Gideon threshing in the winepress, they wonder where that age-old deliverance is now, when freedom will come, and when the Exile will truly be over.[134] They wonder when they will finally be sovereign over their homeland once more—out from under the hand of their gentile oppressors. They wonder where their god is and when he will come to rescue them again.

Peter had been a fisherman. It was the family business. He knew the fish, the boats, the makeup of the storms, the rise and fall of the sea, the pull of the moon. He was not one to dismiss mariner miracles when he saw them, though he knew they were rare. And so, when Peter dropped his nets and followed Jesus at his call, it was not an uninformed or impulsive decision. Something deeply profound was afoot. Peter understood the turn of the tide. "You are a fisherman, now you can fish for men"[135]—this was his moment, and Peter, a leader, captain of his own ship and his own life, would surrender both commissions to Jesus.

Wonder after astonishing wonder, Peter had now seen many miracles, everything from healing the man with the withered hand, to exorcising demons; restoring sight, sound; calming storms; walking on water; and multiplying bread for thousands. Even with such, caution reigned among all the disciples. Hesitant to believe, there was no rush to assign Jesus a title despite all they had seen and heard. It had been centuries since a prophet had been seen on Israel's soil, much less anything more. But finally, Peter took the lead and boldly proclaimed, "You are the messiah," the king we have been waiting for.[136]

But then it appeared as though Jesus hedged. He seemed to retreat—retreat from kingship, retreat from his calling, retreat from the boldness required to be the messiah, just when Peter put his name on the line for him with the others. Jesus instead spoke of death, of dying, of giving in to Roman tyranny; he immersed in the affliction of Yom Kippur and let it dominate. Like Saul waiting for Samuel at Gilgal, watching his soldiers fall away one by one, it seemed that Jesus would forfeit the moment.[137]

People would lose interest in his revolution if he kept talking of suffering and death instead of victory. Saul had taken it upon himself to offer the necessary sacrifice when Samuel seemed to delay and minutes mattered; so, too, Peter took charge of a situation rapidly spiraling out of control. He took Jesus aside, an inspirational moment, one leader to another, a gentle hand on the shoulder, motivational words. But it went badly, very badly. Jesus doubled down, rejected Peter's advice, went as far as to call him "Satan," and then did the worst thing possible: He told the crowds that their reward for following him would be crucifixion on a Roman cross. Weak, Jesus was weak, too strong to listen but too weak for his own good. And for a week, as Yom Kippur affliction gave way to the Sukkot celebration of god, deliverance, and homeland, Peter was forced to stew.

Six days later... YHWH called to Moses from the midst of the cloud, and Moses entered the mystical fog and haze and basked in divine presence.[138] When he finally emerged, his countenance was changed from the encounter, *glowing* like the full moon on a dark night. So bright and beaming was his shining face that he frightened the onlookers of Israel and had to veil himself, like YHWH covering the eyes of those who would gaze upon him as well. Centuries later, "a prophet like Moses" would beam with similar radiance.

Six days after Jesus tells the crowd they must take up their cross, he takes Peter, James, and John and leads them up a high mountain apart by themselves. It is not the first time these *four* have gone somewhere separate from the rest.[139] Peter, James, and John had gone with him to Jairus' home and watched him raise a child from the dead, a resurrection, done with simplicity and immense power; he didn't even have to raise his voice.[140] For Peter, this is the authority Jesus needs to display now with the crowds.

There are no trumpet blasts on this mountain, and its peaks do not shake and smoke, but far away from Sinai, this spot, too, is forever marked by the extraordinary. Jesus doesn't cover himself to spare their eyes; rather, the veil is removed, and Jesus begins to shine. Unlike Moses, he does not "catch" the glow from YHWH, mirroring what had been cast on him. Jesus generates it. He is no mere reflection; he is the god of Israel himself. "His garments became exceedingly radiant white, such as no cloth refiner on earth could whiten them"[141]—such whitening is its own testimony of purity and holiness. It is only YHWH who can bleach so thoroughly, and he has done it before.

The scene transforms in an instant to another Jesus, another high priest. It is Joshua who takes center stage in Zechariah's vision. The excitement of returning to the land of their ancestors dwindled quickly, the returning exiles now desperate for hope. The younger ones have never known this land; seventy years have passed since this people last dwelt on this soil. It has existed for them like a myth, the patchwork of stories from the older generation leaving them in a state of limbo, keeping home elusive, neither here nor there, but resting solely in their communal memory. The elders passed down a picture of what safety and belonging should be, and it could never be Babylon or Persia. But the actual return to the land of Israel is sobering. The temple, destroyed, lies in shambles, the terrain trampled, overgrown, and devastated. Home will have to be remade, religious practice nearly impossible to conceive of in such a state. Confusion, aimlessness, uncertainty, and guilt dominate the practical reality of worshipping their God in their homeland once again. Sin drove them into exile; do they still carry it?

Dirty, Joshua stands in filthy rags, tainted by the individual and communal transgression, unclean in exile, unable to cleanse himself, his very presence in the vision a stand-in for everything—the nation, the individual, and every religious office that must function in society. What happens to him happens to them all. Is he even recognized as acceptable to YHWH? He, too, is new, of that younger generation raised in a foreign land; can they just pick up where they left off, filling the old offices with an interrupted line?

Joshua's story is a Yom Kippur fairy tale that ends happily ever after, though, like most, it begins with chaos and tragedy. The high priest who represents the nation stands before YHWH afflicted, and he cannot come clean.[142] The people of the kingdom the same and they, too, helpless to atone for their sin. Seventy years they have all suffered, but their sin still stains. Yet none of them are destroyed before the presence of this holy god. Rather, Joshua's filthy rags are removed and his guilt gone in parallel; he is clothed in the purest of white garments (מַחֲלָצוֹת).[143] YHWH has cleansed him from his sin and atoned for him despite his inability to participate in his own salvation or the salvation of the nation. Particularly poignant, the name Joshua literally means *salvation*, and yet he is utterly unable to save anyone, including himself. Once again like Moses' glowing face, this Joshua reflects through his bright white robes the salvation and restoration of his god rather than any salvation that he himself can generate. Moreover, YHWH promises to cleanse the entire land in a single day.[144] But while Zechariah closes with this hope, there is no fulfillment—hope deferred to the faraway future.

Shining with radiance, Jesus stands on the mountain. There is no stain on this Joshua, and he needs nobody to cleanse him. Salvation incarnate, he is his name. Jesus himself generates the whiteness that transforms his own garments. There is no Satan to accuse him on this mountain as with Joshua in his filthy rags. Jesus, the god of Israel, dealt with him in the wilderness.

The empyreal character of this event quickens as Elijah and Moses join the party and begin conversing with Jesus. They are a particular pair, being the only two prophets to have caught a glimpse, a real, palatable glimpse of the glory of YHWH on Mount Sinai. Now they stand together on this new mountain, both witnessing, their very presence validation. Uniting them even further is the manner of their departure from their powerful earthly lives; both were taken up by God, and neither tasted death, even after seeing the glory of YHWH.[145] But what they saw only in part, covered through the cleft of a rock, experienced only on the whisper on the wind, now they see in full and without danger or fear of exposure—the god of Israel in the flesh, with light resplendent on his human form. "Show me your Glory," Moses had asked of YHWH.[146] Peter didn't even have to ask. It took centuries and to heaven and back again for Moses to finally see that glory on earth unhindered; it only took Peter six days.

Zechariah's lampstand, an iconic projection of temple imagery into the redemptive future, mixes in and corresponds to Jesus on this mountain: "I see and behold, a lampstand, all of it gold. . . . And two olive trees over it, one on the right of the bowl, and one on its left."[147] This lampstand, reminiscent of the one designed for the original sanctuary, also with seven lamps, was designed not only to adorn beautifully as decoration but to produce light for sacred space.[148] Originally placed in proximity to cast its light on the tabernacle, each one fashioned with pure gold, both the lampstand and the tabernacle represent some aspect of the god of Israel.

A talisman of hope, the lampstand symbolizes home. Like finding the family seal in the toppled ruins of a generational estate or a precious heirloom, long ago ransacked and thought lost, discovered in the dusty back room of some antique market far away, thus is the significance of this lampstand in Zechariah's vision. Against all odds, through providence alone, what was lost has been found and put to its original designated use again.

"What are these two clusters of olive branches that empty into the [lampstand's] two golden pipes?"[149] Zechariah rightly wonders. The angel responds, "These are the two sons of the oil who are standing by the Lord *of the whole earth*."[150] Long before, in the original temple with all its various assigned duties, responsibility for care of the tabernacle and its items fell to the Levites. More particularly, it was the sons of Izhar (oil) who were specifically tasked with the lampstand—the sons of oil in charge of the oil. They were to keep its flame perpetually lit before the tabernacle of YHWH.

The sons of Korah, the ones swallowed by the earth because of their rebellion against Moses, Aaron, and God, were also sons of Izhar.[151] It was their longing for what they thought was a more elevated role, their desire to abandon the menial task of the lampstand, that instigated their grumbling and eventually caused their deaths. As such, it is not just Joshua, the high priest rebuilding the temple, who is cleansed and restored but the light-bringers, the sons of the oil (Izhar), the everyday ministers who take care of the seemingly ordinary tasks. They, too, will be reinstituted and minister to their god once again. It is not just the sacrifices, the elevated priestly duties, that make the spotlight and are considered essential that matter but the entirety of temple ministry. The sin of the past will no longer stain the future.

Jesus is both the high priest glowing in sparkling white and the god who cleanses those garments as well. He is the branch and the lampstand too. The legends of old, Moses and Elijah, both notably Levites as well,[152] stand before their god and pour their oil into him, conversing with him while he lights the world. Sacred space has expanded, no longer just illuminating the tabernacle, and Jesus the lampstand, the god of Israel, lights the mountain as he did in the days of old. The job that had been so menial, so odious to the sons of Korah, now becomes a point of honor as the two greats, representing the Law and the Prophets among other things, take on the task of the ministry of oil—their perpetual ministries fueling the lampstand, Jesus, restoring light not just to the temple but to the world.

Zechariah brings it all back around to Sukkot. A fall harvest festival from the beginning, Sukkot celebrates the relationship between the people and their land. The relationship is symbiotic, both a gift of YHWH to the other. As such, the tragedy of the Exile was not just about the people being in a foreign land away from home but about the homeland, empty of its people, suffering as well: "I flung them with whirlwind across all the nations which they did not know, and the land was desolate after them."[153]

Restoration from exile is not just simply escape from foreign lands but about bringing the people back to their land and is not just about being back in the land but being back Home:

> Thus says YHWH, I have returned to Zion, and will dwell in the midst of Jerusalem . . . and the mountain of YHWH of Hosts will be called Holy. . . . Thus says YHWH of Hosts, behold, I am saving my people from the land of the east and the land of the west. And they shall be my people and I shall be their god. . . . For there will be a seed of peace, and the vine shall give its fruit, and the land will give its produce, and the heavens will give their dew, and I will cause the remnant of this people to inherit all these things.
>
> Zech 8:3, 7–8, 12

Home is where one's god is present, dwelling with his people. Sukkot, then, is a festival about home. It recalls deliverance, the rescue out of slavery in Egypt, but then it settles into homeland, the promise to the ancestors and the place that their very own god has led them. Sukkot celebrates produce and harvest, yes, but it is about YHWH dwelling with, community, memory, thankfulness, and belonging. Those in exile far away could still celebrate Sukkot, recognizing that it is god and kin that make home, that the god of Israel is the god of the universe, and the whole earth and all its crops are his. But for true shalom, perfect completeness, home includes homeland, which means Jerusalem, Israel, Judah, and sovereignty. Peter and his countrymen are longing for sovereignty in their homeland.

So when Zechariah sees a vision of YHWH becoming king of the whole earth and a time when YHWH will be one and his name one just like the daily affirmation in the Sh'ma,[154] only now not just for Israel but for the entire world, it is no surprise that this unification of the nations under this one god would begin with Sukkot, in Jerusalem: "And all the remnant of all the nations who came against Jerusalem shall go up year after year to worship the king, YHWH of Hosts, and to celebrate the feast of Sukkot." Israel's god is drawing the whole world, all the nations, home to himself.[155]

Fearful or not, Peter is no fool. Six days after Yom Kippur with YHWH standing in his glory upon a mountain near Jerusalem, ready to dwell with the people from all the ages, can only mean Sukkot; Peter, too, has been waiting for end of the Exile. Peter understands Zechariah and can read the signs. Moreover, Peter is that leader, one of the ones Jesus relies on, taking stock of any situation and anticipating the need. "Rabbi," Peter says, "it is good for us to be here; let us make three booths, one for you, one for Moses, and one for Elijah."[156] For Peter, this is indeed good, their presence an inauguration of the Parousia. He imagines that this can in fact be the eschatological Sukkot.

Peter has seen the miraculous and knows who Jesus is. Perhaps Jesus' scandalizing suggestion of a cross, not just for himself but for all who would follow him, was just a test of devotion. Perhaps even yet, it will not come to pass. Moreover, if this is the moment that Zechariah is to be fulfilled and YHWH establishes his kingdom, then all the nations, Rome included, will come to pay homage to Jesus on the mountain in Jerusalem. The nations will in fact be subject to Israel and its messiah, its king. And as Jesus' right-hand man, Peter knows what needs to be done: booths. If this is Sukkot, booths must be built.

As if perfectly timed to respond to Peter's new momentum, the cloud descends, the same cloud that covered Sinai the first time Moses walked the earth. The Father in heaven is present and affirms Jesus the way he did at the baptism, only this time, everyone can hear. His voice rings out of the cloud addressing all present, most especially Peter: "This is *my son, the beloved*, listen to him."[157] And with that declaration, the Father in heaven makes clear for all present that Jesus is not without the fortitude needed for a messianic campaign, but that despite appearances, Jesus is doing heaven's will, and the Father has every confidence in him.

Among the Israelite patriarchs, Isaac was always the weak link. Abraham was called directly by YHWH to leave his father's house and go to the land that this god would show. YHWH had promised him land and progeny. Despite famine in the land and no sign of children,

Abraham believed YHWH when he reiterated the promise, and it was counted to him as righteousness. Jacob, too, though deceptive and shrewd, understood the worth of both blessing and birthright, and he took it all. Isaac, however, did very little. He was almost entirely unassertive.

Jacob fled Canaan, Esau's wrath, and went back to Haran. On the way there, he met the god of Israel and found the ladder leading up to the heavens. When he arrived in Haran, he met the love of his life. He worked for her in total fourteen years, never giving her up. On his way back home, full of all that he accomplished and acquired abroad, he met the god of Israel again, and this time prevailed against him with such vigor that this god cheated and dislocated Jacob's hip. Still, Jacob persevered and would not relent: "I will not let you go unless you bless me."[158] Years had only made him more fervent when it came to blessing. Jacob was aggressive, going after what he wanted, and striving not just with man but with YHWH to get it.

Isaac, however, was not a mover; he was moved upon. When god tested Abraham, Isaac seemed to be a passive participant.[159] Even in human affairs, Isaac was able to sit back and let things happen to him. His wife was chosen by his father's servant and brought to him.[160] Regarding his children, YHWH spoke to Rebekah, not to Isaac, telling her that the older would serve the younger.[161] Isaac was lied to, had the blessing he intended to give his favorite son, Esau, stolen by Jacob, Rebekah's favorite. His only response was to shake violently in shock and panic at the mishap.[162] So impotent were his effects that when Jacob hesitated at the plan to steal Esau's blessing, thinking he would bring upon himself a curse from his father rather than a blessing, Rebekah interfered, saying that Isaac's curse would land on her, not on him, deflecting Isaac's only mode of reciprocal paternal action.[163]

But the later rabbis, all too aware of the seeming patriarchal lethargy of Isaac, come to his rescue. When Ishmael, seeking to shame Isaac, highlights his own superiority as one who actively chose covenant obedience in contrast to Isaac, who once again came passively, Isaac responds with force. Ishmael derides him, saying, "I am greater than you in regard to the commandments, as you were circumcised at eight days and I at thirteen years," stressing that circumcision was inflicted upon Isaac as a baby and not willingly chosen. Isaac, however, is no pushover, and he will not be bested. Instead, he invokes heaven: "You taunt me with one organ, but if the Holy One, Blessed be he, were say to me, 'Sacrifice yourself before me,' I would sacrifice myself."[164] And Abraham's god hears Isaac. It is for this reason that Abraham was tested, not for his own sake but for Isaac's, to see if Isaac would indeed keep his word and give his life, shifting the mover and motivation in this story from Abraham to Isaac. Moreover, when Abraham sought to bind his son Isaac with the intent of taking his life, Isaac said to him, "I am concerned lest my body shake from fear of the knife . . . and it will not be considered a sacrifice for you. Rather tie me up very well."[165] Assuming Isaac to be a young man and not a child, and that the aging Abraham would be unable to restrain and sacrifice a fit Isaac against his will, it is clear then that Isaac was a voluntary participant, willing to give his life for his father and his god.

On this mountain of transfiguration, father and son are back. Isaac, far from being the weak link, is at the forefront. Overlaid with the other personas shimmering in and out of focus in the actions of Jesus, Isaac heads up the mountain. Isaac leads the other men. And once there, the father, YHWH in heaven, who once stopped the father Abraham, the father of nations, from sacrificing his son, now turns it all over to his son. Isaac is no longer passive; Isaac is in charge: "This is my son, the beloved, listen to him."[166]

Peter had hoped to bypass the suffering, to go straight to the eschatological Sukkot where all the nations would be subject to the god of Israel. But before that can happen, this Isaac offers himself to be the sacrifice that his Father of all the nations desires. He had just told them, before climbing the mountain, that the messiah must suffer, that they must take up their cross if they wish to follow; like Israel at Yom Kippur, the nation of priests, they will all participate in atonement. And here on this mountain, it all peaks and mixes: Moses and his glowing face, the cleansing of that other Jesus—Joshua in his filthy robes—the bright and shining lampstand that illuminates that place where the presence of their god dwells, the restoration of the temple and all its major and minor functions, the end of the Exile, and that final fulfillment of Sukkot involving all the nations. Everything hinges on this father and this son, the new Isaac. There will be no ram, no substitution this time. This father will sacrifice his beloved. This Isaac will die, just as John the Baptist pointed the way. And through his death, not simply through a war of the messiah, all the nations of the earth will come to the god of Israel, the Father of the nations. This is what Jesus brought Peter to see, the affirmation of heaven and the greats of earth, Moses and Elijah, all confirming for Peter that Jesus is not a weak link but has this well in hand.

And just as quickly as it began, the light shining through the kaleidoscope, refracting prism all over the mountain, simply turns off; the shining robes, the cloud, the voice from heaven, Moses and Elijah, all of it ceases, and what is left is the man Jesus, the one whom they know. The mountaintop experience is not a dream or a waking vision, it is the meeting of heaven and earth, heaven's will spoken clearly, "Listen to him." The memory of it will carry them through the nightmare that is coming. They will go down the mountain, carry on with ministry, until that moment that this Isaac, Jesus, dies—for all the nations and for their Father, their god. But just as Abraham knew that the promise of his god was binding—if Isaac truly died, this god would raise him up again—so, too, the same with this Isaac. This Isaac will die, and this Isaac, Jesus, will raise up again too.

The tradition informs at every step. The messiah is the anointed king and the anointed priest, both. But even more, Israel's king, from the beginning, was always to be YHWH, the god of Israel himself. YHWH, taking his rightful place as Israel's king, became Israel's messiah—the one to save them, recognizable through the replication of his past deeds.[167] But the cycle turns once again; one last time, the lords of Shechem will have their way, and one last time, they will turn to the bramble. Once more, there is a righteous one to suffer for their god, but this time, it is YHWH. YHWH, the tamer of the waters of chaos, the deliverer of Israel, will deliver not just Israel but the entire world from sin, suffering, darkness, and Satan. The kingdom of god has indeed come, and it has come to take dominion over this YHWH's kingdom on earth as well.[168]

CHAPTER 3

YHWH Repents

Redressing the Judgments of Old

That YHWH has a temper is no secret to those familiar with Israel's Scripture. There are fights of old that have caused tension between YHWH and YHWH's people, between the god of Israel and his wife. No longer. YHWH takes responsibility, owns the breach, and mends it all.

Sheep in the Wilderness

Manna in the wilderness. It should have been wedding bliss, but instead it became one of their earliest quarrels, one that never quite went away. Israel complained, and YHWH took offense. Moreover, when Moses passed away, the one like him, promised and hoped for, never came. The shepherds of Israel lacked, so much so that YHWH promised that he would come and shepherd the sheep himself. The promise remained unfulfilled, until now.

Mark 6:30–44

Hosea 2; Joshua 7–8; Numbers 11

John the Baptist stood at the Jordan proclaiming a baptism of repentance, and the god of Israel showed up. His participation puzzling. "God is not a man, that he should lie, or a human being, that he should repent (נחם) or change his mind . . . the splendor of Israel does not break faith . . . he is not a human to repent"—except that he is.[1] YHWH has come as a man of Israel and answered the Baptist's call. YHWH will say sorry for many things but begins with the flood.

Darkness covered the face of the deep before god spoke at creation. "Let there be light," and brightness illuminated the cosmos as this god set to work taming the chaotic waters.[2] The god of Israel established its boundaries, above, below, from land, securing space for all flesh—humankind, animals, creeping things, birds of the air. This god made the earth habitable to life, but disappointment soon followed: "YHWH saw that the evil of humans was great in the earth, and that every inclination of the thoughts of their heart was evil all the day. YHWH was sorry that he made humankind on the earth, it hurt his feelings to his heart."[3]

Regret. YHWH *repented* of making humankind.[4] Releasing the boundaries that held back the waters—a simple matter, almost too easy—all would be lifeless again: "I will wipe out the man who I have created from upon the face of the earth, from man to beast to creeping thing and the birds of the heavens, for I *regret* that I have made them." At YHWH's bidding, all the springs of the great deep split apart, the windows of the heavens were opened, and the rain fell on the earth for forty days and forty nights, destroying all except that which rode the waves upon Noah's boat.

"The waters were so very very strong over the earth, that all the high mountains which are under the heavens were covered. . . . All flesh died; YHWH wiped out every living thing." Yet, when it was all over, there was hint of a different regret. "Never again," YHWH said. "Never again will I curse the ground because of humankind, for the inclination of the human heart is evil from its youth and I will never again smite all life as I have just done."[5] It was the dove, sent out of Noah's boat, that flew back with tidings of good news—life, leaves that grew on trees, the first signs that the chaotic waters were tamed once again, boundaries back in place. Death and destruction passed, the world as a whole safe again.

Jesus plunges beneath the water, under the Baptist's hand, the same waters that consumed the unrighteous in Noah's day, the same chaotic tumult that drowned Egypt's charioteers. He doesn't command; he doesn't subdue; he doesn't tame. Jesus repents. He repents of YHWH's anger, YHWH's destruction, YHWH's temper. Jesus allows the waters to swallow him as they once swallowed Jonah, relinquishing himself to that which had long ago enacted YHWH's judgment.[6] A king of Israel keeping proper form, he submits to the prophet, who prepares the god of Israel to meet his people in the same way that he prepared the people to meet their god.[7]

Jesus rises from the Jordan, that same river that had split at YHWH's command thrice before, and his direction is clear.[8] He will make his way to the Galilee, the sea claimed by Jews and gentiles alike. The dove flies once again, this time swooping down from heaven with its good news. No longer rains of judgment, born from the broken heart of a regretful god, but rather life for death, repentance, the undoing of past destructions. At the Galilee, Jesus recruits fishermen, not theologians but mariners, experts on the water: "You will become fishers of humans."[9] Their expertise, honed for a new catch, will rescue the damned from the watery abyss—all the people that ever were. YHWH has come to make amends for his past doings.

Trained, taught, discipled, Jesus had sent out his twelve as ambassadors of YHWH's kingdom. They returned with elaborate tales, true stories, the excitement of miracles done through their own ordinary hands. Demons obeyed, sickness healed—confirming without doubt, YHWH's power flowed through them as well. But Jesus knows how such ministry wearies, and so he beckons, "*Come away,* to our particular *place in the wilderness,* and rest awhile."[10]

A century after Ahab, Jezebel, and Omri, Hosea personifies the god of Israel as husband married to the unfaithful wife.[11] Elijah's victory over the prophets of Baal was short-lived. Jezebel and Ahab disappeared, but the Baals did not. Amid the judgment and sadness, sin and failure, the prophet speaks words of hope. Israel's god has not abandoned her. YHWH will not let her go; rather, YHWH whispers affections for all to hear:

Therefore, behold, I am alluring her,
and I will bring her into the wilderness,
and speak over her heart.
From there I will give to her vineyards,
and make the *Valley of Achor* a door of hope.
There she shall respond as in the days of her youth,
as at the time when she came out of the land of Egypt.
Hos 2:14–15[12]

The words that Jesus has for his disciples are the words of a god for his people: "*Come away, to our wilderness place.*" The wilderness conjures memory of Israel and her god in the early days of their marriage, before the problems of everyday living crept in. Hosea, however, recalls that even at the beginning, not everything was wonderful. The Valley of Achor stands out as the place of old animosity. More than just a marital spat, Achor remained a deep rift, never quite resolved. Israel fails, and her husband's temper lashes out against her. Sin. Sin makes her vulnerable. Sin makes Israel fall before her enemies. Sin separates her from her god, and YHWH's anger from that sin causes her to wince.

The sacking of Jericho emerged iconic. It began with the spectacular parting of the Jordan, marking Israel's invasion of Canaan with glamour. News of this supernatural event caused the hearts of the people of Jericho to melt with fear. With the blast of the trumpets and the heavenly hosts on their side, the walls of Jericho fell, and Israel took the city. This first victory announced to all that the god of Israel was at war for his people once again. It proved a massive blow to the inhabitants of Canaan, striking terror throughout. If this could happen to Jericho, the rest have little hope.[13]

YHWH declared Jericho to be devoted to destruction (ḥerem). All of it to be destroyed—every item, every animal, every person. Nothing to be taken as spoils of war. This was understood by all Israel. But Achan broke faith, quietly, secretly, one man among all the people of Israel.[14]

Israel's confidence following the defeat of Jericho was contagious. Their god stood with them. They could not lose. The whole of Israel need not go to subdue the smaller town of Ai. Three thousand of Israel's men would be more than sufficient. But then something went wrong, dreadfully wrong. They failed to take the city and shamefully fled. Thirty-six men killed on the fields of battle, a small casualty, but for Israel, it was devastation. A reversal of Jericho, now Israel caught by fear: "The hearts of the people melted and turned to water."[15]

Nothing to explain such defeat. Their god was supposed to be with them. How could they possibly lose? To make matters worse, only silent treatment from YHWH. Joshua, the commander, along with the elders of Israel, tore their clothes, covered themselves in dust, fell on their faces on the ground before the ark of the LORD until evening, and they waited. They waited for YHWH to speak.[16]

But YHWH persisted in his silence. Finally, Joshua dared to initiate, "Alas, Lord YHWH, why did you bring this people to pass over the Jordan at all? . . . What do I say now that Israel has turned his back before his enemies?" After hours quiet, even the beginning of this speech was too much. "Stand up!" YHWH said to Joshua. "Why are you falling on your face? Israel has sinned. . . . They have taken from those things devoted for destruction; they have stolen, deceived, put among their equipment . . . and have become a thing devoted for destruction themselves."[17]

The items were found to be with Achan. *Two hundred* shekels of silver were among his spoils. He, his children, his livestock, and all his possessions were brought to the Valley of Achor, where they were stoned to death, burned with fire, and then heaped with stones—a monument forever. The lavishness of judgment, the heat of the LORD's temper, and the punctuation of a second stoning all stand out. The place, both in history and locale, lives in Israel's consciousness as an Event: the infamous Valley of Achor, where YHWH had to turn from his burning anger against Israel. Hosea, however, sees something new in the tragic event of the past; he envisions hope coming out of failure, a renewed relationship out of previous contention.[18]

It was exhaustion from relentless ministry, not an encounter with Satan, that drove Jesus and his disciples out into the wild this time: "For those *coming and going* were many, and *they had no opportunity even to eat*. And [Jesus and his disciples] went away on the boat *to a wilderness place* by themselves." But that crowd—so desperate: "Now many saw them going away and *recognized* (ἐπέγνωσαν) them, and they ran together there from all the towns and went ahead of them on foot."[19] "On that day . . . ," Hosea continues, "I betroth you for my wife in faithfulness; and you shall *recognize* (ἐπιγνώσῃ) *YHWH*."[20]

Their private spot compromised, thousands await their arrival. Despite the failed retreat, Jesus embraces the throngs rather than turn the boat around: "He saw a great crowd; and he had *pity* for them, because they were like *sheep without a shepherd*; and he began to teach them many things." YHWH had long ago promised, "I will *have pity* . . . and I will say . . . you are my people."[21] Moses, too, worried over Israel; what would happen to them when he was gone? "Let YHWH, the god of all the spirits of all flesh appoint someone over this congregation who will go out before them and come in before them . . . so that the congregation will not be *like a sheep without a shepherd*."[22]

Long years later, on the other side of conquest and kings, the prophet Micaiah would see Israel, scattered upon the mountains, *like sheep without a shepherd*.[23] Evil King Ahab would summon Israel to battle to take back Ramoth Gilead from Aram, forging forward defiantly, despite being warned of doom by the prophet. The battle would end in defeat and cost him his life. But regarding the warriors, YHWH said, "These do not have a lord. Let each man return to his house in peace."[24] As the monarchies declined and gentiles dominated, the sheep of Israel would scatter farther and farther, strewn across the nations. They would remain there until their god brought them home. Even then, they would yearn for a shepherd.

From the beginning of his ministry, Jesus set himself in contrast to the other shepherds of Israel. He dined with the tax collectors and sinners, reaching out to the lost, while the scribes and Pharisees criticized from afar. "Why does he eat with them?" they would chide.[25] "I have not come to call the righteous but sinners," Jesus replied to them. "Why do your disciples not fast?" the disciples of John and the Pharisees had asked him; they would refrain from food for piety's sake. Jesus and his disciples, however, would be so busy in ministry, healing, teaching, and casting out evil spirits, that although they basked in supernatural power, *they would not have time even to eat*, fasting by circumstance rather than religious observance.[26]

Ezekiel, too, had watched the neglect of the sheep with distaste; it was the same in his day. He looked ahead to hope:

> Thus says the Lord YHWH (אֲדֹנָי יְהוִה): Ah, shepherds of Israel *who have been feeding themselves!* Should the shepherds not be feeding the sheep?[3] You eat the fat, you wear the wool, you sacrifice the fatlings; but you do not feed the sheep.[4] The weak you have not strengthened, the sick you have not healed, the broken you have not bound up, the banished you have not returned, the lost you have not sought, but with force and ruthlessness you have followed them. Thus says the Lord YHWH, Behold, I am against the shepherds; and I will seek my sheep from their hand. . . . For thus says the Lord YHWH: Behold, I myself will search for my sheep, and will seek them.[12] As a shepherd seeks his flock in the day of his being in the midst of the scattering of his sheep, thus I will care for my sheep. I will deliver them from all the places where they were scattered on a day of clouds and thick darkness.[13] I will bring them out from the peoples and I will gather them from the lands, and will bring them into their own land.
>
> Ezek 34:2–4, 10–13

The shepherds of Israel have fallen short, and YHWH himself has taken over.[27] It was YHWH who scattered Israel in judgment, and yet now, as promised, he himself personally seeks them out. Jesus has come to find the lost. He has gone from village to village tending to them where they live, healing, offering hope, touching the unclean, and seeking those scattered.

"His disciples came to him saying, 'This place is deserted, and the hour already late; send them away in order that they might go into the surrounding country and villages and buy something for themselves something to eat.' But he answered them and said, 'You give them something to eat yourselves.'"[28] Themselves. Their very words rebound upon them with obligation. The exhausted disciples had come back to Jesus to regroup. It was their time together, in privacy, in fellowship—their turn to be cared for. The disciples themselves had had no time to eat. But Jesus is not like the other shepherds of Israel. He and his are not elites who live apart from the sheep. Unlike Ezekiel's shepherds, Jesus' shepherds will make sure the sheep are fed before they themselves eat. Jesus will make sure of it.

"Ἀπόλυσον (Apolouson)," the disciples implore. "Send them away—*Dismiss* them, *release* them, *divorce* them."[29] Hosea's god, the god of Israel, has not come to this place to put away his wayward wife, to dismiss or divorce her, but to take her back. Making amends for Achor, it is reconciliation that he seeks.

The disciples said to him, "Are we to go away and buy *two hundred denarii* worth of bread and give it to them to eat?"[30] Two hundred. Two hundred denarii. Two hundred shekels hiding under Achan's tent. Two hundred silver coins, separated by centuries. Those two hundred coins cost Achan and his family their lives. Those two hundred coins cost the children of Israel thirty-six men and the battle with Ai. Those two hundred coins have remained a point of contention between Israel and her god since the beginning. The god of Israel today fulfills Hosea. The Valley of Achor has indeed become a door of hope. The sting from that altercation is being undone, and it is not on Israel to fix it. It is her god; YHWH has allured her, and YHWH will now lavish blessing, not judgment, on her and make her forget the strife of old. Two hundred denarii worth of bread—for the god of Israel, this is nothing, but it is everything.

"And [Jesus] said to them, 'How many loaves do you have? Go and see.' And having discovered, they said, '*Five*, and *two fish*.' Then he ordered them all *to recline in parties on the green grass*. So *they sat down group by group by hundreds and by fifties*."[31] When Israel came out of Egypt and found themselves in the desolate nowhere, it was YHWH alone who provided for them. There was no produce of the land, not in the desert. It was YHWH who rained manna from the sky. This is the sweet side of the romance in the wilderness that Hosea remembers, when Israel was provided for by her god. Miracles that spoke of love, commitment, and covenant.

"A man came from Baal-shalishah, and he brought to the man of god bread from the first fruits, twenty loaves of barley and fresh ears of grain in his sack."[32] Elisha turned the occasion into a party, all the men in proximity invited. He used the gifts given to YHWH to feed the people. Neither Jesus nor Elisha caused bread to rain from heaven. The bread is the offering of the people, multiplied with mysterious subtlety, and given back to the people by the man of god. The mediators are in the know—the servant, the disciples, the ones in charge of logistics. They stand between undeniable lack and the man of god who confidently tells them that there will be enough to feed the crowd.

"How can I set this before a hundred people?" Elisha's servant boldly asks. Jesus' disciples similarly suggest, "Do you want us to take two hundred denarii to buy bread for these people?"[33] Whether its twenty loaves for one hundred men or five loaves for five thousand men, the problem remains the same: There is not enough food for this crowd. And yet, the man of god knows, there is not only enough, but there will be food left over.

Moses was overwhelmed and could not bear the weight of all the people himself. It was Jethro, his father-in-law, who suggested, "Set men over them as officers *over thousands, hundreds, fifties, and tens*. . . . It will be easier with you, and they will bear the burden with you."[34] The crowd here with Jesus are the children of Israel in the wilderness again, a distinctly Jewish crowd, and the disciples share his burden; they will take over when he is gone. Ezekiel remembers how it used to be and looks to the future for such again:

> And *I will feed them* on the mountains of Israel, by the streams, and in all the dwelling places of the land. *With good pasture I will feed them,* and on the mountain heights of Israel there will be pasture for them; *there they shall lie down in good grazing land*, and on rich pasture they will pasture on the mountains of Israel. *I myself will be the shepherd of my sheep, and I will make them lie down, says the Lord YHWH.* I will seek the lost, and I will bring back the strayed, and I will bind up the injured, and I will strengthen the weak, but the fat and the strong I will destroy. I will feed them with justice.[35]
>
> Ezek 34:13–16

Jesus is Ezekiel's shepherd, the god of Israel himself, YHWH, "who makes Israel lie down in *green pastures*, who leads Israel beside still waters, and restores their soul."[36] Even when Jairus' daughter walked through the valley of the shadow of death, Jesus was there. Herod, the "king," threw his fancy dinner and invited only the elite but ignored the poor, the hurt, the lost, the outcast.[37] In contrast to Herod's royal spread, Jesus drew all of them to a table in the wilderness. The true king and shepherd of Israel fed them in their favorite picnic spot of old and renewed his love for them there.[38]

The interaction between Herod and John spotlighted Jesus as the authentic king of Israel.

Hosea continues, making the claim even stronger: "The children of Israel will dwell for many days and there will be no king and there will be no prince . . . after they will return and *seek the Lord*, and *David their king*." Ezekiel similarly goes on to say, "And I will establish over them one shepherd, *my servant David*, and he will feed them and will be for them a shepherd. And I YHWH will be for them a god."[39] Jesus is one and the same, the god of Israel and the king from the line of David. YHWH has become a descendant of David, the messiah, and ushers in his own kingdom.[40]

The bread had already been raining from heaven. There was provision, water, nourishment in the desert, but it became rote and boring. Bread from heaven got old. "If only we had meat!" they said. "We remember *the fish*. . . . There is nothing but this manna to look at."[41]

The contagious murmuring of discontent spread. It is no wonder YHWH's anger burned, but it burned surprisingly hot. Moses himself was displeased, not just with the complaining of Israel but with the anger of YHWH. YHWH commanded Moses to tell the people, "YHWH will give you meat! You shall eat not only one day, or two days, or five days, or ten days, or twenty days, but for a whole month of days—until it comes out of your nostrils and becomes nauseating to you! Because you have rejected YHWH *who is in your midst*." YHWH's nostrils were inflamed with heat from his anger (וַיִּחַר־אַף) and thus would fill their nostrils with quail, though they had asked for fish. This event would strain the relationship throughout their days. While quail in the wilderness would forever after evoke provision in the midst of ungratefulness, it would also trigger a cringe to YHWH's overwhelming anger, even more so because the quail was plagued and killed many who ate it.[42]

Jesus reconciles not just over Achor but over a hot temper and plagued quail as well. The sheep with him in this wilderness have not rejected *YHWH in their midst*; they have hunted Jesus down, eager, desperate, running on foot just to be in his presence. They have clung to his every word, even in the desert. He collects the five loaves and uses them to provide bread in the wilderness for the children of Israel, divided into camps just like the earliest days. But the fish, the fish is something special.[43] The Israelites of old did not ask for *quail*, much less plagued quail; they longed *for fish*, from the only "home" they had ever known. The fish is a redo. The fish says, "Let's try again." The god of Israel stands in their special place in the wilderness, repenting for the past, offering them a token from memory, making up to them for the fights of old.

"Taking the five loaves and the two fish, [Jesus] *looked up to heaven*, and blessed and broke the loaves, and gave them to his disciples to set before the people; and he divided the two fish among them all."[44] Hosea had understood that heaven and earth would not only witness but participate in the reconciliation between Israel and her husband: "I will answer the heavens, and they shall answer the earth; and the earth shall answer the grain."[45]

"*And all ate and were filled*; and they took up *twelve* baskets full of fragments and fish. Those who had eaten the loaves numbered *five thousand men*"[46]—not people, not humans, not "men, women, and children," but men. *Twelve* baskets left over, one basket for each tribe. When the manna first fell, YHWH had told the Israelites, the only time where more than the day's needs could be collected would be for the Sabbath. Now there are twelve baskets, enough for much rest.

After the loss of the first battle with Ai and the tragedy with Achan, YHWH told Joshua to try again. This time Israel would take Ai just like they took Jericho, only the spoils and livestock would be theirs to keep. Joshua took *five thousand men* and set them in ambush. At the right moment, Joshua stretched out his sword toward Ai, and the men took the city and burned it with fire. Not a single person of Ai, man, woman, or child, was left alive; *twelve thousand people* were killed in the open wilderness outside the city.[47] *Five thousand* Israelite *men* took the city, *twelve* thousand people of Ai destroyed; *five thousand men* fed by Jesus in the wilderness, *twelve baskets of bread* left over.[48]

Hosea continues, "I will make for you a covenant on that day . . . I will abolish the bow, the sword, and war from the land; and I will make you lie down in safety."[49] Jesus, the god of Israel, the new Joshua, brings Israel out in the desert and feeds them. They need not take the land, nor does Jesus need Joshua's sword. There is no more war to be had. The fighting men need not take the city and destroy its inhabitants. Their overflow is no longer the dead bodies of gentiles collected on the field of battle but baskets of bread, manna, provided by their god, their commander, the messiah. Unlike Ahab's men, wandering and scattered, these men have a lord, YHWH, who once again commissions them to peace. It is a new mission, the mission for the future, not just reminiscence and reconciliation for the past.

Psalm 78 remembers Israel in the wilderness, recalling specifically the story of the plagued quail and Israel's failure to trust and appreciate their god. It is a warning not to be "like their fathers' generation, a stubborn and rebellious generation":[50]

> They tested god in their hearts by asking for food for their souls.
> They spoke against god saying, Is god able to *spread a table in the wilderness*?
> Therefore YHWH heard and was angry and fire kindled against Jacob and also anger rose against Israel.
> They did not believe in god and did not trust in his salvation.
> Yet he commanded the skies from above,
>   And the doors of heaven he opened;
> he rained down on them manna to eat,
>   and the grain of heaven he gave them.
> Man ate the bread of the mighty;
>   Food he sent them in abundance.
> He caused the east wind to journey in the heavens,
>   and he drove out by his power the south wind;
> he rained flesh upon them like dust,

like the sand of the seas winged birds;
he caused them fall within the midst of their camp,
all around their dwellings.
And they ate and were well filled,
for their craving he gave them. (Ps 78: 18–19, 21–29)

"They ate and were filled."[51] Almost a happy ending, except the psalm continues with death:

But they before they satisfied their craving,
while the food was still in their mouths,
the anger of god rose against them
and he killed the fat ones of them,
and laid low the young men of Israel. (Ps 78: 30–31)

The five thousand men in the wilderness with Jesus "*ate and were well filled.*" The old event of punishment and death now rewritten. Jesus has made amends, making a fairy-tale ending of the past tragedy. The former memory can be put away, a new one formed to replace it. This story ever after ends here, happily.

After the city of Ai was ambushed by Israel's five thousand men, and every last one of its inhabitants slaughtered in the wilderness just outside the city, Joshua burned Ai and made it a heap of ruins, just like with Achan. Then he hanged the king of Ai on a tree until evening, and at sunset, they took his body from the tree, threw it down at the entrance of the gate of the city, and raised over it a great heap of stones.[52] As Jesus' ministry continues, it is not some small-town gentile king who will die on a tree so that Israel can take the promised land. Jesus shepherds a much larger flock. He feeds Israel, sends the warriors home in peace, and later will take the place of that gentile enemy. Jesus is the one who will be hanged on a tree. He will be taken down by evening. He, too, will be sealed in death with stone. But as one greater than Elisha, his bones do not remain in his tomb, and in contrast to the king of Ai, his stone will not remain as a memorial. Instead, it is the lack of stone, the stone rolled away, that will remain in this new memory.[54]

"Come away to the wilderness, the place all our own," where YHWH repents for the harsh past, where the god of Israel makes offerings and wins hearts once again.[53] The Valley of Achor has indeed become a door of hope. But even still, there are more amends to make, other fights to fix. The golden calf episode at the foot of Sinai is another that stings in memory.

Help My Unbelief

Israel lacks faith—failing repeatedly, sure of abandonment, running after other gods and other leaders; it has been so since the beginning and in the most important moments. Despite the desire to be better, to trust YHWH and follow his ways, Israel and Judah simply seem unable. Rather than hide or deny, Israel owns their own failure and approaches their god, not with faith generic or faith in themselves but hope in YHWH to fix their lack of faith.

Mark 9:14–29

Exodus 32–34; 1 Kings 8–9; Joshua 10

The cloud of the divine had enveloped the top of that mountain where Jesus was transfigured, and the Father in heaven declared for the second time that Jesus was his son. Only this time, he allowed others to hear.[55]

It was because of Israel's sin that Moses climbed down from Mount Sinai, his visit with God cut short, mere days after sealing their covenant with YHWH. Satan incited them to idolatry, leading them to cast their eyes upon that calf of gold, the creation of their own hands, and worship it as their deliverer and their god.[56] Moses had begged YHWH to relent from his wrath, but when he saw up close with his own eyes what YHWH had already seen from the mountaintop—the dancing, the celebration, all in worship of another—his own nose flared from the anger of it. Still holding in his arms the tablets written by YHWH's own hand, Moses flung them down hard, breaking them at the foot of the mountain, a temporal reflection of the existential reality.

Both Moses' and YHWH's anger would abate, but it would not be without severe punishment. Moses took the golden calf they had made, burned it with fire, ground it to dust, scattered it on the water, and forced the Israelites to drink it.[57] Then standing at the entrance to the camp, he sounded a battle cry: "Who is on YHWH's side and on my side!" It was his immediate tribesmen, the Levites, his own family, who answered the call. At Moses' command, they went through the camp, slashing with their swords, and slaughtered three thousand of their own kinsmen, a culling. Through their bloodshed, they secured their identity, their vocation, their ordination. Forevermore, the Levites would be set apart for holy service to YHWH, service that began with blood.[58]

Once again, Moses trekked back up that mountain to YHWH, soliciting favor and forgiveness for the people, traces of the slaughter, no doubt, still on his sandals. Then YHWH *descended in a cloud*, proclaiming not only this god's name but character: "YHWH, YHWH, a god tender and merciful, slow to anger, and great lovingkindness and truth. Looking after lovingkindness for thousands. Lifting iniquity, offenses and sin, surely not leaving [the guilty] unpunished, [*visiting*] *the iniquity of the father upon the children* until the third and fourth [generation]."[59]

The cloud itself was a shroud of mystery. Both natural and supernatural, it was a locus of divine presence in the temporal, the transcendent in the immanent.[60] It was contradiction. Three thousand were slaughtered by their brothers to pacify the god in this cloud, and yet YHWH self-identified as merciful—a strange sort of clemency.

Many generations later, that same *cloud* would fill the house of YHWH that Solomon built. So thick, so potent, so other was its effect that when he dedicated the temple, the priests could not stand before it. The cloud of YHWH disrupted all of his own official worship and, for those moments, removed all human religious hierarchy. Solomon's prayer was long, patterned, and reminded this god of all god's responsibilities as a deity. But then he veered to the intimate, the particular, the vulnerable: "YHWH our god be with us . . . may he not leave us . . . but incline our hearts to him to walk in all his ways . . . so that all the peoples of the earth may know that YHWH is God and there is no other."[61]

Solomon seemed to know that Israel would need divine help keeping their commitment and that YHWH was always interested in the nations and what they thought about YHWH. When the celebrations were over and all the people were sent home happy from the occasion, YHWH responded back to Solomon in private, "I have heard your prayer, con secrated this house . . . but if you surely turn from following me, you or your children, then I will cut off Israel from the land, cast the house I have consecrated out of my sight, and Israel will become a joke and a taunt among the peoples."[62] There at the establishment of the temple cult, so long anticipated, YHWH offered Solomon very little assurance to assuage his fears. Mercy was once again not the last word of the divine; rather, judgment ended the day.[63]

The punishments all came to pass. Moreover, it was not necessary to wait on future generations for failure to occur; Solomon himself transgressed and fell away. It was his own heart he feared when he prayed help and mercy for them all. Israel did indeed become a taunt, their temple destroyed, and the people sent into exile from their homeland. And though they eventually returned and rebuilt their devastated temple, it was never the same.

But now the god of Israel dons his familiar cloak and enters temporal history once again. *The cloud* notably bypasses the new temple where piety and religious hierarchy abound.[64] It settles instead on the mountain, out in the wild, far beyond the railings, resting once again where the god of Israel once declared that he was full of lovingkindness, and it hovers now over Jesus, his son.

On this mountain, Moses would become a witness to divine paternity. It is not sinful Israel that he sees this time, fathers and sons with their iniquity and punishment being passed down for generations; it is YHWH, the Father in heaven, and Jesus, his Son. YHWH's words on Sinai bear themselves out here; this god does indeed lift iniquity and forgive sin. Last time, YHWH's temper flared, and three thousand Israelites died as Moses tried to appease this god's wrath. But YHWH allows sons to suffer for the actions of their fathers, even YHWH's own. As Jesus descends from this mountain, he bears the consequences of his father's past dealings. He will work out his father's relenting and live up to his name. In place of those three thousand Israelites, Jesus will die. Rather than the people being punished, they will be forgiven, healed, and saved by this merciful god who is slow to anger and abounding in lovingkindness. The scourge of the golden calf event will be done differently this time as the son makes amends for his father.[65]

The last vestiges of the mountaintop experience give way to earthly chaos as Jesus, Peter, James, and John step off the incline onto level ground. A crowd swarms the other disciples who had remained, just as the children of Israel had crowded around Aaron when Moses and Joshua disappeared on their mountain. The exchange between Aaron and the people had not gone well. Aaron was ill-equipped to lead. There was nothing he really had to do; vested with authority, like a familiar uncle watching the children, his only responsibility was to ensure they did not burn the house down. But he could not manage them. The disciples seem no more competent than Aaron. But unlike Moses, who is gone long enough for terrible trouble to ensue, Jesus returns in time to rescue the disciples from both the scribes and the crowd—and Satan, as well, as it seems that he showed up once again too.[66]

The animosity between Jesus and the scribes had begun immediately. His early teaching had astounded the crowds; the reputation that Jesus "taught as one with authority, and not like the scribes," only exasperated things. When news traveled that he was home in Capernaum, the scribes joined the crowds and were scandalized to see him playing god. "Son, your sins are forgiven" was an incantation that went too far, and yet miracle sprung forth from the blasphemy.[67]

When Jesus dined with tax collectors and sinners—the broken and downtrodden longing for acceptance—the scribes scrutinized his love, charity, and inclusion, counting his virtue as vice, his love as licentiousness. With similar inversion, they attributed his power over demons to demon possession, giving credit to Beelzebub and infernal fraternizations for YHWH's mighty power to exorcise. But Jesus pushed back. Teaching openly during the High Holy Days before heading up the mountain, he not only publicly identified himself as the Son of Man but he riled the masses, predicting that the chief priests and scribes would reject and even kill him, going as far as to say that YHWH would shame them for their rejection of him. No doubt this provoked the scribes once again, drawing them to the foot of this mountain.[68]

This motley mayhem—the crowds, the scribes, and the overwhelmed disciples—greets Jesus and the three on their descent, offering sober, earthly counterbalance to their heavenly experience. When the crowds see him returned, *they run to greet him, awestruck*. The Israelites did the same when Moses descended aglow from his mountain.[69] Jesus' words cut through the sea of chaos: "What are you debating about?" One would expect the answer to be some point of law or scriptural interpretation. But neither the scribes nor the disciples answer Jesus' question. It is a father, a simple, earthly father, and it is human need, not theological inquiry, that drives him: "Teacher, I brought you *my son*, he has a mute spirit."[70]

Fathers and sons. On the mountain of transfiguration, it was again fathers and sons, Abraham and Isaac, YHWH and Jesus. But YHWH has another son. Before Sinai, before the golden calf, YHWH sent Moses to Pharaoh, saying, "*Israel is my* firstborn *son*, let my son go that he may worship me." When Pharaoh refused time and again, requital was eventually an assault on the firstborn sons of Egypt, all of them, from the least to the greatest. If Pharaoh had left it alone, it would have ended there, with the god of Israel walking away. Only when Pharaoh pursued

Israel out into the wilderness did YHWH unleash the fullness of the "eye for an eye" response, drowning Egypt's sons, without any regard to birth order, in the very way Pharaoh had drowned his.[71]

When Moses initially resisted the god of Israel, saying he was slow of speech and slow of tongue, YHWH retorted, "Who sets the mouth to man; or who makes *mute* or deaf, seeing or blind. Is it not I, YHWH?"[72] YHWH claims ownership of these things; they are in YHWH's domain; they do not, should not, fall under the purview of Satan. Yet here is a father and son, oppressed not by Egypt, and not even acutely by Rome, but by Satan. It is otherworldly evil, a demon, that oppresses and makes this son mute. It is for this reason that the kingdom of god has come, to liberate YHWH's son from the oppressor, just like in the past. But the lines are drawn differently this time. The god of Israel doesn't simply take sides in human disputes. YHWH has come to side with all of humanity, against the evil that oppresses them all.

"And whenever it takes him, *it throws him down* and *he foams, gnashes his teeth, and becomes dried-up rigid*."[73] The argument between Job and his friends continues. "The wicked *writhe* in pain,"[74] says Eliphaz, deducing Job's sinfulness from his suffering state. "They are marked for the sword . . . because they stretched out their hand against god, and were strong against the almighty, running stubbornly against him."[75] The taste is familiar even with the generic claims, the rebellion in mind akin to the golden calf and the Levites' slaughter. There is a certain audacity to Eliphaz' speech as he considers Job's terrible anguish and leans to accuse rather than comfort. But history and tradition are on his side, and it is safer than the alternative. Job, who desires death over his tortured life, has almost nothing left to lose. He dares what Eliphaz will not—to blame YHWH and not his own sin for his torment: "Surely now, he has made me weary . . . and *dried me up* . . . his wrath has torn me . . . he has *gnashed his teeth* at me."[76]

The beginning of Job's story, though, makes clear that like the boy before Jesus, it is Satan that immediately afflicts him. Satan *made him weary, dried him up, and gnashed his teeth at him.* But in the end, Job spoke what was right about YHWH, unlike his friends. Job was right that YHWH was both ultimately responsible, having given Satan both power and permission to afflict him. YHWH did indeed let the righteous suffer, not for his own sin but for YHWH.[77] With the boy, however, the mute spirit oppresses without permission. Evil is off its leash.

"I asked your disciples to cast it out, but they could not do so." They had cast out demons before, even in Jesus' absence, but this one was different. It would not comply, and the disciples couldn't make it. They were powerful, but it had strength to resist. Later, when all the excitement died, in private, Jesus would explain to them that this type only comes out through prayer. Gehazi, Elisha's servant, had found similarly he was not able to do what Elisha could do. Even with Elisha's staff, Elisha's explicit instructions, and the authority and experience to act in his stead, the Shunammite's son did not respond to Gehazi. It was Elisha himself who wielded power. It was Elisha's prayer, his breath, his flesh on the boy's flesh, that brought about seven sneezes and his restoration. It was Elisha and this mother, no intermediary, just like Jesus and this father.[78]

"*You faithless generation. How long* will I be with you? *How long will I bear you?*" Jesus' frustration is with them all. Ten plagues, the exodus out of Egypt, and the promise of finally settling into the land promised to their forefathers. Israel had watched miracle after miracle, and seen their enemies drowned in the sea, warfare that YHWH fought on their behalf. And now YHWH wants them to fight with him. The spies had been sent in to scope out the land, and after forty days, they brought a bad report: "The land is indeed flowing with milk and honey, and fruit grows, but the people are strong, the cities fortified, and we saw the giants." It was Caleb and Joshua who stood their ground and compelled the people back to rationality when they threatened to appoint a captain and take their families back to Egypt. And as if the squabbling on the ground was not enough, escalating this giant family fight to epic proportions was the weigh-in of the divine. "*How long*," YHWH would cry out over the din of the crowd, "will they refuse to believe in me, *despite all the signs I have done in their midst?*" Miracle after miracle, and Jesus now asks the same.[79]

The memory of Israel in the wilderness figures into Moses' last speech as well: "[YHWH] found him in a desert land, in the formless howling wilderness. He circled him and considered him and guarded him the center of his eye . . . YHWH alone guided him and there was not with him a foreign god . . . but [Israel] abandoned the god who made him . . . YHWH saw and despised, because of anger, his sons and daughters. He said . . . *They are a perverse generation, children with no faithfulness in them.*"[80]

The time in the wilderness was iconic and definitional—Israel, both son and wife, with their god being both loving and frustrated, merciful and harsh, father and husband. The memory of YHWH's protection and provision through miraculous wonders constantly paired with Israel's inability to believe that the past would have any bearing on the future. They did not believe that YHWH's care of them was reliable, something they could count on and trust, not just a fluke, the passing whim of a fickle god. As such, over and over they insult the character of their god. YHWH's faithfulness so often met with Israel's unfaithfulness that the tradition harbors laments for the past with constant warnings and prescriptions to do better in the future. Yet, despite their many efforts, Israel always seems to doubt. The words of YHWH on the lips of Jesus suggest nothing has changed for them. And yet something is different. The god of Israel walks in their midst again, and though temper flares, this time YHWH does not destroy; rather, YHWH heals, the present and the past.

"They brought [the boy] to [Jesus]. And seeing [Jesus], the spirit immediately threw [the boy] into *convulsions*. And falling upon the ground, *he rolled around foaming*. And [Jesus] asked his father, 'How long has he been like this?' 'From *childhood*,' he replied."[81]

Hosea weighs in again, speaking for the god of Israel, recalling a long pattern of idolatrous indiscretions going back *to childhood*: "When Israel *was a lad*, I loved him, and out of Egypt I called *my son* . . . but they kept offering incense to idols."[82] The tradition had always mocked idolatry. The idols were deaf; the work of human hands, they certainly did not make man, spread the skies, or hear prayers.[83] Moreover, people became like their gods. Those who worshipped the god of Israel became holy like their god, and those who worshipped idols became like them: "They went after empty breath, and became empty breath."[84] "What use is an idol," Habakkuk would say, "for the one forming trusts in what he has formed, the product is a *mute* idol."[85] In that last speech to Israel, Moses recalled, "They made him jealous with strange gods, with abominations they made him angry. They sacrificed to demons and not YHWH."[86] The boy, *writhing* and thrashing on the ground before Jesus, is Israel, *mute* and oppressed, under the dominion of Satan, possessed by a *demon*.

The boy's father continues: "[The spirit] has often *cast him into the fire and into the water* to destroy him." Moses had taken that calf of gold and *cast it into the fire, destroying it*, and then he ground it to dust and scattered it *into the water*. The demons that Israel had worshipped, the idol of temptation prompted by Satan himself, were rendered immediately impotent by Moses' flaming anger.[87] In the midst of Isaiah's idol parodies, God had promised, "Do not fear. I have redeemed you, I have called you by your name. When you pass through the *midst of the waters*, I will be with you . . . and when you walk *through the flame*, you will not be burned; the flame will not burn you, for I am YHWH your god."[88] But now this spirit takes revenge, mocking this history and these promises, until the god that made them shows up. With this lad, thrashing about under evil oppression, Jesus fulfills Isaiah's promise made so long ago, making powerless the evil that thwarted his disciples but, even more than that, rescuing those who have been oppressed by Satan rather than adding to their suffering and punishment.

"'If you are able to do anything,' the father said, '*help us, have compassion upon us.*'" It was no time before the covenant that the Gibeonites made with Joshua, and Israel was tested.[89] These Canaanites had wound a tale of deception and caught Israel unaware, tricking them into a relationship that violated YHWH's mandate. The Gibeonites were condemned to servanthood, water carriers before YHWH, but they had saved their very lives, which had been destined for destruction. YHWH had watched silently while all this happened, allowing inhabitants of the land, gentiles, to be saved, even though it was YHWH's own directive that had condemned them to death. Perhaps he was looking for reasons, for opportunities to save, to have compassion.

Five kings from the surrounding Canaanite peoples encamped against Gibeon in response to their covenant with Israel. They gathered their armies and prepared to make war. Desperate, the men of Gibeon sent urgent word to Joshua (Ἰησοῦς), "Come up quickly, *save us and help us.*"[90] Joshua and the men of Israel, men of valor, set out immediately to rescue Gibeon at YHWH's command. Had Israel not marched through the night, by morning the Gibeonites would have been slain. Their deaths might have seemed like the providential answer to the hasty covenant that Israel had ignorantly made with the people of the land, people who would no doubt draw them into idolatry, a correction putting Israel back on track with YHWH's initial directive. But YHWH did not abandon the Gibeonites; rather, he saved them. There was no going back, only forward; YHWH intervened and promised Israel victory to go to their aid.

The god of Israel caused a panic among those encamped against Gibeon, and Israel dealt them a great blow. As they fled, YHWH hurled down upon them great stones from heaven such that more died from the stones than the sword of Israel. Moreover, Joshua commanded the sun and moon to stand still in the sky so that a whole extra day was given to Israel to continue the battle to its triumphant end. Time stood still, a miracle unmatched in the history of Israel, performed to save gentiles.

YHWH fought for Israel, who fought for Gibeon. Mighty miracles came to these gentiles by virtue of their association with Israel; friends of Israel are friends of YHWH.[91]

"Jesus responded to him, 'If you are able! All things are possible to the one believing.' Immediately, the father of the child cried out said, 'I believe, help my unbelief!'" Aaron, too, had told Moses, "Let not the anger of my lord be harsh. You know the people are righteous, but the evil inclination has led them astray."[92] "They believe," Aaron implores Moses, "until they don't believe."

After all this time, Israel still doesn't have faith, and their god, once again in their midst, is still frustrated over it. From the fiasco of the golden calf, to the failure to trust and take the land, through the ages to the present, Israel does not trust their god. They fail in faith more often than not. Yet this father, this desperate spokesman of Israel, does not flinch from his inadequacy but comes face to face before the god of Israel, owning the real problem of the ages: "My faith, do something about my faith." Everything else, the healings, the repentance, body and soul being made right, comes from trusting in YHWH. And this father, like Solomon, knows his lack—he is unable in himself to have faith, and because of it, just as YHWH explained on Sinai, his child suffers.[93] "Jesus, seeing that a crowd was gathering together rapidly, rebuked the unclean spirit saying to it, 'Mute and deaf spirit, I command you, come out of him and do not enter him again.' And crying out and throwing him into convulsions terribly, it came out. And [the boy] became like a corpse. So that many said 'He is dead.' But Jesus *grasping him by his hand* lifted him and he stood."[94]

It is not just a mockery of the idols, their nothingness, their bondage and evil, but the contrast. The god of Israel is life compared to their death, animation to their hollow, dawn to their dusk, the refreshing wind that blows away their stagnant air: "Thus says god, YHWH, the one creating the heavens and stretching them out, who spread out the earth and its offspring, giving breath to the people upon it, and spirit to those walking upon it. I am YHWH who has called you in righteousness, and *I grasp you by your hand* and keep you. I give you *a covenant for people as a light for nations* . . . . I am YHWH, it is my name, and I do not give my glory to another nor my praise to idols."[95]

The boy and his father are Israel before her god.[96] Despite all the past failure to trust in YHWH and YHWH alone, they are still his. Three thousand died at the foot of Sinai, but though appearing to be dead, this boy will not be counted among them—things are different this time. Jesus, YHWH, grasps Israel, this boy's hand, and saves him from both Satan and death. But it is not just about reconciliation between YHWH and Israel, the faithful and the faithless, a do-over of the golden calf episode. Salvation of Israel, this boy's life and his father's faith, is also about saving the world—like the Gibeonites, who would be destroyed save their association with Israel. Solomon in all of his wisdom knew this, that Israel could not keep faith without their god's help and that it was tied to the rest of the world. Israel in covenant was always to be a light to the nations, drawing them all into YHWH's salvation as well.

On those mountains, YHWH proclaimed his name as Mercy and then introduced his son. Jesus will suffer both to rescue YHWH's other son, Israel, and to save the world, proclaiming YHWH's name as true. YHWH takes responsibility and makes amends—for Israel's faithlessness and his own past anger over it.[97] But just as there is a shift in divine policy, so there is a shift in the temporal establishment. There will be no more sword-wielding Levites, those who zealously ferret out sin and slaughter those guilty of it. Jesus has already told his disciples, and any who would follow him, that they would have to take up their cross in place of their swords.

Beware of the Leaven

The ramifications of YHWH's temper, especially in light of the Exile, impacted certain shepherds of Israel with an overzealousness, resulting in a departure from law rather than the upholding of it. Despite YHWH's intention that law was for humans and not humans for law, the shepherds went to extremes. YHWH not only repents of his own temper but also reschools the shepherds of Israel regarding piety and grace.

Mark 8:14–21

1 Samuel 21–22; Deuteronomy 15:7–11; Leviticus 7:12, 23:27

The posture of Ezra and Nehemiah had set the tone for those particular religious leaders who would follow with similar rigidity in Jesus' day. It was no surprise that they would tiptoe around the deity known for reacting with temper, having just returned to their homeland after nearly a century of punishment in exile.[98] Anxiety reigned. While the prophets interspersed mercy and grace with judgment, for some, caution dominated. It seemed that any infraction could frustrate the tenuous generosity of their god, and the favor of restoration and return would once again give way to punishment. Reflection and regret fueled rigor—a strict adherence to the letter of laws.

Strife with certain Pharisees and scribes had long been building. Their perception of Jesus' seeming disregard for the law combined with his lack of deference to them provoked. They were scandalized.

But their disquiet is part of his aim. Jesus came to do more than just repent for YHWH and his occasions of temper. He has come to transform the religious hierarchy that evolved as a reaction to it—those who walk on eggshells and teach others to do the same out of genuine holy fear, as well as those who have used the reputation of YHWH's untamed harshness as an excuse to dominate and control the sheep, thus securing power.

It was just after another miraculous feeding of thousands in the barren wild, this one resulting in seven baskets brimming with leftover bread. Lavish overflow. Even one of those baskets would have been enough to sustain them on their subsequent journey. Perhaps the chaos, perhaps charity, whatever the reason, "they forgot to take bread, except for *one loaf*, they did not have any with them on the boat."[99] The occasion provides metaphor. "*Watch*," Jesus says. "Beware of the leaven of the Pharisees, and the leaven of Herod."[100] The disciples, however, retreat to the literal, missing his allusive pun. They imagine Jesus to be fixated on their mishap, agitated over their forgetfulness, as if the one who provided bread for thousands could ever be wanting for provision. But it is not the lack of bread that has drawn Jesus' ire. It is the hostility and hard heart of the religious leaders that risk being a possible contagion to the disciples. Despite miracle after miracle, they still demand yet another sign, and the god of Israel has a history of temper when tested in the wilderness.

The tension had begun early in the ministry: "It was a Sabbath, and Jesus was going through the grainfields, and his disciples began to make their way plucking the heads of grain." The Pharisees had been observing, noting, paying attention. "*Watch* (ἴδε/ὁράω)," they said regarding the disciples. "Why do they do on the Sabbath that which is not lawful?" Jesus pulls a story from the tradition: "Have you never read what David did when he had need and was hungry, and those with him? How they went into the house of god, Abiathar was high priest, and he ate the bread of the presence, which is not permitted to eat except for priests, and he gave also to those with him."[101] And so old tensions inform the new.

It was a dark time in Israel. Hope had been diminishing; they had never quite taken the land promised to them by YHWH. Israel had grown tired of the tribal skirmishes, the petty and not-so-petty assaults against them by outsiders, the appalling lack of leadership during the time of the judges. They had begged Samuel, their judge and prophet, for a king. They wanted to stand on the international scene like the other nations around them.[102] Both Samuel and YHWH disapproved, feeling it a slap of rejection. Yet the people's request prevailed. Saul the Benjamite was chosen by YHWH and anointed by Samuel.[103] Standing a head and shoulders above the rest, Saul looked every bit like a king.[104] But Saul's prominence was short-lived.

The baton of Joshua fell to Saul—the mandate to finish the conquest of Canaan, including the annihilation of the people in each city and village that Israel took—but Saul was no Joshua. Disobeying both god and prophet, Saul was insubordinate in his task to completely destroy the Amalekites and all their possessions. Instead, he devoted to destruction all the people, but he spared Agag the king and the best of the sheep, oxen, calves, and lambs. Adding insult to injury, he hid, just as he had conspicuously among the luggage when initially chosen, a child covering his own eyes and thinking himself invisible. He blamed the "sparing of the best" on his people, claiming it was for sacrifice. Ego masked by religiosity, prompting Samuel's words, "Does Yhwh delight in burnt offerings and sacrifices as in obeying the voice of Yhwh? Behold, to obey is better than sacrifice."[105] Through this failed campaign, Saul's false piety and weak leadership were exposed.

This grave error in judgment cost Saul the kingship. It wasn't just his future line that was denied, but the kingdom was ripped from him in an instant. His successor, the young David, was anointed king in his stead, even before Saul's death.[106] David entered into Saul's service, and for a while, all was well. But soon the situation became tense and created uncomfortable conflict. Saul, still alive, was not going to relinquish the kingship to David, and as his emotional stability devolved, Saul became paranoid and threatened. David had long served Saul as a warrior, but his charisma, popularity, and ambition became untenable. Saul, thinking that David would act to take the kingdom, began to aggressively hunt him down as a threat to the monarchy and his own personal being.

For all his later faults, though, David was no fool. What protection would he himself have if he set the precedent before all that the new "favorite," the new chosen, could cut down the old one?[107] David instead fled from Saul, from the sin crouching at his door, from assassination and insurrection. Finding himself and his men out in the wilderness and out of provisions, it seems that someone then *forgot to bring bread* too. David came to Nob, to Ahimelech the priest, claiming to be on a secret mission from Saul. "Give me five loaves of bread, or whatever is to be found," David said. "There is no common bread . . . but there is holy bread," and so Ahimelech gave them holy bread, the bread of the Presence, *bread with no leaven in it.*[108]

This is the story Jesus invokes to defend his disciples against the Pharisees' accusation. "The Sabbath was made for humankind," Jesus punctuates, "not humankind for the Sabbath."[109] The memory of God's creation swirls into focus. Humankind, the pinnacle, made on the sixth day in the image of God, was empowered to rule and have dominion and then rest.[110] The Sabbath safeguards that rest.[111] It completes and buffers the week. It is shalom. The Sabbath was about ceasing from work for humankind's sake, not simply for rest's sake. The Sabbath, then, is not a god in itself, nor an arbitrary line not to be crossed—a day to be honored more than the humans for whom it was created. Humankind came before the Sabbath.[112]

David and his companions were not the only ones at the house of YHWH in Nob that day. Doeg the Edomite, the chief of Saul's shepherds, was there as well, and he was paying attention. He returned to his master and served as informant, prompting Saul to summon the priests from Nob and accuse them of treachery against the crown. Despite the protests and rightful claims of loyalty from Ahimelech, the ranking priest, Saul ordered not only his death but also that of all his father's house as well. The servants of Saul, however, Israelites with a fear of YHWH, would not raise their hands against his priests. So, rather, Saul commanded the foreigner, Doeg the Edomite, the informant, to strike down the priests. With the hand of this gentile, Saul, the rejected king, killed with efficiency not only the eighty-five men who wore the linen ephod of the priesthood but every man, woman, child, infant, ox, donkey, and sheep in Nob. Only Abiathar escaped. Saul wiped out his own kinsmen, the priests of Nob and all their families, with more vigor than he did the Amalekites at the commandment of YHWH, his treachery fueled by his selfish and vengeful obsession to destroy David.[113]

Another Sabbath, another altercation. A man in the synagogue suffering with a withered hand. Once again, like Doeg, the Pharisees are watching. They do not wonder at Jesus' power to heal; they know he can. They wonder if he will—if he will "transgress" the Sabbath to restore this man. "Is it lawful," Jesus asks them directly, "to do good or *to do evil* on the Sabbath, to save a soul, or kill it?"[114] Deuteronomy weighs in, having overheard their inner thoughts:

> If there is a needy one among you, one of your brothers, among any of your towns, in your land which YHWH your god is giving you, you will not *harden your heart* or shut your hand from your needy brother. For you shall surely *open your hand* to him and surely lend to him enough for his need, whatever there is lacking to him. *Watch* (הִשָּׁמֶר)! Lest there be a worthless word in your heart saying, "The seventh year, the year of remission, is near," and your eye *does evil* on your needy brother, and *you do not give to him*, and he cries concerning you to YHWH, and sin will be with you. . . . For there will not cease to be needy ones among the land and so I command you saying, "You will surely *open wide your hand* to the needy and the afflicted in your land."[115]
>
> Deut 15:7–9, 11

Healing on the Sabbath. These Pharisees would prefer that Jesus not heal on the Sabbath. They seem to consider the calendar, the week, and think, "One more day. What's one more day? The afflicted man can wait one more day; 'the time of remission,' is close." And as this unworthy thought takes hold of them, their *hearts are hardened*. In their effort to keep the letter of the law, they sin against their neighbor and, thus, their god.[116] "Open wide your hand," Deuteronomy says, noting that to keep it closed is to *do evil*. But these Pharisees keep their hands closed. Though Jesus has what this needy one among them needs, a miracle, they would rather him withhold; they would rather him close his hand too.

Jesus heals despite them, grieved at their *hardness of heart*. These leaders of Israel should be known by their open hands rather than their clean tight fists, which give them repute.[117] Yet it is the needy one, the man with the withered hand, who opens wide his hand—made whole by the god of Israel himself, who, too, opened wide his hand as he healed on the Sabbath. And like Doeg the Edomite, who long before informed and then conspired with Saul the declining king to murder the innocent, these Pharisees too run and inform Herod "the king."[118] They conspire with the Herodians to destroy Jesus.[119]

The Herodians had their own unique brand of leaven to avoid. More political than religious, the dynasty of Herod ruled Palestine under Rome, as "kings" at the turn of the century. Herod the Great (37–4 BCE) at least held the title, while his son Herod (Antipas) the Tetrarch (4 BCE–39 CE) never officially did. Herod the Great kept the Jewish dietary laws of kashrut but was famous for killing off rivals to the throne. Their religious devotion fooled no one as even the gentiles mocked. Emperor Augustus was famously rumored to have played the pun that he would rather be Herod's pig (ὑς) than his son (ὑιος).[120] Similarly, Herod the Tetrarch seemed to genuinely enjoy conversing with John the Baptist but was easily manipulated and had him beheaded by the shrewd opportunism of his wife. Jesus' warning suggests that the Pharisees, too, will get their way with Herod. It will not be hard, especially if they whisper suggestions that the "Lord of the Sabbath," who compares himself to King David, might be a threat to the throne.

The Herods were pious, if not for their own sake, then for the support of the populace. Between their pedigree and their affiliation with Rome, the Herods needed all the positive perception and popular good will that they could muster. The Herods were converts to Judaism going back to the time of Herod the Great's father, Antipater. Antipater was an Idumaean, the Roman name for an Edomite. The parallel rich with ease. As Saul needed the hand of the Edomite to kill those his men would not, so the Pharisees need the hand and the political power of the

Edomite to kill as well.[121] As Saul murdered his kinfolk with the hand of the Edomite, so, too, will these Pharisees follow suit.

"*Watch*!" Jesus tells the disciples, the same command the Pharisees voiced to accuse the disciples eating grain, the same warning that Deuteronomy gives regarding hearts. "*Watch*, for the leaven of the Pharisees, and the leaven of Herod." Leaven. Leaven is complicated.[122] Leaven in itself is not forbidden. Israel was allowed to use leaven in their bread. In fact, worshippers were encouraged to bring leaven before YHWH in their thanksgiving offerings and their first fruit offerings, the full and fluffy loaves raised up before their god, acknowledging YHWH's provision and blessing.[123] Leaven, however, is not permitted to be burned on the altar, not a smidgen, ever. It is forbidden at Passover as Israel remembers deliverance from Egypt and bondage, and it is forbidden from the grain offering that smokes and burns before YHWH as it is completely consumed by fire.[124]

Thanksgiving. Praise. Leaven before the god of Israel is gratitude for grace. Not demanded or obligatory. Not a poor person's offering as the poor have nothing extra. Leaven acknowledges the special moments of YHWH's particular care—the lightness of heart reflected in buoyancy of the bread. A trip embarked upon with a safe return. An illness recovered from. Redemption from the pit and being crowned with love and compassion.[125] The over and above, given for the over and above.

Leaven rises above the formulaic. Leaven a celebration. Leaven makes levity, but prescribed levity falls flat. These Pharisees have attempted to make the "over and above" the norm in all things. Piety has been ratcheted up. They thought it was better for one to go hungry rather than to "violate" sacred time. They thought it was preferable for one to remain afflicted rather than impose upon the holy day of rest. They safeguarded the Sabbath to such a degree that they denied the Sabbath itself the ability to participate in goodness, healing, and restoration. Instead, they bound and constricted it with an overzealous adherence to misunderstood law.[126] And here, Jesus targets their leaven, the clear sign of the thanksgiving and first fruits offering, indicative of these "over and above" offerings and consistent with these Pharisees' "over and above" practice, a vice, only because they ruined its virtue.

The leavened bread of the offering must be treated carefully, guarded, lest it contaminate the grain offering, one of the options for prescribed worship. A portion of this grain offering would be burned on the altar, turned into smoke to rise before YHWH. If leaven were to brush against the grain offering, it would not only nullify the offering, but it would defile, violating the prohibition against leaven being burned on the altar. One loaf is what makes a grain offering, one unleavened loaf. Only one loaf in the boat with Jesus and his disciples and a warning over leaven. Beware.

The leaven of the Pharisees, their "over and above," has not been contained. Its overuse, its systemization, is no longer about thankfulness. It lost its joy and, thus, its very purpose. Their rigid piety has not achieved what they desired; instead, it has contaminated their everyday living before their god and neighbor.

For the disciples, it all comes down to the bread. They had seen Jesus like a ghost, walking on the surface of the sea, come to rescue them from hostile waters. But they were confused, and not grateful or encouraged, because they didn't *understand* (συνῆκαν) about the loaves; instead, their *hearts were hardened*. "Why are you discussing that you have no bread?" Jesus probes. "You have the one who multiplies bread," he implies. "*Still* do you not perceive? *Still* do you not understand? Do you have *your* hearts hardened? Having eyes do *you* not see? And having ears, do *you* not hear?"[127]

Behind the scenes, watching the details of the miracle manifest in real time, the disciples had seen Jesus feed the crowd of Jewish men in the wilderness with their own eyes, yet they didn't understand what it meant. Now again, after seeing a second feeding close up, they still don't understand.

"Do you not remember?"[128] The intimacy of the question alone should melt their hardening hearts. "You were there with me, you saw,"

Jesus' question implies. But the question does more; it once again invokes the past, the tradition that informs. This is what the thanksgiving offering was about, remembering who YHWH is and what he has done. This is what unleavened bread at the Passover was about, *remembering* that children of Israel were slaves in Egypt and that their god delivered them.[129] This is how the commandment regarding the seventh day begins, "*Remember.*" "*Remember* the Sabbath and keep it holy."[130] "Remember," lest you forget.

The god of Israel remembers too. YHWH remembered Noah and all the living creatures and beasts that were with him on the ark. YHWH remembers his promise never to flood the earth again every time he sees the rainbow in the sky. YHWH remembered Abraham and thus spared his nephew Lot from the destruction of Sodom. YHWH remembered Rachel and Hannah, brokenhearted, barren women, and gave them children. YHWH remembered his covenant with Abraham, Isaac, and Jacob when hearing the groaning of the children of Israel enslaved in Egypt. YHWH remembered to soften his own heart, plunge into the Jordan, and repent.[131]

And now the god of Israel remembers the fights of old, Achor, Achan, quail in the wilderness, bloodshed at Sinai, and he walks them back. YHWH has come, in person, to make amends, to live out his name—to have mercy and save. Moreover, Jesus has undertaken to reform the shepherds, that they, too, would remember YHWH's grace, YHWH's lovingkindness, YHWH's compassion, and lean into that rather than his moments of anger.

CHAPTER 4

Yhwh, God of Israel

Ministry to the Gentiles

The gentiles are not the enemy. Over time, evil and the humans who got mixed up with evil became conflated—all to be destroyed. Part of the surprising work of the messiah is the decoupling of the two. Evil is the enemy—evil that has afflicted Jew and gentile alike. The gentiles no longer a casualty of the war with evil, rather, they, too, are to be saved.

A Different Plane of Battle

Through the centuries, as the different gentile oppressors took their turns dominating Israel, the battle lines were drawn. The expectation of the messiah was clear—he would rescue Israel from oppression, turning the tables to dominate the gentiles. The messiah would lead Israel into battle against the nations, and Israel would win. The mission of this messiah, though, is different than expected. Jesus' war is not with the gentiles but with evil that oppresses with no regard for national boundaries.

Mark 4:37–5:20

1 Kings 18:21–29; Jonah 1

It was back in the old days that the first Joshua showed up at this same river, the border to the land of promise. He, too, was there to usher in Yhwh's rule—the kingdom of god as it would manifest on earth through Israel. Yhwh's heavenly armies even showed up to assist. It is no surprise, then, that when the new Joshua shows up announcing conquest, it is at this same spot, though the kingdom he ushers is not earthly and its parameters not exclusive.

Jesus inaugurates his ministry at Capernaum. The people marvel at the authority with which he teaches. They see the effects but are unaware that before coming here, Jesus faced down the unseen powers of the world—Satan himself. A different plane of battle.[1] *An unclean spirit* recognizes what the crowd does not. "I know who you are," it screams through its host. Strange. Disconcerting. Power acknowledging Power. In the synagogue on the Sabbath, sacred space and time jarred. Even evil must bear witness. "The holy one of YHWH" is present in their midst. Jesus casts out the *unclean* spirit, *rebuking it* (ἐπετίμησεν) and *commanding its silence* (φιμώθητι). Fame of Jesus ripples.[2]

By sundown, the "whole city has gathered together at his door." Hope has been roused. Jesus heals the sick and vanquishes demons, continuing to silence the evil spirits because they know who he is. His presence means their time of dark dominance is over. Not just Jerusalem and Judea; word has spread. They come from beyond the Jordan, even gentile territories, Idumea, Tyre, and Sidon. The whole world, desperate with need, seeks him, and Jesus does not turn any of them away. A new flag flies. The kingdom of god is here.[3]

Jesus has the disciples ready a boat off the coast lest they be crushed by the crowds. Before long, he simply teaches from the water. With evening, the exhaustion, long at his heels, finally catches up. Rather than face the multitude, Jesus crosses the sea. Finally, he finds rest. Jesus *crawls in the stern and falls asleep*, leaving the task of sailing to the experts.[4] Rest, however, remains short-lived.

"A *great windstorm* arose"—a creature of the elements, it pummels with torrents of seawater, pounding against the boat, looking to destroy all flesh in its path. It floods, the fountains of the great deep bursting forth to lend it aid. Yet Jesus sleeps, soundly enough to be unaware of it or decidedly enough to ignore it. Panic seizes these seasoned mariners. Uncanny and menacing, they know this storm is beyond their skill. They intrude on Jesus' much-needed slumber: "Teacher, do you not care *that we are perishing* (ἀπολλύμεθα)?" Alert in an instant, Jesus once again *rebukes* (ἐπετίμησεν) and silences (πεφίμωσο)—last time the spirit in the synagogue, this time the angry wind and treacherous sea.[5] The water, emptied of all its uproar, melts into serene calm, smooth as glass, no hint of its previous mayhem. But Jesus knows their thoughts. "Why are you so cowardly?" he asks his disciples. "Still, you have no faith?"[6]

It was a showdown for the ages: the god of Israel versus Baal, the storm god of Old Canaan and Phoenicia; Elijah versus Jezebel's 850 prophets. Elijah was making a point. When he won, there would be no question, no doubt, no excuse. Every concession made for Baal—the contest on Mount Carmel (Baal territory), the test deferring to Baal's strength. Sacrifices readied, the god that consumed with fire from the sky, was God. Baal, by reputation, carried lightning in his right hand. All odds in his favor, yet, when implored by his horde of prophets, he answered with silence, muzzled perhaps. Elijah relished the moment, taunting, "Perhaps he is *sleeping* and must be awakened."[7] But Jesus is not Baal. Sleeping or awake, he was always in control.

Another man of god. Another boat. Another sea. "Go to Nineveh," YHWH told Jonah. "Cry out against it; for their wickedness has come up before me." That the stench of their evil had wafted to the highest heavens is no surprise; that the god of Israel wanted to save an entire city of gentiles, is. Jonah hoped that YHWH would destroy the Ninevites, but he knew better.[8] This god named himself Mercy. There would be no death or destruction. So Jonah finds a ship to take him as far from Nineveh as possible. He *crawls in its hold and disappears for a nap.*[9]

But the god of Israel knows the face of these waters. He has hovered over them before, and his will is not so easily thwarted. YHWH hurls a storm upon the sea, the very windows of heaven open to weigh in on Jonah's disregard. The judgment Jonah desires for Nineveh rains down hard upon him instead with no rainbow to mediate.[10]

The tempest rages, threatening to break apart the boat and drown not only Jonah but the gentile mariners with him. Jonah, however, slumbers on. The cargo is thrown overboard in the last-ditch efforts to survive. And yet, Jonah does not stir. Finally, the captain rouses him: "Arise, call out to your god! Perhaps the god will give a thought to us, *that we may not perish* (ἀπολώμεθα)." Jonah, however, knows exactly how to still the storm. "What is this that you have done?" the mariners exclaim when they learn he is fleeing from his god—a question asked before to those hiding from the divine. "Pick me up and throw me into the sea," Jonah advises, "for I know, that it is on my account that this tempest is upon you."[11]

These foreign sailors try to save his life, rowing with all their might back to land. But the sea overwhelms their efforts. They pray to YHWH, Jonah's god and not their own, begging for their lives, "Lay not on us innocent blood." Finally, reluctantly, when all other options have run out, they acquiesce and toss him into the sea.[12]

Jonah descends into the graveyard of the drowned, the company of the damned—like all those before consumed by the waters of YHWH's judgment. The gentile mariners, however, remain secure on the boat, safe now, like Noah on his ark, as the tempest ceases from its raging. They *fear a great fear* (ἐφοβήθησαν φόβῳ μεγάλῳ) over this god who controls the storm. They offer an offering and vow vows to the god of Israel, who spared their lives as he demanded Jonah's.[13]

These seamen recognize the one who calms the sea as the god in charge. When Jesus quiets the storm, the disciples also *fear a great fear* (ἐφοβήθησαν φόβῳ μεγάλῳ). But instead of recognizing Jesus as the god of Israel, the god of the universe, they look to one another and ask, "Who is this that even the wind and the waves obey him?" Who indeed! Jonah's gentile sailors know.[14]

For three days and three nights, Jonah remains in the depths, safeguarded by his god in the belly of a sea monster, protected from the waters of judgment and death. Then YHWH once again sets him on the path to preach a message to foreigners, setting a new precedent—an Israelite prophet sent by the god of Israel to save gentiles.[15] Jesus will go even further than Jonah, crossing into death's domain to rescue all held captive by it, Jew and gentile alike.

At baptism, Jesus emerged from Noah's waters empowered. Not only is he master of those waters here but also the realm of judgment and damnation that they have governed. As the fish vomits up Jonah to continue YHWH's mission of salvation to the gentiles of Nineveh, so Sheol will vomit Jesus from the grave. National borders did not constrain YHWH's plan to save; with Jesus, even metaphysical borders give way. But he does not himself go down to the depths and take on Sheol quite yet. Death has encroached upon the land of the living and must be dealt with here first.

Gerasenes. Fresh from the sea, Jesus, like Jonah, disembarks onto gentile territory. They moor by the graveyard where Jesus and his disciples can slip in unnoticed, avoiding the crowds. But there is more. Jesus has business here with the "Baals"—those demonic thugs bold enough to pick a fight, flinging the storm from afar.[16] "Immediately," a man who dwells in the tombs meets them.[17] It is as if Jesus was expected, as if the man was waiting for them, as if his wards to keep Jesus away failed, and now he guards his borders.

Alone. Isolated. Surrounded by shadows. Darkness fills him from within. He lives in between, neither living nor dead. Not one house for one demon; he hosts a legion.[18] He is far outnumbered in the body that was once his own. "It is not good for man to be alone," but for this man, it would be better.[19]

His life is hard, harder than *the stones* he uses to *gash himself.* The prophets of Baal had *cut themselves,* too, shedding blood to curry favor in Elijah's contest, but to no avail.[20] This demoniac howls, forlorn on his mountain, *crying out* in a loud voice, the same as those prophets *calling out* to Baal, all desperate for a break in the silence.[21] Like Baal himself, these demons act as though the tempest is theirs to wield, conjuring it to keep the holy one at bay. The god of Israel, however, still commands the storm. Last time not only was Baal defeated but his prophets slain.[22] Things have changed; Jesus has not come to destroy the people but to save them from the evil that uses and torments them.[23]

Everything about this place screams unclean—gentiles, graveyards, demons, pigs. It matters not. Jesus makes the unclean clean; it is for this purpose he has come. "Come out of the man," he commands. The demoniac runs to Jesus from a distance, falling to the ground in worship, the spirit realm once again testifying to what the natural realm does not yet know: "What is this between me and you, Jesus, son of the Most High God? I adjure you by god, do not torment me."[24] By god. The spirit claims rights. It knows Jesus' name, his title, his reputation, his power.

"What is your name?" Jesus asks. "Legion." The name chosen to display power now gives them away. The spokesman begs Jesus not to send them out of the country: "Send us to the pigs." The herd, numbering two thousand, rushes off the cliff, headlong into the sea that did evil's earlier bidding, both the unclean spirits and unclean animals expelled.[25] Legion's former host begs to go with Jesus, but Jesus instead restores him to his people, his life. "Go home," he says, "and tell your friends." The man goes further, proclaiming throughout the entire Decapolis how much Jesus has done for him, amazing all who hear.[26] When Jesus returns later to gentile territory, his reputation will have grown and his ability to exorcise will be known.

Ministry to foreigners easily dismissible as happenstance, exceptions, and asides. Jonah's mariners less about gentiles and more about identifying Jesus with the god of Israel. The demoniac from Gerasene, too, a legion of demons put in their place rather than the suffering foreigner set free from them—Jesus' identity and supernatural power primary. That those involved with the god of Israel happen to be gentiles more incidental than purpose or policy. Or so it once seemed.

Jonah's gentile mariners no longer exception but precedent. The proponents of Baal no longer simply enemies but also victims. Evil no longer simply human vice but mingled with supernatural influence. And the redemption of all, the aim of the kingdom of god come near—no longer exclusive for Israel but for all humanity, no longer harsh with judgment but graceful with mercy.

All Foods Clean

Clean and unclean foods, long a barely veiled metaphor. Unclean foods come from unclean people, the gentiles. But Jesus cuts to the heart of the matter. It is not food that makes one clean and unclean. In Jesus, YHWH has come to save, opening the doors to those long thought forbidden as a matter of policy, especially in light of the Exile.

Mark 7:1–7:30

Isaiah 29:14; Jonah 3; 1 Kings 17, 21

The whole region rushed to grasp the fringe of Jesus' cloak when he came to Gennesaret. Israel's disinherited re-inherited.[27] Those once sold to the nations being restored from their exile. The god of Israel has come near and drawn close. The commandments of YHWH healed any who efforted to brush against them, revealing them to be a balm rather than just a taskmaster. Word of this must have spread, drawing the attention of the religious elite: "And the Pharisees and some scribes having come from Jerusalem gathered around him; they were noticing that some of his disciples eat their *bread* with common hands, that is unwashed—for the Pharisees and all the Jews do not eat unless they wash their hands *with their fists*, observing the tradition of the elders. And unless they wash (baptize/βαπτίσωνται) [those things] from the market, they don't eat, and there are many other traditions which they observe and grasp hold of (κρατεῖν), the washing (baptizing) of cups and pots and beds (κλινῶν)."[28]

The tension remains an insider debate. Jews policing Jews on piety and devotion. Certain Pharisees visited John as well on a similar fact-finding mission. They notably did not participate in his baptism, though Jesus did. Jesus marked his entrance onto the public stage by descending into the same ancient waters as his sheep, defining his ministry from the onset as one of communion, not separation, and setting its point of origin at the place where Israel both came into their inheritance and lost it again. These Pharisees and scribes instead remained aloof, setting themselves apart, the separate ones, as their name defines. They would like all Jews to be separate as they are—separate from what is foreign, unclean, and even common.

"Why aren't your disciples walking in the tradition of the elders but with common hands they eat their bread?" Common hands. Only the priests are commanded to wash, required to have clean, purified hands and not common hands.[29] These Pharisees, serious about being a nation of priests, demand such for all. Yet Moses himself did not require this. Commoners do not need to wash for purification. Common people are allowed common hands before the god of Israel. "Hypocrites!" Jesus calls them. "Isaiah prophesied rightly about you, as it is written, 'this people honor me with their lips, but their hearts are far off from me. In vain do they worship me, teaching the teaching of men as doctrine. You reject the commandment of god and *grasp* the tradition of men."[30] The sick at Gennesaret *grasping* the tassels of law are still in recent memory: "For Moses said, 'Honor your father and your mother, and he who speaks evil to his father or mother is to surely die.' But you say if a man says to his father or mother whatever you would have gained from me is 'Corban' (that is gift *for God*), no longer do you permit him to do anything for his father or his mother, rendering powerless the word of God by your tradition which you have handed down. And many similar such things you do."[31]

Only one commandment of the ten is overtly tied to Israel's promised inheritance: "Honor your father and your mother . . . *that it may go well with you in the land that YHWH your god is giving you*."[32] This and their permissive attitude toward the violation of it are what Jesus highlights—the mistaken practice that the same act that deprives and dishonors their parents can in any way honor YHWH, that divine piety can be separated and then prioritized over love of neighbor. Standing on Naphtali, the very soil that witnesses to Israel's past failure in this regard, these leaders do not understand what it was that got them sent into exile in the first place. The very meaning of "corban" derives from "nearness," an offering designed to draw their god close, but one cannot simultaneously draw close to YHWH and far from neighbor. Their befuddled attempts at nearness result in farness. Corban, misappropriated, has not given them the restoration they sought.

Isaiah's chastisement of hypocrisy offers surprising resolution, proclaiming judgment that looks like grace: "For thus, behold, I will again deal amazingly with this people, and the wisdom of their wise will perish, and the discernment of their discerning shall be concealed."[33] Confused and derailed, yet diligent in their devotion, the religious elite's own wisdom needs revision, revelation, restoration. It is what YHWH offers to do. Isaiah saw not only the problems that afflicted religious observance but also the hope and solution for change.

Here in this debate, in the shadow of the Exile, looming questions and anxieties govern—the nuances of punishment and suffering and how to prevent them again. Fear from individual and communal trauma manifests in misunderstanding and misappropriation of law. The policing of one's neighbor governs, lest like Achan, one man's "sin" dooms the entire nation.

Jesus has already been retuning their understanding of Sabbath, fasting, and keeping the commandments: "He was saying to them, listen to me, everyone, and understand. There is nothing outside of a man going into him, which is able to defile. But those things coming out of a man are what defile him."[34] What has been here and there mentioned, and everywhere implied, becomes explicit with the Jerusalem entourage; what has operated until now quietly in everyday acts of mercy and restoration by Jesus now becomes policy.

In private, the disciples ask for the interpretation of this "parable" as it cannot be face value. But Jesus scolds them too: "Are you also without understanding?" The disciples' misunderstanding might be even worse than the Pharisees' and the scribes'. The authorities at least practice what they believe, washing everything fastidiously for piety's sake.[35] Jesus' disciples, on the other hand, are not washing their hands but also cannot believe that Jesus is making unwashed hands licit: "Do you not understand that anything which goes into a person from outside is not able to defile him, for it does not enter to the heart, but to the stomach and it goes out to the sewer? (Thus, he cleansed all the foods)."[36]

Lying on the tanner's roof in Joppa, Simon Peter had a vision. It was the very city where Jonah had tried to flee from Yhwh; Jonah's intent had been to escape the call to preach a message of repentance to the gentiles. The smell of burning hides wafted up to Peter as he fell into a trance, the scents mingling with his ecstatic experience, governing the images he would see. The heavens dangled a strange and repulsive banquet for him, unclean and common foods, four-footed creatures, reptiles, and birds of the air, laid out on a blanket for Peter to partake. "Arise Peter, kill and eat," a voice said. While Peter protested, saying, "By no means Lord, never have I eaten anything common or unclean," the voice responded back, "What god has made clean, you must not call common." As Peter puzzled over the vision, the answer literally came knocking at his gate: gentiles—the tie between unclean foods and unclean people—a long-known pairing.[37]

From Gennesaret, Jesus quietly slips across the border. Gennesaret raised the issue of inheritance. Jesus (Joshua) walked their towns, villages, and fields, reclaiming for them what had long ago been promised. The question of inheritance looms even here outside of Judea. Jesus arrives in the region of Tyre and Sidon looking to escape. Rest has been elusive in Judea. When Elijah needed to hide, Yhwh sent him to this same place.[38]

Immediately, he is found. It should be no surprise; the man who had been set free from Legion not far from here went around telling everyone about Jesus. Another gentile, a Syrophoenician woman, seems to have heard and appears in his house of refuge uninvited. Desperation compels her to bypass normal etiquette and decorum, her daughter too afflicted by an unclean spirit.[39] Unclean, like the spirit in the synagogue. Unclean, like the woman with the issue of blood. Unclean, like Jairus' dead daughter. Unclean, like all the foods Jesus has just made clean. Unclean, like this entire place where Jesus seeks refuge.

Jesus has stepped in time with Jonah before. He was both the man of god asleep on the boat and the god who calmed the seas.[40] The Syrophoenician begs Jesus to cast the demon out of her daughter.[41] But Jonah's lack of compassion, his ethnocentric bias, governs his mood. "Let the children be fed first," he retorts—the Jewish children, the ones he escapes by hiding here.

Hard, nationalistic Jonah. "Forty days and Nineveh will be overturned," Jonah called out, conveniently leaving out the "unless," "unless you repent, unless you change your evil ways." But from the beginning Jonah knew, thus his frustration at the end.[42] The god of Israel sent Jonah to Nineveh to save, not to destroy. But even in his eventual reluctant compliance, Jonah only preached the bare minimum—destruction—and he was no advocate.

"It is not right to take the children's bread," Jesus continues, gliding along the path that Jonah has plotted out before. But by the time Jesus arrives at this moment, the five thousand men of Israel have already been fed, with twelve baskets left over. The daughters of Israel have received their healing, one even rescued from the long covetous fingers of death and given food. There is no lack for the children; in fact, there is abundance. Even the Jewish parent has been touched, cared for, precedent for this encounter. Jairus, too, would have been a victim had his child remained dead. Ministry has seen that the Jews, the children, have received their bread and have been filled. Finally, before the Jewish religious authorities, Jesus declared all food clean. All is in order.

Still, Jesus resists her desperation: "It is not good to take the children's bread (ἄρτον) *and throw it to the dogs.*"[43] Jesus brings up the past, her history, her genealogy, recalling the sin of her foremother, another Syrophoenician woman who did in fact steal Israel's inheritance. It was usurpation. That Jesus voices this offense betrays grudge.[44]

Ahab was easily manipulated. Immature, managed, he was not the leader he should have been. Rather, Ahab was a petulant child occupying the king's throne, evil like his father before him. Ahab wanted a vegetable garden. In the tradition of Esau, he thought vegetables were reason enough to solicit the exchange of one's birthright. When Naboth balked indignantly at trading his family vineyard, his ancestral plot next to the palace, for a "better one," Ahab went home and pouted. "YHWH forbid that I should give you the inheritance of my fathers," Naboth had said. He did not despise his birthright. Naboth understood what it meant to be a child of Israel.[45]

Ahab's wife, Jezebel, was shrewd. She was a Sidonian princess, a Syrophoenician woman. Jezebel knew power; the daughter of King Ethbaal of the Sidonians, she had been close to it her whole life. Her power was foreign. Her power was corrupt. It polluted the hands that wielded it, but it was power nonetheless. She saw her crestfallen and ineffective husband. The plan she hatched would gain him both Naboth's vineyard and, hopefully, the backbone he lacked as well. Her plan was not without repercussions. She did not realize that to make a move against Naboth, to make a move against his land, to steal his inheritance, was to tangle with the god of Israel directly. She did not realize that this plan would cost her her life.

"Do you govern Israel?" Jezebel said to her husband, the king. "I will give you the vineyard of Naboth." With lesser men, treachery, lies, and the murder of both reputation and body, Jezebel's lackeys removed Naboth not only from his land and inheritance, but they hauled him outside the city. They stoned him and let his innocent blood flow. The dogs would lick up his blood, the physical world punctuating and making blatantly corporeal what had already happened in the metaphysical world. The gentile dogs had in fact licked up poor Naboth's blood on Israel's soil. When the news reached Ahab that Naboth was dead, he would descend on Naboth's vineyard. He would not go down to mourn, to tear his clothes at injustice, to be appalled at the violation of one of his own by a foreigner, or to confess guilt for his failure to guard one he was charged to protect. He would go down instead to take possession of that which was not his, that which could never be his. It would turn out that in fact Ahab did not govern Israel; Jezebel did.[46]

It is with this memory that Jesus accuses this Syrophoenician woman. Dogs licking blood. What response can she give? It is no mere puppy that Jesus names her. To call a woman "dog" to her face carries the same deliberate sting no matter what time or place one lives.[47] She is of the same stock as that notorious feminine villain of old, Jezebel, the gentile dog who stole the children's bread. This Syrophoenician before Jesus is guilty, by people, by blood, by association.

But she did not come this far to flinch, crumble, and fail. Like Jairus, she, too, has a daughter, and her daughter is in need. This Jewish man can cast out demons, and he has done it for gentiles before: "Sir, Lord, even the dogs under the table eat the children's crumbs (ψιχίων)."[48] Dogs. She takes control. She is not one of the mangy, disgusting, wandering street dogs known in Israel but perhaps the pampered and adored, small household dogs prevalent here in Tyre and Sidon, dogs that would be treated to *crumbs*.[49] She, too, invokes Elijah. She, too, has a claim to make against Jesus, and her claim is equally valid.

Jezebel's sway had infiltrated the land. Baal, the god of the storm, had taken over Israel. Asserting dominance, YHWH's prophet Elijah proclaimed a directive: "As YHWH the god of Israel lives, before whom I stand, there shall be neither dew nor rain these years, except by the word. Of my mouth."[50] Elijah's situation became more and more precarious as the scarcity of water impacted Israel and her king; he needed to be scarce. He hid in the last place Jezebel would search for him.

"Arise," YHWH told Elijah. "Go to Zarephath, which belongs to Sidon and dwell there. I have commanded a widow there to feed you." So Elijah went and hid in Jezebel's hometown and found this widow at the city gate: "Bring me a little water in a vessel . . . *and a crumb of bread* (ψωμὸν ἄρτου)."[51] She didn't have even a crumb of bread to offer, just the last bit of flour to cook the last meal for her and her son. "Make me little cake first . . . the jar flour shall not be spent, and the jug of oil shall not be empty, until YHWH sends rain upon the earth." She believed this foreign prophet. She fed him. She gave him a place to hide.[52]

Not long after, the widow's son became ill; his breath was stolen from him. The widow, recognizing Elijah as a man of god, charged him, "You have brought my sin to remembrance to cause the death of my son!" Elijah prayed on behalf of the mother for the life of the child and *laid the child on his own bed*.[53] Gentiles—Elijah prayed for gentiles. The widow of Zarephath, a Syrophoenician woman, offered him kindness, refuge, *and crumbs*. It would not be forgotten. YHWH listened to the voice of Elijah, saved the child, and thus saved the mother.

Crumbs. It is these crumbs, banked for her long ago by the widow of Zarepheth, that this Syrophoenician woman now claims as her right before Jesus. Like the Ninevites before her, she needs no mediator. She presents her claim before the god of Israel, with no advocate. Jonah retreats. Compassion takes over. Jesus changes his mind. The god of Israel relishes a reason to relent from judgment and offer grace, even and especially for gentiles; Jonah always knew this. It is not a ruse; it is not a game; it was never just a test of her faith. Just like Jesus repented at the Jordan, and the god of Israel relented from his plan to destroy the Ninevites, so Jesus changes his mind here, and it has real consequence.[54]

"Because you have said this, you may go—the demon has left your daughter."[55] She believed, like the widow of Zarephath before her. She went home to her child *lying on the bed*, healed of the demon.[56] But the interchange was never just about her. It was a collision of purpose. The back-and-forth between the Syrophoenician woman and Jesus brings to the forefront the tradition's argument with itself over what to do about the gentiles. This gentile did in fact influence Jesus. But unlike Solomon, who lost his heart because of foreign women, this woman helped Jesus find his in the midst of exhaustion. Thus, the answer to the question of what to do with the gentiles. Save them. Save them all. As Jonah and Elijah experienced, for the god of Israel, this was always the plan.

A Gentile Prophet

The promises of old regarding the gentiles are coming to pass. Recognition of what the gentiles can and cannot do is being refashioned. Exception—Balaam, Job, Cyrus—becoming rule. Not only will the gentiles be saved, but they will also become emissaries, ministers of YHWH.

Mark 7:31–37

Isaiah 6, 66; Leviticus 8, 14

The encounter with the Syrophoenician became a path to another world, the gentile world. The trajectory of Jesus' ministry altered. Instead of leaving the way he came, he went through. Rather than taking the straight path back home, he went roundabout, going to Sidon, throughout the region of the Decapolis, toward the Sea of Galilee.[57] With each step, he healed those in his path, restoring the broken to wholeness—his trek beyond the borders mirroring the ministry of home, distinction between Jew and gentile melting away. The gentiles had suffered no less. The massive powers did not crush Israel and Judah alone. *Tyre and Sidon* were devastated by exile as well: "For to YHWH belongs the capital of Aram, as do all the tribes of Israel . . . *Tyre and Sidon*, for they are very wise. Tyre has built a fortress for herself, and she has heaped up silver like dust and gold like the dirt outside. Behold, YHWH will dispossess her and hurl into the sea her outer ramparts and it will be eaten by fire (בָּאֵשׁ תֵּאָכֵל)."[58]

It is not just Israel and Judah for whom YHWH had judgment; the god of Israel governs all the nations. Isaiah casts the vision of siege towers leaning in on Tyre to tear down her palaces. She would be ruined, so desolate that the desert-dwelling animals would find their home in her. Tyre would be forgotten for seventy years. But hope would remain. At the end of those seventy years, *YHWH would visit her.*[59] Jesus' very steps through Tyre and Sidon, gentile kingdoms that the god of Israel had long ago claimed, announce the redressing of their sins and the end of the Exile, just as for Naphtali.

The man they bring to Jesus is deaf and cannot speak without handicap. Moses himself had encountered the presence of YHWH with his own speech impediment: "Who sets a mouth in a man? Or who makes mute or deaf or seeing or blind?" YHWH had owned, "Is it not I, YHWH?" They beg Jesus to place his hand upon this man. Rumors of miracle have reached them, convincing them that a simple touch from Jesus will heal their friend; they are right: "Taking him aside from the crowd to himself, Jesus thrust his fingers in the man's ears and spitting he *touched, lit, ignited* (ἥψατο) his tongue."[60]

"Bring forth the people who are blind though they have eyes, and *deaf though they have ears*. Let *all the gentiles* gather together and let the people assemble."[61] The gentiles were long marked by their spiritual deafness throughout the tradition, having become living images of their own gods—idols that can neither see nor hear. The gentiles unable to hear the true god, the god of Israel, despite the ears he gave them.[62]

Spit. Divine spit. Jesus smears his own spit in the man's mouth. Shamanesque, primal, primitive, en vogue, the saliva of magic men known to cure.[63] Yet a paradox, something wholly other—human residue of the God Most High, more precious and potent than the mystical balm of Gilead, an ointment like no other. The god of Israel had established precedent long ago, swearing by himself when making the promise to Abraham—nothing greater than godself to bind, to heal.[64] "Woe is me!" Isaiah cried when he saw Yhwh enthroned in his heavenly temple. "I am lost, I am a *man of unclean lips* and I am *dwelling amidst a people of unclean lips; yet my eyes have seen the king, Yhwh of hosts.*" With Isaiah's cry, the heavenly seraph took a *live coal* from the altar and *touched, lit, ignited* (ἥψατο) Isaiah's mouth, blotting out his sin and causing his guilt to depart. Cleansed before the god of Israel, Isaiah hears the call, "Whom shall we send?" and he answers, "Here I am, send me."[65]

Isaiah's sin renders him unclean; that he is a citizen of that holy nation set apart for Yhwh does not ameliorate. The man before Jesus, even more so. He is a gentile, truly a man of unclean lips, living among people of unclean lips. Isaiah reveals a particular sameness between Israel and the nations; it is not just the gentiles who are unclean—all are unclean before Yhwh. Israel is not clean; Israel is chosen. It is the presence of the living god that touches both tongues to purify and loose, cleansing sin and enabling speech. Like Isaiah, this gentile, too, has seen Yhwh, the god of Israel.

Isaiah's initial task is to warn—of judgment, of oppression, of displacement. The divine has his own siege ramps: "Keep hearing, but do not understand, keep seeing but do not know, make the heart of this people grow fat. Make their ears heavy and their eyes sealed tight. Lest they see with their eyes and hear with their ears and understand with their heart and turn and are healed."[66] The dulling of their senses will make judgment sure. Yhwh will not recant and change his mind because they will not repent and change their hearts. He has made sure of this.

"How long?" Isaiah asks. How long is this judgment to last? "Until the cities lie in waste . . . and the land is desolate from desolation."[67] Isaiah pronounced seventy years of devastation for Tyre, but judgment would eventually run out and make way for restoration. There would be an after, this deaf man witnesses to the after. Not only will he be a sign of the end of the Exile, but, like Isaiah, he will become one who announces it.

Jesus looks up to heaven and sighs (ἐστέναξεν); ancient memory floods.[68] Ezekiel sighed too: "And you son of man, sigh (καταστέναξον) . . . and in bitter grief, sigh before their eyes. And it will be when they say to you, 'Why do you sigh?' And you will say, 'Over the report which comes, *every heart will melt and all hands will be feeble, every spirit will faint and all knees will go to water.*'"[69]

Ezekiel's message was for everyone, everyone in the region. They would all be devastated. Babylon comes for them all. In his oracle against Tyre, Isaiah pointedly blames YHWH for Tyre's destruction: "Who has purposed against Tyre . . . YHWH of Hosts counseled this to defile the pride of all the glory, to shame all the honored of the earth." But Isaiah continues to have hope for Lebanon, the larger region of Tyre and Sidon:

> The wilderness and dry land will be glad, the desert shall rejoice and blossom like the lily. It will surely blossom and rejoice with rejoicing and singing. The glory of Lebanon shall be given to her, the splendor of Carmel and Sharon. They[70] will see the glory of YHWH, the splendor of our god. *Make strong the feeble hands and strengthen the stumbling knees. Say to those anxious of heart,* "Be strong, do not fear! Behold, your god will come with a vengeance, with recompence of god, *he himself will come and save you. Then the eyes of the blind will be opened and the ears of the deaf unstopped. Then the lame will leap like a deer and the tongue of the stammerer sing for joy.*[71]
>
> Isa 35:1–6a

Jesus stands on these gentile lands, sighing at the devastation before him. The deaf man stands as both a simple individual needing healing and as a representative of the nations of the world beyond Israel that have suffered judgment but who, too, belong to the god of the universe. This god comes in person to bring freedom to all his people: "And the ransomed of YHWH shall return and come to Zion with a cry of jubilation and everlasting joy will be on their heads. They shall obtain joy and gladness, and *sorrow and sighing* (στεναγμός) will flee away."[72]

They begged Jesus to "*lay his hand*," and he thrust his fingers in the man's ears.

It was a new era, a new covenant made with the god of their fathers, the god who delivered them from the oppression of Egypt. The very first consecration of Israel's priests, a model forever more. Moses took oil and poured it on Aaron's head, making him *Christos*, an anointed one.[73] Aaron and his sons then *laid their hands* on the ram of ordination, and the animal was slaughtered. Moses took some of the blood of the ram and *put it in the lobe of Aaron's right ear*, as well as his sons'.[74]

When a leper, one who had been unclean and *separated* from the camp, was brought to the priest to be declared clean, the priest slaughtered a lamb on his behalf and took the blood and put it on leper's earlobe and then did the same with oil that had been brought with the lamb as an offering. With this and the confirmation that the leprosy was gone, the unclean one was declared clean.[75] The Levites had been designated to serve as priests, ministers before Yhwh in his temple. But no Levite with any sort of physical blemish (blind, lame, mutilated, etc.) was permitted before the altar; these were excluded from serving.[76] Curious that the miracle-working, mighty god of Israel wouldn't just heal the afflicted Levite so that he could serve. This didn't happen, though, not during Moses' and Aaron's time.

But now a double ceremony. Both the cleansing of the unclean and the consecration of the priest, though no animal need be slaughtered. The god of Israel is present, the one who gives potency to the coals from the altar and cleanses this man with unclean lips. Jesus draws him away from the crowd, but instead of banishing him, he draws him to himself. Jesus heals this gentile of his blemish, makes him clean, then consecrates him. The fingers that touch this man's ears, coated with Jesus' own spit—more powerful than the blood of any ram: "For I know their works and their thoughts, and *I come to gather all the nations (gentiles) and tongues*, and they shall come and they shall see my glory . . . *From them I will send survivors to the nations* . . . And they will declare my glory among the nations. And they shall bring all your brothers from the nations as an offering to YHWH . . . *And also from them I will take to be priests and Levites says YHWH.*"[77]

The deaf and stammering man will go out to the nations healed, fulfilling the mission for which YHWH has consecrated him, to draw the gentiles to the god of Israel. Yet, with his newfound speech and mission, "[Jesus] ordered them that they might not tell anyone, but the more he ordered them, the more zealous they proclaimed (ἐκήρυσσον/κηρύσσω)."[78] If Jesus had truly prioritized silence, he need only have refused to heal, refused to unlock this man's speech. But instead, he restores his words, enabling him, giving this man full capacity and his compatriots full reason to proclaim. The god of Israel has been in their midst, and like Isaiah, they are all not only willing but desiring to be sent to proclaim his salvation to all the nations of the world.

Feeding Four Thousand Gentiles

One gentile, two gentiles, four thousand gentiles fed in the wilderness. The god of Israel feeds them bread, just like Israel, his own. God of the universe, the gentiles are his own.

Mark 8:1–10

1 Samuel 4–6; Jonah 3–4; Joshua 9

There had been exceptions made for gentiles before. Rahab, Ruth, Naaman. The widow of Zarepheth, the man at the tombs, the Syrophoenician woman. Here and there, the god of Israel allowed for one, two, a few. Sometimes even more, sometimes many. But those stories inflected, qualified, particular, never top of mind. They were the exceptions.

"*In those days* . . . while Jesus was walking about the area of the Decapolis, there was again a great crowd having nothing to eat."[79] The previous crowd had reclined in the green grass of Judea. Joshua's warriors fed and sent home without a fight. Israel's past made right, an old story with a new ending. But not so simple. Now another feeding. The presence of the second redefines the first, the Jewish feeding no longer the "only" but "another." The two symbiotic, both halves of a whole.[80]

This crowd is a gentile crowd. The Jewish crowd had tugged at Jesus' heart, compelling him to interrupt his own plans for rest to feed them.[81] They were sheep without a shepherd, and the true shepherd of Israel would not leave them alone to fend for themselves.[82] This crowd also needs a shepherd: "Jesus calling his disciples to him said to them, 'I have *compassion* (σπλαγχνίζομαι) on the crowd for already they have remained with me *three days* and they have nothing to eat. If I send them away hungry, *fasting* (νήστεις), to their homes, they will faint along the way.'"[83]

Long ago, another gentile crowd tugged at YHWH's heart, to the prophet's dismay. *Three days* Jonah was in the belly of the fish, stewing, stubborn, angry at YHWH's mercy to the Ninevites. Their evil *had risen to the heavens*, calling for destruction. *Three days' walk* it was across that gentile town, a trek Jonah had been called to make to preach warning to the entire city. But Jonah never makes it that far. One day in, and the people of Nineveh believe this foreign god and proclaim *a fast* (νηστείαν). They repent of their evil, moving YHWH to repent (וַיִּנָּחֶם) of his destruction. Jonah fumes, "This is why I fled to Tarshish; for I knew that you are a *gracious god, merciful, slow to anger, great in loving kindness, and relenting from evil*."[84] Virtue turned to vice in Jonah's indignant speech.

Jonah's gripe recalls verbatim YHWH's poetic self-revelation from ages prior on Mount Sinai. Communing with YHWH at the time of the golden calf episode, Moses was not at all culpable in Israel's idolatry. Yet, in their moment of crisis, guilty before the divine, he stood with them, not against them. "Let me alone," YHWH had said to Moses, "so that my wrath may burn hot, that I may consume them, and I will make of you a great nation."[85] But Moses placed himself between the people of Israel and their god, a force, a stumbling block, allowing YHWH to rage without consequence. Moses compelled YHWH to remember both his promises to the patriarchs and his reputation among the nations, going as far as to say, "What you do to them, do to me."[86] "YHWH repented (וַיִּנָּחֶם) of his anger and the evil he had said he would do against the people."[87]

YHWH desired Jonah to play the role of Moses. Jonah was to stand in YHWH's way so that YHWH could rage over the sin of the Ninevites and not wipe them out. Jonah instead stole YHWH's role. Jonah was the one to rage, hoping for judgment instead of mercy and requiring this god to be the one compelling graciousness from a man, leaving the Ninevites with no mediator.[88]

The Ninevites improvised as best they could. Moses had the Israelites strip off their ornaments as a result of their sin. The Ninevites stripped not just their ornaments but their clothes, too, putting on sackcloth as they sat in the dust.[89] They *fasted,* called out to this god, repented, and hoped it would be enough to avert destruction. It was.

When Jesus decides to feed this second crowd, the disciples react, "How (from where) is one able to feed these people with bread in this desolate place?"[90] They have already seen Jesus miraculously feed five thousand Jewish men, mirroring the god of Israel's manna in the wilderness. They cannot doubt his abilities. The question is deceptive. It is not about feeding a crowd; it is about feeding gentiles. "From where (πόθεν) do you get the *right* to feed *these* people, to give the children's bread to the dogs?"

The god of Israel now stands before a herd of Jonahs. "I have compassion for this crowd," Jesus began the conversation with the disciples. YHWH had similarly said to Jonah, "*Should I not pity* (אָחוּס) Nineveh?"[91] Jesus does not chastise the disciples for their lack of compassion, for resisting this gentile crowd. He simply bypasses their question and sets for them an example. "How many loaves do you have?" he asks. "*Seven . . . There were about four thousand people.*"[92]

"*In those days*, the Philistines marshalled for war against Israel, and Israel went out to war against them . . . but Israel was struck down before the face of the Philistines." Long after Joshua but before the era of the kings, in a battle against the gentiles, the gentiles won. The casualties devastating, *about four thousand* Israelites slain. Far worse than the thirty-six at Ai.[93] Israel, however, had a "secret weapon."

The ark of the covenant was an enigma. It seemed like a "what," but was really a "who"—the glory of the god of Israel, whose presence dwelt on that ark. Its demand for ritual purity and fastidious care far more than empty observance. They brought the ark from its resting place at Shiloh to the midst of the battleground so that it, YHWH, could save Israel from her foes. At the noise of Israel's cheering, the Philistines panicked. The reputation of Israel's god had long gone before. "These are them!" they cried out. "The gods who smote the Egyptians with every wound in the wilderness."[94] The ark its own kind of psychological warfare.

The Philistines fought hard "like men." They knew what was at stake: death and servitude. Curiously, their fighting paid off. Israel was defeated and fled, "*everyone to his home* (לְאֹהָלָיו)," the ark of YHWH taken.[95] Neither Israel nor the Philistines understood the ark or the god of Israel's relation to it. They thought it to be a talisman, a totem, a tool. A supernatural force to be wielded. A power to be owned, not a personality to be revered. Both parties were equally shocked at the outcome of this battle. Neither suspected that Israel could lose. Nor that this was only the beginning.

Once in Philistine territory, the ark was by no means owned, dominated, or docile. The ark was not a captive but rather an unruly guest. The god of Israel continued to glorify himself, terrifying the Philistines, striking them with unseemly tumors, and subjugating their god Dagon. From town to town, they ferried the ark, but Israel's god cast affliction wherever they went. In Ekron, the people revolted. Deathly panic spread as his hand laid heavily upon them. *Their cry for help ascended to heaven*. Finally, the Philistines reasoned to send the ark back to its place, Israel.[96]

Their own priests and diviners deliberated as best they could *with no priest or prophet of Israel to mediate*: "Return to him a guilt offering . . . give glory to the god of Israel . . . why should you harden your hearts as the Egyptians and Pharaoh hardened their hearts?" YHWH had moved through their land, killing, inflicting plagues, eliciting fear, and finally soliciting worship—the appeasement of guilt from these gentile captors. The Philistines could not get rid of the ark fast enough. It had remained with them for *seven* months. When the ark finally made it back into Israelite territory, it wreaked havoc there, too, killing seventy men in Beth Shemesh for not rejoicing at its return.[97] Both the Philistines and Israel found that this god is no good luck charm.[98] His fearful holiness would inflict upon all, gentile and Israelite alike, with equal recourse and sometimes minimal distinction.

"Some of them *have come from afar* (ἀπὸ μακρόθεν ἥκασιν),"[99] Jesus said regarding this gentile crowd. Their distance traveled added to his compassion toward them. Foreigners flocked to find Israel's holy one. The first Joshua had been moved by such as well.

Both Jericho and Ai had been decimated, but they were only the beginning. All the inhabitants of Canaan would be utterly destroyed to make way for Israel. Rumors rush across the land. The people of Canaan know their time is limited. Many of the gentile tribes band together, thinking that, united, they might have a chance against Joshua and Israel.[100] Some, however, hatch a different sort of plan.

The Gibeonites approach Joshua with a rouse. Innovative. Cunning. They pretend. They dress in worn-out shoes, pack moldy bread, and spin a story: "We *have come from a far* country (ἀπὸ μακρόθεν ἥκαμεν) . . . because we have heard a report of all that YHWH your God did in Egypt; make a treaty with us."[101] Double-talk—but the plain value of their words do not lie. They heard of YHWH's reputation, that it meant death for them, and they came to thwart that plan. They came to save their very lives.

The leaders of Israel partake of the Gibeonites' provisions (צֵידָם), eager to solidify friendly relations in otherwise hostile territory. Nobody consults YHWH, the only one in their midst who would know anything about these foreigners, and strangely, YHWH does not offer. YHWH seems to want to save them, keeping their confidence throughout their deception. Joshua himself makes a covenant with the Gibeonites guaranteeing their lives. The leaders of Israel swear an oath to them. But only *three days* after the covenant of peace had been made, the Israelites learn that the Gibeonites are actually close neighbors, living among them. When Joshua confronts, they confess, "We heard . . . and we feared for our lives."[102] Rightly so. Were it not for the covenant that they secured through deception, the Gibeonites would already be dead.

Joshua honored the covenant of peace despite their trickery, even saving their lives from the Israelites who wanted to disregard it. Moreover, though Joshua imposed upon them servitude, "you will be hewers of wood and water carriers," the water carriers would be providing water for the altar of YHWH. These foreigners would live in very close proximity to the god they sought, a blessing cloaked within their servitude. Joshua went as far as to say, "Cursed are you, but not cut off," he, too, acknowledging the merit in their plan.[103] They are alive.[104]

Before in the wilderness of Judea, Jesus had employed the disciples to organize the seating. It hearkened back to the days of Moses, people in groups of thousands, hundreds, fifties, and tens, particularly appropriate for a Jewish crowd. Here, Jesus does not summon the disciples as such. Instead, he keeps pace with the god of Israel's past dealings with the Philistines, the Gibeonites, and the Ninevites. Jesus deals with these gentiles directly without mediator; he himself orders the crowd to sit on the ground.[105]

After giving thanks (εὐχαριστήσας), Jesus gives the loaves to his disciples to distribute to the crowd. And lest this crowd be treated any differently than the Jewish crowd who was fed first with both bread and fish, this crowd, too, gets fish.[106] Moreover, they, too, "ate and were filled," this time with *seven* baskets left over.[107]

About four thousand Israelites were slain in that battle with the Philistines. Jesus repays with kindness, feeding *about four thousand* in the wilderness, bringing the gentiles into his fold.[108] For every Israelite who was lost in that battle with the Philistines, Jesus feeds a gentile in an otherwise desolate place. For every month that the god of Israel made war, Jesus fills a basket with bread, feeding the hungry with abundance and making peace.[109]

Akin to the god of Israel with the Ninevites, Jesus' compassion for foreigners stings the still open wounds of Israel's memory. These are not just gentiles but gentiles who killed Israelites, YHWH's chosen. Like the gentiles of old, these have listened to Jesus' teaching, fasting before him the same as those Ninevites. They have remained with him for *three days*, the amount of time it took Joshua and the Israelites to find out the Gibeonites were their neighbors, the amount of time Jonah resisted YHWH in the belly of the sea monster. The god of Israel made clear with the ark of the covenant that divine holiness could strike out at gentiles and Jews alike. YHWH makes clear with the Ninevites that the opposite is also true; YHWH could have *mercy* on Jew and gentile alike.[110] Jesus acts in kind, feeding both crowds the same with bread and fish, sending them both away fed, with leftovers and with no more need to fight for their lives or for inheritance—in YHWH's kingdom, there is enough for all.

CHAPTER 5

YHWH, God of the Nations

Salvation for All

Distinction between peoples no longer divide. Even in and from Sheol, YHWH finds, rescues, and redeems—Jew, gentile, chosen, unchosen, past, future, dead, alive. YHWH, God Most High, has come to save all, for all ages—everyone everywhere.

Dalmanutha

Mystery. The places of legend are called to witness to YHWH's reach and YHWH's desire and ability to save, YHWH's attention to gentiles once again in the forefront. Nobody is beyond YHWH's reach, and the powers of old bend to his power.

Mark 8:10–13

Job 28, 30, 38; Psalm 78[1]

"And immediately, he embarked on the boat with his disciples and went to the area of Dalmanutha."[2] The Pharisees converge there too; signs and wonders draw them. They are among the guardians of the nation, governing the things of the god of Israel, protecting—often overprotecting. Their scrutinizing presence transforms this place into crucible. They showed up before, just after the healing of the masses at Gennesaret, following the feeding of the five thousand men in the Judean wild.[3] Here they appear again, just after the breaking of bread for this second crowd. News traveled fast. Jesus has crossed the boundaries of Israel, feeding gentiles with miracle. The Pharisees have come to test.[4]

It is not the first time Israel has tested their god regarding food in the wilderness. "Prove your authority"—the unsaid, and real, meaning of their demand for a *sign from the heavens*. "Just like your fathers," Psalm 78 mutters. The psalm, longwinded and with ancient memory, has much to say about Israel trying God's patience. "They *tested* God in their heart," the psalm remembers. "They murmured against him saying, 'Is god able to arrange a table in the wilderness? . . . Can he also give bread, and provide meat for his people?'"[5]

The familiar words of the children of Israel now nuanced on the lips of the Pharisees to ask about Jesus: "Can he set up a table in the wilderness . . . for them?" The miracle is the sign, about four thousand fed from seven loaves. But these reject it with suspicion, raising the bar of belief to the point of doubt. They have good reason, though. The stakes are too high. Mingling with the gentiles led to the Exile. The undercurrents of the tradition that emerge with contradiction invite complication; they dangle as forbidden fruit with dangerous consequences—exceptions to long-established rule. Simple separation is safer. The Pharisees' very identity built on this.

When last they met, Jesus had declared all foods clean.[6] Even then, it had been about gentiles. No longer theory, now practice, the Pharisees' piqued concern not at all misplaced. Jesus dares exactly what they fear. For better or for worse, the wilderness is Israel's special place with their god. YHWH's firstborn, no other children need be acknowledged, certainly not invited there. It is not just the god of Israel who is jealous; his wife is possessive of him as well.

Jesus *groaned deeply in his spirit*.[7] "*My soul grieved* for the needy,"[8] Job had cried out in his own defense, moving past mere appearance and religious civility to expose the integrity of his heart. Job *groaned* over the distress of his fellow man, and it was recalled in his own acute suffering. True piety, through and through, but it fell upon deaf ears. The compassion of Job should have been the bulwark defending him against misfortune. Rather, it made him all the more the target of it and heightened the tragedy of his undeserved affliction. Jesus, too, sighs at the suffering of the gentiles, at the never-ending argument with the Pharisees. He sighs, foreshadowing.

"Why does *this generation ask for a sign*?" Jesus considers aloud.[9] Only Noah was righteous in *this generation*. Only Noah and his family were saved from the floodwaters of destruction.[10] The muffled cries of the drowning must have reached heaven as they disappeared into the depths of their watery grave. But after the darkness—the clouds, the rain, black skies, and catastrophic death—light bursts forth. The sun, from its inception *a sign in the heavens* marking the seasons, now proclaims a season of mercy and grace. Emerging like a bridegroom from his chamber; there is nothing that can hide from its glow.[11] It dispels the darkness, shining through the droplets of water, announcing the end of judgment with the array of color—Apollo's shafts called upon to hold future destructive waters at bay: "The Lord god said, '*This* is the *sign* of the covenant that I give between me and you and between *every living being* that is with you, and to unending *generations*.[12] I have set my bow in the cloud, and it shall be a *sign* of the covenant between me and the earth . . . and I will remember my covenant . . . and the water shall no more become a flood to wipe out all flesh."[13]

Bread multiplied for the multitude in the wilderness is a sign from heaven. But these Pharisees desire a different sign, one with different implications, something celestial, focusing perhaps on the hereafter rather than the here and now.[14] Yet their very words summon the sign that undermines them, the rainbow, *the sign from the heavens* that the god of Israel had with all flesh—the gentiles included.

The precedent for the god of Israel caring for those outside the fold of Israel stretches back to the earliest days of humanity. Before Israel was, all the peoples were his. Deeper magic—its ancientness gives it priority over subsequent particularity, before the covenants with Moses and even Abraham. The confirmation of it not on stone or even flesh but as the many colors bursting forth in splendor, painted on the sky for both heaven and earth to see, reflecting the humans it would serve to protect.

The sign of Noah appears to be the only sign Jesus will offer before his thoughts wander. "Truly I say to you, if *this generation* is given a sign,"[15] he begins and then he trails off. No more is said. He climbs on his boat and sails away. But the rainbow is not the only sign.

Job takes his friends to the deep and dark recesses of the earth to expound on the elusiveness of wisdom. True wisdom has disconcerting things to say about the suffering of man, things beyond the simplicity of sin and punishment. Few dare tread there. Job casts the vision of a mining scene, the searching for precious metals and stones. His winding tour through the underworld of gold, silver, copper, diamonds, and sapphires eventually peaks with analogy. Wisdom cannot be found in the same way as valuable gems, digging and sifting the recesses of the earth where few living souls go. But someone does amble those paths; a figure moves about this strange, hidden place, buried deep in the mountains: "[The miner] sets an end to the darkness and searches out to the end of all the extreme limits, a [precious] stone in the darkness—the *darkness of death* (צַלְמָוֶת). He breaks through [the mountain] with torrents, rivers, far from where [any person] dwells; [there] the forgotten ones [are], far apart from [the path of] those traveling—(דַּלּוּ מֵאֱנוֹשׁ)[16] Dalu menosh / Dalmanutha *they hang, away from people*—trembling/wandering."[17]

Dalmanutha tells of a tragedy, one desperate for remedy. There are those in exile, hanging, forgotten and alone, in shadow and gloom, in the darkness of death.[18] Job tells of one who knows exactly where they are and is able to rescue them. Dalmanutha is a place but not on the shores of the Galilee; it does not exist in the temporal/physical realm. It is liminal space, more real perhaps than a coastal town with its waves beating on the shore. Jesus did not go there on his boat, but he will go there. Dalmanutha is the true test, the real mission. Dalmanutha is the sign.

The figure moving through Job's mountain mines is master of his domain. He knows the hidden corners: "The place of sapphires . . . and the dust of gold are his. The *pathway* is his alone; even the keen-eyed birds of prey and the kite have not spied it . . . In flint he stretches out his hand; he overturns the mountains from the roots. In the rocks he cleaves rivers, and his eyes see every precious thing . . . the hidden thing he brings to light."[19] But neither the gemstone treasures nor the hidden paths are the aim of this quest. As unique and rare as the gems and precious metals are—those items with the most worth of all the substances of the earth—wisdom is rarer, more evasive, and remains the mystery.

The powers of the earth and beyond offer hearsay. Has anyone seen wisdom? Abaddon and Death, those mighty forces that wait for physical bodies to take their final resting place in the earth, entities that own mankind at the last, weigh in like the butcher and the baker, saying simply, "We've heard she's around . . . but haven't seen her." *The Deep*, that endless cavern, present with the god of Israel at the creation of the world, powerful with mystery, pipes in and says, "She is not in me." Similarly, the *Sea*, which houses all the fish, the ruins of old, and whose moods control the fate of the ships that sail it, also affirms, "Neither is she with me."[20]

Those ancient forces of the universe reprise as chorus in YHWH's pinnacle speech back to Job the humbling conversation before his restoration. It is the breaking of divine silence, the official "dressing down," the day with YHWH for which Job had long been asking. "Where were you when I laid the foundations of the earth?" YHWH questions Job from the storm. "Who determined its measurements? Who shut the *sea* with doors and said here your proud waves shall stop?"[21]

This divine reckoning wholly unsatisfying. The inquisition reversed; it is YHWH's questions that pour forth, with none of Job's answered: "Have you come to the springs of the *sea* and have you walked around in search of *the deep*? Have the gates of *death* been uncovered for you and have you seen the gates of the *darkness of death*? . . . Where is the way to the dwelling of light, and the darkness, where is its place? That you may take it to its borders and that you may understand the *paths* to its house."[22]

That old, curious miner is alluded to again, his jaunts in the deepest parts of the earth confirming as well that this gentile has been privileged with truths shrouded from most mortals. Wisdom has whispered her secrets to Job even as she has remained elusive to the age-old forces of the world. But while some may be in the know, only one has walked the paths.

YHWH's speech sobers, making clear that nobody but YHWH knows the mysteries of the universe, and while YHWH deigns to respond, YHWH is beyond summoning. There is no force, no entity, and certainly no man that has any comprehensive understanding of, much less control over, *the sea*, *the deep*, *death*, or any of the *pathways* except YHWH himself. The elusive figure from Job's tour through the underworld is no mere miner. The figure is the god of Israel, the god of the universe, the same god who would challenge Job and humble his presumption. Job acquiesces with the rightful response to such divine chastening, "I have declared but I did not understand things too wonderful for me, and I did not know . . . therefore I despise myself and I repent in dust and ashes."[23] If only the Pharisees before Jesus concluded the same.

The god who sweeps majestically through the cosmos is also the one to walk with his people in the cool of the day. Death and Abaddon bow to this god, yet the Israelites complain in the wilderness and vex. YHWH is both grand and awe-inspiring, familiar and moody, designer of the universe, and yet concerned over desires of his creation. The god that declares ownership over the east winds then employs those very same winds to blow in the heavens and rain flesh upon the Israelites in the wilderness.[24] The god who knows where the doors of heaven are also commanded that they be opened to rain down manna and feed Israel in the desert.[25] The god who caused rivers to stream from stone and made a way for the voice of the thunderbolts in the deep mountainous mines then also struck a rock in the wilderness so that water flowed in order to provide drink for the Israelites in the desert.[26] YHWH's role as creator and his attentive governing of the archaic elements of the universe do not make him distant or impede his intimacy toward man, who is "but flesh, a wind that goes and does not return."[27] Rather, with all YHWH's divinity, he tends to humankind's most basic and intimate needs.[28]

The Pharisees understand far more than it would seem about what is at stake as they ask Jesus for a sign from the heavens. Miracles on the ground manifest divine intent. Cycles and seasons, sun and rain are gifts to the earth, generic, to all without reserve. The meddling of such, favor bending what nature governs, is reserved for the chosen. If all are chosen, then none are chosen: "You who feed these gentiles in the wilderness, do you have rights to the heavens as well?" Their assumption, their hope, is that Jesus has overstepped, that there is a disjoint between fraternizing with the gentiles and being in the employ of the god of Israel.

But the god of Israel conversed with Job, a man from the East, a foreigner. Before he was the sinless sufferer, Job was just another gentile. YHWH marked him as righteous and confided to him wisdom—the power of the cosmos in the particular on the earth. Job complicates the uncomplicated. With litany, Israel's god gave Job sign after sign to explain that his ruling of the cosmos is his unquestionable universal authority. The god of Israel's recitation of credentials to a righteous gentile disrupts the nationalistic priority so dear to these Pharisees. YHWH's feeding of four thousand gentiles in that special wilderness place reserved for YHWH and YHWH's own establishes his care of them not as exception but norm, not accident but rule.

Jesus' baptism ripped the heavens open, never to be closed again. Not over Zion—the god of Israel's provincial domain—rather, this god tears the sky at the border between Israel and the world. Heaven is not the exclusive property of the chosen but the god who chooses, and he expands his invitation to whomever he pleases. The flood had poured its judgment upon all. Now heaven embraces all, desires all, calls to all in the public square. No particularity to the destruction, now none to salvation.

Jesus feeding the five thousand Jews in the wilderness was never an arbitrary miracle, a generic display of power. It was personal, intimate, relational. A new memory sewn into the old. The continuation of Sinai history, another chapter in the love story between the god of Israel and this god's people. It was the announcement loudly proclaiming that YHWH, who delivered his people from Egypt and fed them in the wilderness, is here again. These Pharisees know that Jesus feeding the four thousand gentiles in the wilderness draws on the same principles, threatening Jewish particularity. It is YHWH, the god of Israel, wielding his divine powers to once again save his own—the gentiles. It is the god of Israel inviting them once again to participate in his-story.

Throughout their time together, YHWH's wrath has over and over again threatened to destroy Israel because of her sin: "They did not trust in his wonders and all their days [disappeared] in a vapor." But though angry for a moment, Israel's god "was compassionate, and covered their iniquity"; YHWH had compassion on his own. But even the tradition recognizes a truth: The whole world is YHWH's, all flesh. So though YHWH destroy the Egyptians, letting loose upon them fierce anger and not sparing them from death, drowning them in the depths of the sea, and though YHWH floods the entire world because of their evil and iniquity, they, too, are still YHWH's, all of them.[29] And it seems he was always able to fish them out again.

"Have you come to the springs of the sea, or walked around in the searching of the deep? Have the gates of death been revealed to you or the gates of the darkness of death?"[30] YHWH himself built the roads to these places, and YHWH knows who dwells there. Dalmanutha is about the lost, wandering, trembling, in need of someone to save them. Dalmanutha is about the drowned of Egypt, the drowned of Noah, the damned of any age that need redemption, the covering of their iniquity, and a pathway made for them, to lead them out of death. Dalmanutha is the sign that the Pharisees provoke, a sign for their future generations. It is the understanding that the god of Israel plans to save the entire world—past, present, future—and not just the Jews. And this happens not in some distant eschatological future but in the now.

Dalmanutha is where Jesus' ministry will end. He, too, will hang, outside the city. The sighing, the groaning comes full circle:

> But I will be their song of mockery, and to them a byword . . . Before me they do not refrain spit . . . Nobody helps concerning them. Terrors are turned upon me . . . And now, my soul is poured out over me, days of affliction have taken hold of me, night bears upon my bones and the gnawing does not take rest. With great strength he searches my garment, by the collar of my tunic he grasps me. He has thrown me in the mire and I have become like dust and ashes. I cry for help, but you do not answer me. I stand, and you understand me. You have turned cruel to me, and with the might of your hand you persecute me. I know death you will bring me and to the appointed house for all living.
>
> Job 30:9–10, 12–13, 15–21, 23

Jesus will suffer like Job, but unlike Job, Jesus will die. For days, weeks, maybe longer, Jesus has been warning, "The son of man will be handed over, he will die, and three days later he will rise." "Take up your cross," he said. But now the time has come: "See, we are going up to Jerusalem, and the son of man will be handed over to the chief priests and the scribes, and they will condemn him to death and hand him over to the gentiles."[31] Like the miner, Jesus will go to the depths of darkness in order to save. He is making amends, not just for Jews or even for gentiles. He is making amends for YHWH, for all who have fallen under the weight of YHWH's judgment since the beginning of time.

Up to Jerusalem

What has been hinted to is now plainly declared. YHWH's messiah, the son of David, YHWH himself, has come to die. The war they all hoped for has not and will not come to pass. This is not failure or timidity—the watering down of promise and fulfillment. It is YHWH's will and redemption on the grandest scale.

Mark 10:32–11:10

Numbers 13–14, 22–24; Genesis 45, 47; 1 Kings 1, 11

Hints to reward in the afterlife have already been made. Jesus told Peter in everyone's hearing that they who give up those things dearest to them in this life would find eternal reward in the age to come. James and John have had glimpses. They were in the room with Jairus' daughter raised from the dead. They were on the mountain with Moses and Elijah when Jesus shimmered with light. They heard the voice proclaim Jesus the beloved son.[32] And now they approach with boldness, like Joshua and Caleb of old, unafraid of the giants, the gentiles, and all that meets them in Jerusalem, their sights set on the world to come.

"Teacher, we want that *whatever we ask* of you that you might do for us." Herod had offered Herodias' daughter *whatever she asked* too.[33] It ended with John the Baptist's head served on a platter. That exchange looming in the background should have given clue. But their request surprises even Jesus: "Grant to us that we might sit, one at your right and one at your left, in your glory." "You do not know what you ask," Jesus offers. "Can you drink the cup which I will drink and be baptized with the baptism which I will be baptized?" But they know exactly what they ask.[34] They have been paying attention.

The spies of old had seen the land, the promise of new life before them, but *ten of the twelve* shrunk from the threat of death and defeat. Despite mighty miracles, proof of YHWH's prowess in earthly battle, and YHWH's faithfulness to come through, the spies brought *a bad report*. The land cannot be taken; there be giants. Only two of the twelve,

Joshua and Caleb, remained confident that Israel could take the land. YHWH was with them.[35]

James and John, too, know what lies before and who it is that travels with them. Rather than tricking Jesus into giving them the best seats of easy honor, their design is the opposite. They plot to coerce him into consenting to their premature suffering, for them to accompany him in death now rather than for him to protect them and die alone. They know Jesus' kingdom and understand its warfare. They know that they will not take the gentiles; they understand that the gentiles, and even some of their own, will eventually take them. What they offer is to move up the timetable on their own suffering: "The cup which I drink you will drink, and the baptism which I am baptized you will be baptized, but to sit at my right and my left is not mine to give but for those it was prepared."[36] The crosses next to Jesus are already taken.

So offensive was Joshua and Caleb's claim of potential victory as it clashed against the people's fear that the congregation desired to stone them. Only the presence of the glory of YHWH, appearing at the tent of meeting, staved communal judgment. The other ten disciples became angry with James and John—at their presumption, their forward momentum without consultation or consensus, their recklessness obligating the whole of them to danger—as the rest would be less loyal now to refuse.[37] Jesus drew the ten close with a lesson: "You know that those considered rulers among the gentiles subdue them and their great ones exercise authority over them. Not so with you. Whoever wishes to be great among you will be the servant, and whoever wishes to be the first will be the slave of all."[38]

Joseph, son of Jacob's first and only love, Rachel, was his father's favorite; he was beloved. Joseph brought *a bad report* of his brothers to his father. Young, foolish, and gloating with shameless ambition, he advertised his dreams of ruling to all. Everyone would bow down to him—his father, mother, brothers, the sun, the moon, and eleven stars. His ten older brothers, incensed by him, sought to end his dreams of grandeur and spare themselves the offense of his very presence. They sold him to the gentiles. Years of servitude, slavery, and prison imposed themselves on Joseph until, one day, Pharaoh took him from prison and made him ruler of all. At the moment of reconciliation with his brothers, he confessed, "God sent me here before you to preserve life." It wasn't just the children of Israel that he saved but the entire gentile world as well: "The son of man came not to be served but to serve, and to give his life a ransom for many."[39] His disciples can expect no less.

They continued on toward Jerusalem. Jesus and his disciples went in and out of Jericho, a large crowd accompanying them on their way out. Rahab and her entire household came out with Israel's spies during that first conquest—gentiles spared for their loyalty to the god of Israel; Rahab, a foreigner, grafted into the very lineage of the messiah.[40] But forty years prior to Rahab, Israel would have dealings with other gentiles while camped in the plains of Jericho.

Israel wandered decades in the wilderness because of those ten spies and the congregation of Israel that they riled to fear and faithlessness. All who murmured would die in the desert. But despite the internal argument between Israel and her god, the family dispute was not on display for outsiders, who saw only the united front.[41] The neighboring nations became unsettled. Moab had seen what Israel did to the Amorites, and they were very afraid.

Balak, king of Moab, sent envoys to the prophet Balaam to curse Israel—a strange and unique event as this gentile seer, unknown to Israel, served YHWH. Balaam had a reputation for results; those he blessed were blessed, and those he cursed were cursed. But when he inquired of YHWH over this particular matter, YHWH made it clear: "You cannot curse this people, because they are blessed." Israel's status guaranteed by YHWH, so much so that others judged by relation, "those who blessed Israel blessed, and those who cursed Israel cursed."[42] The revelation that unfolded, however, was unexpected; the seer could not see. Balaam completely unable to perceive the angel of YHWH with sword drawn, that his donkey saw plain as day, poised and ready to destroy him because of his entertaining of Balak. But then YHWH opened Balaam's eyes so he, too, could see.[43]

Blind Bartimaeus, the son (*bar*) of Timaeus, a gentile name, sat on the Jericho road there in the Jordan Valley, collecting alms. When he heard that Jesus of Nazareth was passing by, he screamed aloud and would not stop, despite the crowd demanding his quiet. "Jesus, *son of David, Have mercy on me*," echoing the words of Tobit, who also claimed God's mercy in the restoration of his sight. Jesus stopped and had him brought: "What do you want me to do for you?" "That I might see," Bartimaeus urged. "Go, your faith has saved you."[44]

After Balaam's sight was retuned by the angel of YHWH, four oracles poured forth from him, all pronouncing blessing upon Israel, despite their sin in the wilderness. He spoke "the utterance of a strong man whose eye is clear . . . who sees the vision of the Almighty." He looked ahead and said, "I see him, but not now, I behold him but not near—a star shall tread the path from Jacob, and a scepter shall rise out of Israel . . . one out of Jacob shall rule."[45] Bartimaeus' sight restored, he now sees the one that Balaam had long ago glimpsed in the far away future..

Despite the importance of the Davidic line, only one king was ever called the *son of David*, Solomon.[46] He was also the last to ride through Jerusalem on a colt, his father's colt, announcing to all during that tumultuous time of monarchic succession that Solomon was David's choice for the throne. Solomon was a man of peace, unlike his father, David, who had been forbidden from building the house of YHWH because of the blood of war on his hands. Solomon secured that peace for the land in part by his alliances with foreigners; he was friend to the gentiles. His love of foreign women certainly alarmed the tradition, which blamed him in part for the Exile. Jesus, son of David, engages and invites the gentiles as well, drawing all to himself.[47]

Jesus, too, rides into Jerusalem on a colt, a colt never ridden by anyone before. There is no king before him to pass succession; he is the king who comes out of nowhere, fulfilling promise: "Go into the village . . . you will find a *colt tied* there." Jacob, Israel, saw this colt from his deathbed, giving his final blessing to his children. "The scepter will not depart from Judah," he had said. Visions and scepters from the past coalesce upon Jesus in the present. Jacob's blessing continues, "Binding his foal to the vine, and to the choice vine *the colt* of a donkey, he washes his clothes in wine and in the blood of wine berries his clothes."[48] Rule of the messiah would eventually require blood, but Jesus, son of David, son of Judah, has known that all along.

Fig Trees and Vineyards

Fig trees and vineyards, the parable of old no longer about disobedience but about power and the attempt to usurp it. YHWH has meddled in this story before and is practiced at making good from the evil. Death at the hands of the envious and power-hungry will not result in defeat but redemption and life.

Mark 11:11–12:10

Isaiah 5, 56:3–5, 7–8; Jeremiah 7–8

> They were nearing Jerusalem, at Bethpage and Bethany, near the Mount of Olives. . . . And he entered Jerusalem, and the temple, and having looked around at everything, the hours were already late, he went out to Bethany with the twelve. And on the next day as they were going out from Bethany, he was hungry. Seeing a fig tree in leaf from afar, he went in case he might find anything on it. He came upon it and he found nothing except leaves. For it was not the season for figs. And answering he said to it, May no one ever eat fruit from you again. And his disciples heard.
>
> Mark 11:11–14

The very name Bethpage announces; it is the place of unripe figs. That Jesus came up emptyhanded in his search should be no surprise. But figs still mark the time and the occasion. Entering Jerusalem on that colt and welcomed with praise and palm branches, the countdown begins. Time, in fact, is very short.

Jesus makes his way back to the Jerusalem temple after the night spent in Bethany, "the house of affliction." It's not as if the peddlers, those money changers, dove sellers, and the like, making a profit on the business of temple sacrifice, showed up overnight. They had long been there, likely Jesus' whole life. But today he makes a scene. Time for them to be driven out:[49] "Is it not written, my house shall be called a house of prayer for all the nations."[50]

What shambles they returned to from the Exile. It was not just the land but the returning people a mess as well. A mix, a mash. Restoring things to the imagined measure of holiness of the past—simply impossible. So much collective damage, so many brutalized people. And not just Judahites. Foreigners in the mix. The question of integration or separation, both fraught with peril. But the words that pour forth from Isaiah are a salve, making no distinctions among the peoples. All welcome as they are, for YHWH has gathered them to himself:

> Let the son of the foreigner who has joined to YHWH not say, "Surely YHWH will separate me from his people." And let not the eunuch say, "I am a dry tree." For thus says YHWH, "To the eunuchs that keep my sabbaths, who choose what delights me and holds strong to my covenant, I will give my house and within my walls a monument and a name better than sons and daughters, a name forever which shall not be cut off . . . I will bring them to my holy mountain and cause them to rejoice in my house of prayer, their burnt offerings and their sacrifices to favor my altar, *for my house will be a house of prayer to all peoples.* For the Lord YHWH, who *gathers* those scattered of

> Israel, declares yet I will *gather* [others] to those already gathered.
>
> Isa 56:3–5, 7–8

The family reunion happening among YHWH, his people, and the land could easily leave out the others, the awkward extras, tagalongs, not tied by blood or earth. YHWH's house is of central importance—the focal point for community life, the litmus for acceptance and rejection. But the god of Israel calls the foreigner close and says, "You belong too." From the earliest dedication of the temple by Solomon, it was to be so: "When a foreigner who is not of your people Israel comes from a far-off country for the sake of your name, and he comes and he prays towards this house, you hear from heaven, your dwelling place, and do according to all of which the foreigner calls to you."[51] The temple was never just for Israel but for the name of YHWH to be renowned throughout the earth and a place where the foreigner could come and know him along with Israel.[52]

The tables continue to turn, Jesus' temper not abated. He knows what this temple was supposed to be and what it has become: "*You have turned it into a den of robbers, of violence, of revolutionaries.*"[53]

It was a tense time in Judah. The northern kingdom of Israel had already been scattered to the nations by Assyria; ten tribes gone, only YHWH could facilitate their return. Babylon, now pushed against Judah's door—the new power in the region, powerful enough to defeat and unseat Assyria. The prophets agreed what Judah needed was hope, even more than truth. And so the rally cry YHWH would never let his precious temple fall—rhetoric that people could believe, despite what their hearts knew. They made the cry for their god synonymous with the cry for battle.

But YHWH raised up his own prophet, a thorn in the side of the religious and political leaders and their wishful propaganda. Jeremiah would not fall in line:

> Do not trust these words of deception, 'the temple of YHWH, the temple of YHWH' . . . If you do not oppress the sojourner, the widow, and the orphan, and innocent blood you do not pour out in this place, and if you do not go after other gods to your own evil, then I will cause you to dwell in this place which I gave to your fathers. Behold, you are trusting in words of a lie without profit . . . *Has this house which is called by my name become a den of robbers in your sight?* (Jer 7:4, 6–8, 11)

The sojourner. Jeremiah, too, notes YHWH's care for the foreigner who dwells among Israel. Isaiah and Jeremiah's concern over gentiles combines with Jeremiah's indictment of the Judean leadership to fuel Jesus' zeal as he cleanses the temple, the notable backdrop to the prophets' concerns as well.

Jeremiah worries not just over the foreigner, though. He is concerned for those alone, with no one to protect them—the widow and the orphan. Soon after, Jesus would accuse the scribes of devouring widows' houses. He would call attention to the poor widow at the treasury in the temple, only two small coins to her name, and yet she puts it all in. The rich, notably the religious leadership, in their abundance give but not to her. They pour money into the temple offering, but the widow has given more.[54] They let their neighbor, the widow, suffer, and it becomes their indictment, as the god of Israel sees. YHWH's house—YHWH has always seen. In Jeremiah's day, he held the leaders to account. Their temple would not be safe from the onslaught because of how they treated the foreigner, the widow, and the orphan. Jesus, too, moves his attention from the widow immediately to the temple, predicting the same: "There is not a stone upon a stone that will not be thrown down."[55]

Jeremiah continues, "Prophet, priest, they all are making a lie. They have healed the fracture of the daughter of my people with curse, saying 'Peace, peace, but there is no peace.' They shall fall among the fallen. When I punish them they shall stumble. *I would surely gather* them declares YHWH . . . but there are no figs on the fig tree. Even the leaves have withered and what I gave to them has passed."[56]

In the morning, Jesus, too, passes by: "They saw the fig tree withered from its roots. And Peter said, 'Rabbi, Look, the fig tree that you cursed has withered.'"[57] Figs and people, then and now. In the days of Jeremiah and the days of Jesus, the god of Israel would gather his own. But neither are there for the gathering.[58]

Jesus' temper at the temple draws attention and ire. The leaders indignant. The field on which Jesus retaliates is Isaiah's vineyard. "Judge between me and my vineyard," the god of Israel had said. The vineyard set upon a very fertile hill, rocks purged, choicest vines planted, along with a vat and watchtower built—all effort made to make the vineyard thrive: "Why, when I hoped for it to yield grapes, did it yield small unripe berries? I will turn aside from its hedge and it shall be devoured, its wall broken, it shall become trampled . . . For the vineyard of YHWH of Hosts is the house of Israel and *the man of Judah* his delightful planting. He hoped for justice and behold, bloodshed; for righteousness, but behold, a cry for help."[59]

Israel did not produce good fruit. Because of their oppression, their land would be devoured—Isaiah's message not at all veiled. Jesus borrows the imagery but shifts the meaning:

> A man planted a vineyard, put around it at fence, dug a winepress, and built a tower, and handed it over to farmers and took a journey. And he sent a slave to the farmers in season in order that he might take from them fruit from the vineyard. And taking him they beat him and sent him away empty. And again they sent to them another slave and even that one they beat over the head and dishonored. And then he sent another and that one they killed, and many others, some they beat, some they killed. Still one more he had, *a beloved son*. Last he sent him to them saying, they will respect my son. But those farmers said to

> one another, this is the heir, *come let us kill him* and the inheritance will be ours. Taking him they killed him and threw him out of the vineyard. And so what will the Lord of the vineyard do? He will come and destroy those farmers and give the vineyard to others.
>
> Mark 12:1–9

The focus is no longer Israel and the vineyard but the stewards. That certain Jewish religious leaders had persecuted the prophets sent by YHWH by no means a new claim. Jesus' declaration that he will be persecuted and killed by the guardians of the vineyard, the religious hierarchy of Israel/Judah also heard before. New, however, is the nuanced accusation that at least some of those who persecute Jesus know exactly who he is. They know he is the son, the beloved son of Israel's god.[60] The tie to Isaac, as well as the words spoken by the heavenly voice at Jesus' baptism and transfiguration, summoned again by the mention of *the beloved son*. These leaders know Jesus is the messiah. It is not in ignorance or piety that they persecute but desire for power. "*Come, let us kill him*," Joseph's brothers had also said, though, unlike Jesus, neither Isaac or Joseph actually died in their moments of crisis.[61] These stewards actively wish to deny the return of Israel's king and god. Because of this, care of YHWH's vineyard is handed to others. Given that it is the gentiles who came to trample the vineyard of Isaiah's parable and that Jesus has already fed four thousand gentiles and consecrated one as a priest, the scandal inherent in Jesus' parable is as brazen as the original. The "others" may be the next generation of Jesus' disciples, but they will no doubt include the gentiles as well.

YHWH Dies

YHWH has come to die. He takes the place of all those in the past who have faced death—Isaac, Joseph, Job, Jonah, even Israel in Exile.

Mark 14:32–16:20

Genesis 15:1–21; 45; Psalm 2, 22; Daniel 7:13

The three had accompanied him everywhere; they boldly desired to stand by him to the end. James and John asked for the places next to him in his suffering glory, and Peter had promised that even if all should desert, he never would.[62] Jesus knew none of them could, or would, follow through.

Betrayal set in motion by Judas, chronos barrels toward kairos. There in the garden of Gethsemane, the last private earthly excursion Peter, James, and John would ever have with Jesus. The predictions no longer future but present, the moment arrives, and it is too much to bear. Jesus, in deep distress, utters a confession to his friends: "My soul is deeply grieved, *to the point of death*, remain here and keep alert." But when Jesus returns from his closeted spot of despairing prayer, they are asleep. Three times he must wake them, each time, eyes so heavy, they leave him to bear his aloneness alone.[63]

Abraham still remained childless. He had been called to the land of Canaan by YHWH and promised children. The land was both occupied and in famine, and he and his wife remained childless. Years passed, and nothing seemed to change until the next encounter with YHWH: "I am YHWH who brought you up from Ur of the Chaldeans to inherit this land." "But how shall I know?" Abraham pressed. *Three* animals, each *three* years old, and a couple of birds. Abraham brought these to YHWH, preparing them as commanded.[64]

"It came to pass as the sun was leaving that a *deep sleep fell upon Abram* and behold, a horrifying darkness . . . and when the sun went and it was dark a smoking oven and a torch of fire passed between these pieces."[65] In that liminal space, sacred ground, that most important moment when agreements between YHWH and humankind were being made, Abram fell asleep.

Eli the priest failed in one particular task, raising decent boys. Privileged and impious, they abused their roles as priests such that when Eli called his sons out on their evil behavior, they didn't heed him because YHWH had already determined to destroy them.[66] Samuel was a miracle child, prayed for in Eli's presence by a barren mother. The prayer granted, in conjunction with Eli's careless assurance, created a bond between mother and priest. Samuel was sent to Eli's care as an offering to YHWH, an offering that God accepted. *One, two, three times he called to Samuel out of sleep*, marking him the next prophet to his people.[67] The time had come. Establishment changing, Eli's sons judged—Samuel, Eli's child apprentice and disciple, the new leader to care for YHWH's people.

Jonah, too, had been *grieved to the point of death* but not over 120,000 gentiles, who didn't know their right hand from their left, and many animals—those he was hoping to see die. Jonah was grieved over a plant, a plant that gave shade and then died at the hands of YHWH's appointed worm.[68] It was Jonah who was to stand in the gap between these gentiles and YHWH's judgment over their sin. But his own prejudice over their past offenses forced YHWH's hand. Jonah had no compassion. It was YHWH who stood between his own judgment and clueless gentiles.

Once again, YHWH stands in the gap, this time *giving himself* as a ransom for many. This time it is he who is *grieved until death over a vine*, Israel. He is the beloved son, put to death by those stewards who wish to inherit without compassion. Joseph is still the model, the one who suffers in order to save the world. Sold into slavery and death, just to be raised from the pit in time to save them all. Jesus, too, sold, betrayed, given to the pit, the pit with no return, only to return and inaugurate YHWH's kingdom.[69]

"You are still sleeping and taking your rest. Enough. Behold, the son of man is betrayed into the hands of sinners." Their hour past, his hour comes. No ram comes to rescue this Isaac. Rather, this beloved son betrayed with a kiss:[70]

> Why do the nations rage, and the peoples plot in vain? The kings of the earth take their stand and the dignitaries counsel together

> against YHWH and against his anointed . . . the one dwelling in heaven laughs, the Lord mocks them . . . He said to me, "You are my son, today I have begotten you . . . Ask of me and I will give the nations as your inheritance, and the ends of the earth as your possession" . . . And now, kings, be wise and instructible, judges of the earth. Serve YHWH in fear and rejoice in trembling. *Kiss the son*, lest he be angry, and you will be lost on the way.[71]
>
> Ps 2:1–2, 4, 7–8, 11–12

"You intended evil against me, but YHWH meant it for good, for the sake of causing many people to live"—Joseph's words to his brothers.[72] This betrayal will bring life—Judas a player in YHWH's drama.[73] In the end, it is not the nations, Israel or the gentiles, that will have their way but YHWH and YHWH's anointed.

The arrest. All of them, his disciples, desert him and flee.[74] First stop, the Jewish council. The priests, the elders, the scribes, all assembled, their plan to put him to death—the hired tenants of the vineyard. If in ignorance before, no longer. They summon witnesses. Less competent than Jezebel's henchmen false witnessing against Naboth, these cannot get their story straight. No matter. The high priest questions Jesus directly, no mincing of words, "Are you the messiah, the son of the blessed one?" The truth will seal Jesus' doom, but it is for this reason he has come. "ἐγώ εἰμι, I am . . . "[75]—the answer to their question and his name both the same. The proof of his guilt, despite his innocence.

"And you will see *the son of man, sitting at the right hand of power, coming with the clouds of heaven*." The metaphysical claims, Daniel's *son of man coming with the clouds of heaven*, it is all too much. "YHWH said to my Lord, *sit at my right hand* until I make your enemies a footstool for your feet."[76] Jesus unveiled. Direct messianic claims.[77] They tear their clothes.[78] The stewards have been told, and they reject. They will kill the beloved son. Like Eli's sons, God wills it to happen.

The mockery begins. "Prophesy," they call to the blindfolded Jesus. But he is one step ahead; his prophecy unfolds as they taunt—Peter denying him three times. They hand him to the gentiles. Accusations fly, but nothing sticks. Pilate recognizes that jealousy drives this internal dispute. Jacob's sons are once again envious of the beloved. "Crucify him." The crowd demands his death, and Pilate satisfies. The soldiers take him. Jacob's vision for Judah, so long ago set in motion, is realized today. The scepter will not depart. He is the king of the Jews. Even the gentiles title him. His cloak, purple like wine, like the blood of grapes. Paid with the homage of mockery. They spit, they strike, they salute, they crown him with thorns.[79] Suffering Job is his kin.

They crucified two thieves with him, one on the right and one on the left, the very seats James and John had wanted. Jesus drove out the robbers, the insurrectionists from the temple, only to share company with them in the end.[80] No longer just Abraham covered by blackness or Peter, James, and John resisting the pull of sleep; as this Isaac dies, darkness falls across the entire land.[81] For three hours, it is Jesus who hangs in between, he himself the Jordan. He hangs between heaven and earth, outside the city between home and away; he hangs like all those in Dalmanutha and like those gentile kings whom Joshua defeated as Israel realized the promises made to Abraham during that first terrible darkness.[82]

"*Eloi Eloi Lama Sabachtani*—My god, my god, why have you forsaken me?"[83] The psalm pulled to inform:

> All who see me mock/deride me,[84] they open their mouths at me and shake their heads . . . Many bulls encircle me, mighty ones of Bashan surround me . . . Like water I am poured out; my bones are all dislocated; my heart melts like wax within my breast. Withered like a potsherd is my mouth and my tongue cleaves to my gums. And in the dust of death you lay me. For dogs surround me; a company of evil doers encircle me. Like a

> lion are my hands and feet. They gloat and stare at me. They divide my clothes and over my garment they cast lots . . . He did not despise or detest the affliction of the afflicted. He did not hide his face from me. And in his cry of help to him he heard.
>
> Ps 22:1, 7–8, 12–18, 24, 27–28

David's ancient lament reframed as prophetic. A last word of protest, claiming victory in what looks like defeat. The god of Israel tormented like Naaman—slandered, shamed, inheritance stolen, blood pouring before the dogs outside the city. But the psalm continues with potency, pushing through to purpose—the purpose of it all: "All the ends of the earth shall remember and turn to YHWH. And all the families of the gentiles shall bow down before you, for dominion belongs to YHWH and he rules over the gentiles."[85]

The gentiles. It is not just about Jesus' present suffering. It is about the suffering that Jesus has warned of all along, gaining speed with the psalm, accomplishing the purpose of bringing the gentiles to worship Israel's God—final dominion, final victory—through self-sacrifice and not war. No longer that small-town gentile king outside of Ai, hanged until dead outside the city so Israel can inherit, but the anointed king of God, hanged outside Jerusalem, city of David, seat of kings, icon of Israel's inheritance, so that *all*, gentiles included, can inherit.

But the psalm is still not spent; there is more: "Before him shall bow down all who go down to dust, and his soul did not preserve alive . . . And they shall come and proclaim his righteousness to a people yet unborn."[86] It is not just Israel and the nations but the dead and those not yet, those future generations. All humanity that ever was or will be will worship YHWH. Dalmanutha. This is why Jesus hangs, to bring to YHWH everyone, past, present, future, Jew, gentile. The kingdom of god has drawn near for this purpose. The whole world is his, and he comes to call his own.

Then Jesus uttered a loud cry and then breathed out his soul. And the curtain in the temple was split in two from top to bottom.[87] King Darius, that old gentile king, had he been here, might have seen the hand from the heavens tear it, the inner sanctum of the temple now open for all, at the moment the son of man gives his life.[88] The first to affirm, the first to speak, the gentile centurion: "Surely this person was the son of god." That Jesus is the beloved not lost on this one. The first movement of the vineyard governance changing hands.[89]

Jesus' body is taken from the cross, wrapped in linen, and laid in a rock tomb, with a stone rolled to seal the opening. Joshua had taken that gentile king, hung him outside of Ai, and buried him in the rocks. His dead body, entombed in that pile of stone, would serve as a memorial of Israel's chosenness.[90] The sign of those defeated so that Israel could inherit. But the god of Israel brought YHWH's kingdom near, in part to rewrite, revise, and move the past forward, to envelop everyone, all the nations, in the blessing of particularity.

The women waited for the Sabbath to pass. And early on the first day of the week, the sun having risen, they went to the tomb. At the dawn of creation, the god of Israel wielded his dominion over the darkness and the chaos of the waters, marking the first day of the week. God spoke light into being, and the darkness dispelled[91]—this sunrise as powerful as the old. The darkness that reasserted itself at Jesus' death, covering all in darkness, is dispelled once again.

The three women arrive with spices. They are too late. The woman with the alabaster jar knew the moment.[92] The anointing of his body must happen before or not at all. A new memorial replaces the old. Still stone, still a tomb, but now empty. Israel's god, king, and messiah took the place of that gentile king and rewrote the story. The stone rolled away—what is now remembered.

There had been a young man wearing only a linen tunic, following from a distance after Jesus' arrest. Discreet but not elusive enough. They seized him, and in his desperate escape, he surrendered the garment, fleeing naked in the dark. The young Joseph, too, left his garment as he fled from Potiphar's wife's advances. The garment proof of his guilt, despite his innocence. Joseph found that his pit could get even deeper. No longer a slave, now thrown in jail with all of his integrity.[93]

But years past, fortunes turned, and those early dreams Joseph had as a boy finally came true. Pharoah himself pulled Joseph from jail and from the pit of death that his brothers had thrown him into so long ago. He made him second in command of the kingdom, clothing him in new robes.[94] As the women approach the tomb, they find the stone rolled away and a young man sitting within on *the right-hand* side of the tomb, dressed in a white robe.[95]

Jesus missing and a stranger sits to the right of his resting place.[96] The women are *alarmed*. "Do not be alarmed," he says. "You search for Jesus the Nazorean, the one who was crucified. He is not here. *Look, the place where they laid him*."[97] At the moment that Joseph reveals himself to his brothers, they find themselves so *troubled and dismayed* at his presence that they were *unable to speak*. He was gone, sold, good as dead, mourned, never to be seen again, and yet, after all that transpired, he stands before them alive. "*Do not be distressed*," he tells his brothers. "*Look, your own eyes see*, and the eyes of my brother *Benjamin*, that it is my own mouth that speaks to you . . . *Tell* my father all my glory . . . hasten and bring my father here."[98] And so Joseph sent his brothers on the journey back, and he warned them, "Do not *tremble* along the way."[99] The young man in Jesus' tomb continues: "*But, go, tell his disciples and Peter, that he goes ahead of you to Galilee*." So the women "went out and fled from the tomb for *trembling and amazement* seized them."[100]

Galilee of the gentiles, where it all began. Death and resurrection, there in his father David's city, his father's mountain, but he goes back to Galilee. It's the meeting place he sets for his friends. Jacob, too, would find his son, long thought dead, ruling in a land occupied by gentiles.[101] Jesus would appear to Mary Magdalene and two more disciples on the road, but none would believe them. Jacob also didn't believe when his sons returned with news of Joseph. Too much. Too much to believe that someone could return from the dead.[102] Or even if they could, in some faraway time and faraway place, not in my time, before my eyes. My grief, my loss after so much devastation, could not be met with life to match it. But that is what the god of Israel has done. All that has died now has a place in life. His very own judgment that swallowed up the earth in flood now consumed by his love and life. The commandment that Jesus gives the disciples when they finally break bread again: "Go, into all the world and proclaim the good news to all creation." Proclaim to Jew and gentile, plant, animal, bird, all the creeping things which creepeth upon the ground, all that was caught in judgment now has good news—"the sacred and incorruptible proclamation of eternal salvation" for all.[103]

Conclusion

The misunderstanding that has long ruled the reading of Mark's Gospel has proven unnecessary. Mark announces from the beginning, and with clarity, what his Gospel project is about. His message is simple, its meaning unveiled. Yet, sometimes, the most straightforward of things cannot be taken at face value. They are too unbelievable. Like staring directly at the sun, one must shift their gaze, looking at all that is illuminated by its rays rather than the flaming orb itself.

This is reflected in the many ways Mark has been appropriated—each use projecting a different image of the Gospel. Mark has been considered the first building block for how the Gospels came to be. Mark has been a mirror held up to reflect what the earliest Christians believed about Jesus. Mark has been a window peering onto the ever-elusive historical Jesus. Mark has been deemed a well-crafted and plotted drama that tells a tale as entertaining as it is unique. Mark as bios, Mark as kerygma, Mark as footnote, Mark as story. Many lenses, many Marks. Each legitimate in its own particular way. But questions of use cannot be so neatly isolated or determined, nor should contemporary concerns define or take precedent. In the end, Mark self-defines. Mark is new, an arche. Mark's originality, Mark's genius, Mark's announcement is Mark's "good news." Analogous to how YHWH's declaration of being turned into a name and title, so, too, Mark's declaration of good news becomes a title and a genre—Mark's gospel becomes Mark's Gospel.

From the beginning, Mark has been peddling hope, grand hope. "Israel's Exile," he seems to be announcing, with all the failed promises of restoration and its never-ending punishment, "is finally over"—a savior has come. The setting was the Jordan. The Exile ends where it began. The Davidic king, the iconic prophet, and the god of Israel himself all show up. But Mark's announcement is not just about that "event" in Israel's past, despite its magnitude, its devastation, and the indelible traumatic mark left on the psyche of an entire people. That event of the past was just the symptom. The crisis was far bigger than the Exile, and thus Israel's return home too small a remedy for the larger, more pervasive, and enduring problem.

This might be why a clear, unambiguous announcement regarding the end of the Exile is conspicuously absent in Mark's Gospel, though the Gospel's many intertextual nods allude to it at every turn. The announcement that Jesus, at long last, has brought the Exile to an end is only the beginning of the good news that constitutes Mark's Gospel. The message that the Baptist preaches simply, loudly, for all to hear—the message that becomes the hallmark of Jesus' own ministry—reveals what is at stake. "The kingdom of god is at hand," John proclaims. Jesus comes after and reveals it has come. The arrival of God's kingdom encompasses so much more than Exile's end. The end of the Exile belongs to the events made only of this world. The arrival of God's kingdom is an event that comes from somewhere else. YHWH's kingdom is over the fence. Mark's gospel that "the kingdom is here" becomes his Gospel, the space where this kingdom becomes manifest.

Despite the splendor of Cyrus' decree sending the Jewish people home, the proclamation by Isaiah referring to Cyrus as YHWH's anointed is deeply perplexing. The messiah of Israel, the "anointed," their deliverer, was supposed to be one of their own, a king from the line of David. That YHWH would maneuver the gentile nations in his punishment of Israel is nothing new. But that YHWH would also choose to use the nations in Israel's restoration is a surprising, fitting, and yet galling bit of poetic justice. While YHWH's inclusion of the gentiles in his plans for Israel could be read as necessary, a necessary predicate to combat Israel's postexilic xenophobia, such a reading seems so wanting—so shallow and meager. Israel's return is so troubled, so piecemeal, so bland that it cannot even be considered a poor substitute for the fulfillment of the grand promises made by YHWH through the prophets.

The reality of return to the homeland was anticlimactic and wholly disappointing. It was nothing like what was expected. Everything about it unreasonably hard—no eagles' wings to mount, no being carried home along a leveled road in YHWH's mighty arms. Trouble and strife plagued the returning exiles every step of the way. Haggai tells that the same god who once waxed poetically to David, explaining that he didn't need a temple, now takes offense over the same, punishing the weary exiles because they built their own houses rather than his. The problem of the temple finally rectified, Ezra reports that the elders who had known the first temple wept at the sight of the second—not from joy but from sadness. The new temple, lacking in every possible measure, would not live up to memory. For that older generation who had seen Solomon's temple, the new one was not redemption and restoration but a reminder of all that had been lost.

But Mark's Gospel assumes that restoration from the Exile is not the biggest problem. Part of the larger problem implicated YHWH. Moses had said, "If your presence does not go before us, do not take us up from here. For how will it be known then that I have found favor in your sight, I and your people, if not for your going with us."[1] Ezekiel had seen the chariot of YHWH's presence leaving the temple in Jerusalem to join his people in exile. The prophets spoke of YHWH himself guiding the exiles home. And yet, when the time came, YHWH seemed absent. Neither Ezra and Nehemiah, nor Haggai spoke of YHWH's grand presence. Rather, they shook in panic at his perceived wrath—beating, berating, and pulling hair out over the continued contemporary failure of YHWH's people. His presence feared but not felt. The problem Mark's Gospel addresses is YHWH's own exile, not just Israel's.

This is Israel and Judah's crisis, not just the Exile in itself but the possibility that YHWH has abandoned. In their most desperate time, in wrath and punishment, YHWH abandoned them, and no amount of prophetic reframing can whitewash this fact. The waves of return to the land happened long ago and ingloriously so, coming and going amid the silence of their god. The pomp and circumstance that was supposed to mark their return never occurred. Restoration, if it could be called that, limped along for a few centuries under gentile domination, never truly complete. This is the truth that Mark confronts. This is the power of his pronouncement, his good news. "The kingdom of God has come," he announces. It is the specific counter to the claim that YHWH and the hope for a kingdom have forsaken them.

Mark, however, points to a different kind of rescue, a different kind of return. It would be easy to become lost to Mark's announcement that Israel's long-hoped Davidic messiah is really here and that Elijah, too, has returned. Mark knows that the fulfillment of these promises matters; no new message can flourish without them. But they signify something far more important—that their god has not forgotten them, that YHWH has come for his own, that YHWH keeps his promises. The secret to Mark's gospel is not that Jesus is the long-awaited Messiah. The true secret is that the long-awaited Messiah is YHWH's presence among his people. Jesus inaugurates the reign of YHWH because YHWH is with Jesus, because YHWH is Jesus. Jesus is not just YHWH's man; he is the man YHWH. The return is not just Israel to her land but YHWH to his people.

It should be no surprise, then, that when YHWH arrives in Jesus, his first order of business is just as scandalous, wild, and unpredictable as the method of his arrival. YHWH participates in an act of communal repentance. Israel's god shows up, and the repentance that he has expected of his people, demanded of his people, is now his own. After the long years of divine silence, YHWH repents; moreover, he redresses the judgments of old. The steps Jesus walks throughout Mark's Gospel make amends for the ways Israel felt slighted by her god. Those times of unrestrained temper are remembered with reparation. The promises so long ago forgotten so as to be thought broken are renewed and kept. The abandonment that broke their hearts and their faith is met with presence, compassion, and cause to hope in their god once again. YHWH has not only come back to them, but he has come as one of them—his solidarity beyond imagination. YHWH is a man of Israel. As the man YHWH, Jesus not only calls Israel to be Israel, but Jesus becomes Israel for Israel.

Mark's Gospel is the good news that YHWH is here, ushering in his kingdom, his presence present in Jesus. But Mark's good news does not end there. Though Jesus' first words, "The time is fulfilled. The kingdom of god has come," were intended for the children, for the chosen, Mark understands their reach. The story is wanting, incomplete, if the beloved child, lost among the orphans of a foreign land—every one of them hoping for rescue, belonging, and family—is finally found by the doting and generous father, only to leave all the other children behind. The fairy tale becomes Faerie and a tale worth telling when the father comes for his beloved and then gathers up all the other orphan children too. He takes them all home with him, saving them all, giving them all family, home, belonging. There is no jealousy; the child relishes their position as a conduit of the father's generosity. The father's kingdom and household are grand, grand enough to make good all the promises of hope his children have made on his behalf.

Election is no longer about keeping people out. The power of election is that the elect gather in all the rest. This is why the return was so unsatisfying, so thin. YHWH, the particular god, the god of Israel, did not even deliver on his promises to his own. Israel in Exile, Israel the divorced, was made no more favored than the other nations. Rather than deliver all, YHWH rejected all, and the return did not overwhelm all with restoration. But the return was not the end; it was only the beginning. Israel was always to be a light to the nations, and YHWH's desire was always to bless the other nations through Israel. Israel is chosen, blessed, but this one god dreams of including all people within his blessing. Mark's Jesus desires to elect everyone, beginning with Israel. YHWH's kingdom has invaded, not to include some and reject others but to welcome all.

The elect are to be gatekeepers who beckon all to come through the gate. They are indeed guardians though they guard not to make sure the gate is kept shut but rather that it always remains open. Chosenness is not that "we prosper while others suffer; we live while everyone else dies." Chosenness is the call to lead others to light and life, most especially outsiders. Mark uses the old tales of Israel to demonstrate that election is not exclusion but rather the very beacon for inclusion. Mark underwrites this fantastical vision of inclusion by narrative fusion. No one text will do. No simple citation will suffice. Mark allows a torrent of texts to flow, combine, and form a grand river of Gospel—a god who repents, a people who enjoy their god's presence in this world once again, and the rest of the world invited into that which was once exclusive, by the people who have become heralds for their god. It is not that Mark points to this text or that text as if to say, "Look, a promise has been fulfilled." Mark opens up the whole of the Scriptures and allows a flood of texts to serve as the colors for the gospel vision he now paints. This underwriting is what turns gospel to Gospel—and Mark's Jesus into a brand-new figure.

There were notable times when YHWH visited, and his mythical realm came near. When his people were most desperate, YHWH showed up—this is Israel's history, not just her hope. The voice that spoke to Moses from the flaming bush confessed, "I have surely seen the affliction of my people . . . and their cry I have heard . . . I know their sufferings . . . . And I have come to deliver them . . . . And have come to bring them to a good and spacious land, a land flowing with milk and honey." Cataclysmic events followed, resulting in miracles and deliverance. When Israel approached the Jordan, coming into their inheritance after forty years of wandering, Joshua was met by the angel of the LORD with his sword in hand. There at the Jordan, the armies of YHWH joined the army of Israel, ushering in inheritance with the power of YHWH's kingdom.

In both of those grand events, YHWH's kingdom broke into Israel's reality. Mark dares the story about Jesus to jump this same fence, to enter into that same untamed place that transcends this worldly limitations and bursts with wild possibility, a place undaunted by the grit and grime of grave clothes and burial spices. Mark taps into this same magic of old but for a new and different purpose. Before, YHWH intervened in earthly matters to side with Israel, YHWH'S own, over the other nations. YHWH'S kingdom now arrives, ushered in by Jesus, for the purpose of saving the nations, not destroying them. YHWH, God of Israel, ministers among the gentiles too.

Cyrus, YHWH's anointed, was more than just a feeble last-minute substitute reappropriated because of YHWH's failure to show. Cyrus was YHWH's own too. YHWH called him, marked him by name. And he was not the sole exception of a gentile belonging to YHWH. The scandal of particularity is not that there is one god and this one god's one people, Israel. The scandal of particularity is that there is one god and this one god's world, and he desires the whole of it, not just a small part of it, be gathered to him as his chosen.

The expectation after the Exile was that the messiah would continue in the ways of the past. David's lineage would return and lead Israel in earthly victory against the gentile nations. But Mark's Jesus refuses to see gentiles as the enemy. When the sky tears open, the world changes. The voices of the other world can be heard, both good and evil, and they testify to YHWH'S desire to save, and his endorsement of the methods and working of his son. Humanity, regardless of gender, ethnicity, or any other human or social construct, is not the enemy. Evil is the enemy. It is evil that oppresses through demonic possession, through sickness and disease, through hard-hearted piety, through a myriad of other things. It is evil that leads to death. Human hosts are to be redeemed, not destroyed. Unchosen, unelected humans are not the problem. The gentiles are not the problem. Evil and the world's captivity to evil are the problem. Mark's Gospel reveals the powerlessness of evil before Jesus, the face of YHWH's kingdom.

Mark has preached a gospel grounded in monotheism and election for a new end. It is not enough for YHWH, for Mark, or Mark's Jesus that all Israel is saved; the desire of Mark is for all the world to be saved. Mark's Gospel is a gospel of universal inclusion, a gospel of universal salvation. It is not that Mark blended existing features in a new way, though he did that. It is that Mark took his narrative cues from another world. Israel sat by the rivers of Babylon and wept as their captors demanded of them song, but Mark sings a new song by the banks of the Jordan, one that includes both captive and captor. Mark achieved a new form and a new claim by a new route. He did not practice pesher or allegory or catchwords. He did not use proof texts or merely echo. No. Mark fused narrative. Mark created a new form that preached a new message.

It is no wonder that Mark practices a strategy of narrative fusion. Mark's Jesus demands it. Mark's Jesus preaches conversion, the conversion of theological imagination. Mark's method must match Mark's message. Both are as improbable as they are totalizing. Mark is a self-defining genre, maybe the very first of its kind. It does not merely announce the improbable has occurred; it makes present the impossible—the kingdom is here. The danger of monotheism, on both the divine and human sides, is exclusion, and such exclusion demands redress. Such a message, such a Gospel, demanded a rereading, a new figure. Citation of text was not enough. Mark fused narrative after narrative after narrative of old, with the new narrative of Jesus, to create this new figure. This is gospel making Gospel.

This reading of Mark's Gospel, of Mark's Jesus, and Israel's god raises theological questions. And rightly so. Such a reading decenters the "idea" of "God," whose many predications of perfection prevent any notion of repentance and recenters YHWH, the named and particular god of Israel, and the scriptures that narrate his being and nature, his actions and opinions. It is on this tradition of YHWH and his relationship with Israel and the world that Mark depends. YHWH arrives with a history of regret and repentance. YHWH has a history of temper and violence. YHWH has a history of siding with gentiles, sometimes over his elect. YHWH has a history of showing up late and sometimes not at all. YHWH has history. But YHWH loves. YHWH loves his own—both Israel and the entire world and all that is in it. YHWH is god of the nations, and his salvation is for all.

Christianity has been implicated—indeed, named as a chief culprit—of a posture of exclusion, othering, a privileging that fosters suspicion, hatred, and even violence. But this posture is not in keeping with the first Gospel. Mark's Jesus depicts YHWH to be a god who draws all and YHWH's kingdom to be a place of hope and joy big enough for all. This Gospel of inclusion contests both the depictions and practices of Christianity that would exclude anyone. Like Jesus, the followers of Mark's Jesus are to embark on a life that welcomes all. Like YHWH, Mark's Jesus reconciles—even YHWH's own previous judgments. Mark solicits its readers to generously and openly embrace everyone, individually and corporately, as a first-order implication of Jesus' words and deeds, primary to a life of holiness. The Gospel of Mark is good news for all, portraying Jesus, as the messiah who opens his hands rather than closes his fists, the embodiment of YHWH, god of the universe, whose name has always been Lovingkindness and Mercy. Mark's Gospel marks a new beginning.

NOTES

PREFACE

1. Maxine Grossman ("Exile," in *The Oxford Dictionary of the Jewish Religion*, ed.Adele Berlin [Oxford: Oxford University Press, 2011], https://www.oxfordreference.com/view/10.1093/acref/9780199730049.001.0001/acref-9780199730049-e-1032) marks four major exiles: the Egyptian exile (Jacob to the Exodus), Assyrian exile, Babylonian exile, and finally the exile after the destruction of the second temple in 70 C.E. until 1948. Grossman notes, "Until the advent of the modern era, exile was regarded variously as an unmitigated evil, a curse, a punishment for Israel's sins, and a redemptive suffering; in all cases as a provisional form of existence, which would be terminated by the ingathering of the exiles and messianic redemption. The latter either had to be patiently awaited or actively prepared for by piety and penitence. In early rabbinic and later mystical theology the notion of Israel's exile was complemented by that of God's own exile (*galut ha-shekhinah*—the exile of the divine presence." Louis Jacobs, ed. ("Exile," in *A Concise Companion to the Jewish Religion* [Oxford: Oxford University Press, 1999], https://www.oxfordreference.com/view/10.1093/acref/9780192800886.001.0001/acref-9780192800886-e-205) defines "exile" simply as "the banishment of the Jewish people from their homeland and the state of mind produced by this." He continues, "On the theological level, exile is interpreted as remoteness from God so that, in some religious sources, redemption from exile means not alone the salvation of the Jews from oppression and persecution, but the restoration, in the individual soul, of the harmony and bliss that are the fruit of nearness to God." The experience of physical and socio-political exile cannot help but instigate individual and communal soul searching regarding the existential state of exile. By Mark's day, this is full force.

My argument is that Mark understands the Assyrian and Babylonian Exile to be but a symptom of the larger problem of exile. Mark's claim is that the god of Israel has come to solve the latter. YHWH redeems from the more sinister and pervasive metaphysical exile, and that all smaller and temporal Exiles are once and for all subsumed into its redemption.

CHAPTER 1: A SAVIOR COMES

1. The very mention of the Jordan ignites anticipation of the extraordinary. Its involvement at key metaphysical moments in Israel's history suggests itself an instigator. Kay Kessler notes in "Setting as Character" (*Encyclopedia of Romance Fiction*, ed. Kristen Ramsdell [Santa Barbara, CA: Greenwood, 2018], 323–324), "A setting can both evoke emotion and strengthen conflict to a degree that it too, significantly shapes the narrative . . . Essentially, the setting becomes a character." Naaman's commentary undergirds such identification nicely as he disparages the waters of Israel, adding that his own land has grander and greater rivers, only to be proven wrong (2 Kgs 5:12). His rivers do not cleanse the leper, the Jordan itself revealed to be an agent of YHWH's grace. Michael Walsh contemplates in "How *The Phantom of the Opera* Led Me to a Long-Lost Musical Treasure in Paris" (*Smithsonian Magazine*, March 2008) why *The Phantom of the Opera*, written in 1909, still resonates: "The reason we still read and watch *Phantom* is its setting: The Opéra itself. Above all, *Phantom* is a story of place." The story of Israel, while no doubt about a people, is also about a place, the land of Canaan as Israel's inheritance, and the Jordan River functions as the front door.
2. Mark 1:1. With "Son of God," Mark provides the reader bookends (1:1 and 15:39). Regardless of what comes and how bad the catastrophic nadir, Mark gives away the happy ending at the beginning—his story is one of "good news." I agree with Donald Juel (*Messianic Exegesis* [Philadelphia: Fortress, 1988], 80), who notes, "At least in Mark, the messianic associations of Son of God are apparent. Particularly striking is the scene before the Jewish court where the high priest asks Jesus in that climactic scene, 'Are you the Christ, the Son of the Blessed?' (14:61)—to which Jesus replies, 'I am, and you will see . . . ' The question and response occur as part of a trial dominated by royal imagery. The

link between 'Son' and 'Messiah' established in the Letter to the Hebrews is present in Mark as well." William Wrede (*Messianic Secret*, trans. J. C. G. Greig [Cambridge: James Clark, 1971], 77) similarly states, "There can be no question here of a proof from linguistic usage, say from the connection of the two expressions in one passage (14:61, 1:1), but if Mark ever identified the Son of God and the Messiah he simply cannot have had an idea of the Messiah inferior to the meaning of the term 'Son of God.'"

3. Isa. 40:9–11. LXX Isaiah 52:7, 60:6, and 61:1 all use εὐαγγελίζω as well. Morna Hooker (*The Gospel According to St. Mark*, BNTC 2 [Peabody, MA: Hendrickson, 1991], 34) does not quite go far enough when explaining Isaiah's usage: "The good news that is proclaimed is the imminent salvation which God is going to work for his people . . . By using this term, Mark claims that this salvation has come in Jesus." This is true. But what Hooker doesn't say is that every Isaiah usage of εὐαγγελίζω is in the specific context of the announcement of the end of the Exile. This is how Mark understands the good news too. Good news is the herald that YHWH himself has come to redeem his people from their specific punishment of Exile and exile. The sentinels can see the return of YHWH to Zion (52:8). The glory of YHWH will once again shine upon Zion as Zion watches all its people, the wealth of the nations, and the nations themselves come back through its gates (60:1–16). Moreover, one specifically anointed by YHWH will announce this good news, news of YHWH's favor to his people (61:1–2).
4. Ps 2:1–2, 4, 6–8. While specifically relevant to this psalm, Joel Marcus (*Mark 1–8*, The Anchor Yale Bible [New Haven, CT: Yale University Press, 1974], 166) captures nicely the overall approach to Mark's utilization of Scripture: "The OT allusions, however, do not just function as scriptural proof texts but contribute importantly to the message of the passage. Psalm 2 was interpreted messianically in early Judaism so that its citation here gives a divine imprimatur to Mark's assertion in 1:1 that Jesus is the Christ."
5. 2 Sam 7:12, 14. No doubt Mark would have picked up on the "I will raise up your offspring" as resurrection language.
6. Juel (*Messianic Exegesis*, 62) points to midrash on Nathan's Oracle in 4QFlor to shed light on how the promise to David of a descendant on

the throne would have been interpreted during the intertestamental period: "The [Dead Sea] scrolls are important because they provide insight into aspects of post biblical Jewish tradition in the Christian and pre-Christian era that were previously unknown . . . The midrash reads Nathan's words to David as a prediction of the coming Messiah at the end of days, and it quotes, without hesitation, the words of God according to which he will call the Messiah his 'son.' The midrash offers a striking comparison with the opening chapter of Hebrews, where both 2 Sam 7:14 and Ps. 2:7 are quoted to speak of Jesus the Messiah as God's son. With the publication of the midrashic fragment, textbooks that spoke about messianic language in postbiblical Judaism have had to be rewritten."

7. 2 Kgs 2:14.
8. Mark's explicit Isaiah citation has perplexed many as it is actually a mix of Isaiah and Malachi 3:1, with the wording most closely resembling LXX Exodus 23:20. And so theories abound. But surely Mark knows that an audience for whom such fulfillment matters would be well aware of the discrepancy. Marcus (*Mark 1–8*, 147) comes close when he says, "Mark's ascription of the whole catena to Isaiah could simply be a mistake, but it is more likely that Mark is deliberately setting his story in an Isaian context." Yes, but more precisely, Mark sets the lens by which to read his passage by citing Isaiah. Richard Hays (*Echoes of Scripture in the Gospels* [Waco, TX: Baylor University Press, 2016], 20–21) rightly notes, "Mark's attribution of the mixed citation to 'the prophet Isaiah' reflects not ignorance but theological intentionality." Isaiah pronounces comfort, the end of the Exile, the end of punishment. Mark establishes priority. The Exodus passage, the undercurrent, does something unique here too. Exile is punishment; captivity in Egypt was not. Yet the god of Israel returns those exiled to their land of promise, the same as those he delivered from slavery in Egypt. Prior guilt does not alter the behavior of YHWH, who forgives sin and washes clean.
9. Mark 1:2–3.
10. Exod 23:20.
11. Isa 40:1–3.
12. This larger passage (40:9–11) was also heard in the initial announcement of good news. There, too, it was YHWH himself who would

comfort and carry his people home. The presence of Yhwh is the sign, the announcement of the end of the Exile. No intermediary necessary. While cautious reading forces ambiguity at first regarding what Mark intends to claim about Jesus, the larger story bolstered by his intertextual allusions seems to make clear that Mark is quite literal with his scriptural interpretation and thus the identity he ascribes to Jesus from the very beginning.

13. Mal 3:1, 5–6; 4:5.
14. The symbolism is subtle. Malachi, already in play in Mark's Gospel, says, "I will rebuke the eater/devourer for you and it will not destroy your fruit of your ground" (3:11). This only works with Hebrew as LXX alters to "I will order for you food and I will not destroy the fruit of your ground." Victor Hurowitz ("Critical Notes: אכל in Malachi 3:11—Caterpillar," *JBL* 121 [2002]: 327–330) explains, "Morphologically the word is to be parsed as an active participle in the *qal* theme of the common root אכל, and etymologically it can be given a literal translation 'eater' or 'devourer.' It is also clear from the context that some sort of agricultural pest is indicated." Hurowitz notes in fn.1, "The LXX seems to reflect a different pointing of the word, not as a participle but as a segholate noun אכל meaning food." This accounts for why the entire LXX translation of this verse is different from the Hebrew. Throughout MT, locusts are tied to devouring. They are the eater, specifically the eater tied to the punishments of covenant infidelity (Deut 28:38). Joel 2:25, in the context of postexilic restoration, says, "I will make peace/restore for you the years that the locust has eaten."
15. There is the new Elijah and the old. In Elijah's confrontation with the prophets of Baal, he tells King Ahab to summon all Israel, "πάντα Ισραηλ." All Israel is mentioned twice (1 Kgs 18:19, 20), while simply "πάντας," "all" (1 Kgs 18:21) or "πᾶς ὁ λαὸς," "all the people" (1 Kgs 18:25, 30, 39) shows up four times. Ben Witherington III (*The Gospel of Mark* [Grand Rapids, MI: Eerdmans, 2001], 73) does not mention the echo when he comments, "We are further told that John attracted a crowd from the whole Judean countryside and even from among the Jerusalemites. This is of course a hyperbolic remark, but its rhetorical purpose is to indicate John's great popularity." Hooker (*The Gospel According to St. Mark*, 37) makes no mention but simply says, "The

statement that the whole of Judea flocked to him, together with everyone from Jerusalem, is clearly an exaggeration." It may be an exaggeration, but it is a very old exaggeration deliberately echoed here. Both cases refer to the whole people in need of repentance, of turning their hearts back to their god.

16. N. T. Wright (*The New Testament and the People of God* [Minneapolis: Fortress, 1992], 268–272), in his oft-quoted definition of Exile, explains, "Most Jews of [the Second Temple] period . . . believed that, in all the sense which mattered, Israel's exile was still in progress. Although she had come back from Babylon, the glorious message of the prophets remained unfulfilled. Israel still remained in the thrall to foreigners; worse, Israel's god had not returned to Zion." Brandt Pitre (*Jesus, the Tribulation, and the End of the Exile* [Tübingen: Mohr Siebeck, 2005], 32–40) disagrees and distinguishes his own understanding of Exile from Wright's: "Unfortunately, what Wright means by 'the end of exile' is inherently flawed. To put it bluntly: while Wright is absolutely right about the importance of the 'exile,' he is fundamentally wrong in his understanding of it." Pitre's disagreement with Wright is threefold: "First, [Wright] is claiming that 'most Jews' of the Second Temple period—even those living in the land of Israel, whose ancestors had in fact returned 'from Babylon'—still considered *themselves* to be 'in exile,' . . . for first century Jews in Palestine . . . the *Babylonian Exile had not yet ended* (33) . . . Second, when Wright speaks of the end of 'exile,' he is *redefining* the meaning of 'exile' so that it *no longer refers to the geographical expulsion and captivity of the Jews* . . . (33) Third . . . in this articulation, Wright appears to be simply equating 'the Jews' of the Second Temple period with all 'Israel' . . . (33) There is little support in the Second Temple Literature that Jews living in the land of Israel considered *themselves* to be in Exile: i.e. that the Babylonian Exile had not ended (35)." Whether or not all Jews considered themselves to be in Exile, Mark considered all Jews living in the land of Israel to still be in the Exile. Mark seems to land somewhere between Wright and Pitre. Those who returned from Babylon are still in Exile as they are still dominated by foreigners and their god has not returned, but they also know that the Northern Kingdom of Israel still remains scattered. The Exile will not be over until the scattered return to the land

and YHWH, too, returns, throwing off foreign domination and setting both Judah and Israel completely free. Mark understands the kingdom of god that John the Baptist announces, and Jesus inaugurates, to be the beginning of the end of the Exile. YHWH has finally come. But it is not this temporal plane that is of primary consequence. The heavens have been ripped open at the baptism and the temple curtain at the crucifixion. Creation is no longer exiled from her god; even death will no longer hold sway. Mark understands restoration to be bigger even than the Exile that has concerned Judah and Israel. Moreover, gentile inclusion, while involving the drawing of the nations to YHWH, God Most High, Lord of the whole earth, is also about drawing back the ten lost tribes that had been thoroughly scattered to the nations. I think Mark knows that to draw the gentiles in is to draw Israel back in. Pitre (263) concurs on this point: "Isaiah explicitly depicts not only the ingathering of the nations but, moreover, a *mission proclamation* to the Gentiles . . . Isaiah 66 provides the much-needed *rationale* for why Jesus stipulates that 'it is necessary' for the good news to first be proclaimed to 'all the nations' (Mark 13:10). In short, *the only way to bring about the End of the Exile*, the ingathering of the lost tribes who had been scattered among the nations, *is to go to the nations* and *to bring the Gentiles to Zion, along with the Israelites scattered among them.*" Jason Staples (*Paul and the Resurrection of Israel: Jews, Former Gentiles, Israelites* [Cambridge: Cambridge University Press, 2023], 324) argues similar logic with Paul's "all Israel will be saved." Staples explains, "When Paul observed uncircumcised Jesus-followers receiving the spirit—the very thing promised not to gentiles but to Israel as part of the new covenant—he turned to his scriptures to understand this unexpected development . . . Paul argues that after being divorced from the covenant for infidelity and behaving like the nations, the bulk of non-Jewish Israel had effectively become *gentilized*, having assimilated among the non-Israelite nations. As such, the bulk of non-Jewish Israel could be reckoned as ethnically dead, having been assimilated and consumed by the nations, no longer ethnically distinct as a people. But the God who brings life from the dead is now doing just that by calling gentiles—truly 'not my people'—his people as Hosea had prophesied. The promise that God would call his people 'from the nations' (ἐξ [τῶν] ἐθνῶν) meant not only 'from among the nations' but 'from gentiles.' Where Israel had become *gentilized*, now gentiles are effectively being *Israelitized*, transformed from one ethnicity to another and integrated into the ethnic people of Israel. The inclusion of physically uncircumcised persons in the promise is therefore not a rejection or replacement of Israel but rather the means by which God is reaching out and saving more of Israel than anyone anticipated, a process analogous to resurrection from the dead. God has not replaced Israel with a new people but is calling, gathering, revivifying, and reconciling even those thought irretrievably lost, having been fully consumed and absorbed by the nations."

17. Paolo Gervasi ("Fetishizing Memories. Emotional Objects in Literature," paper presented at the Emotional Objects: From Lost Amulets to Found Photos event at the Human Being Festival 2017, Queen Mary University, London, November 20, 2017) discusses the potency of literary objects to trigger memory in their reader. The example he uses is the "madeleine scene" from Marcel Proust's *Remembrance of Things Past* (1913–27): "Tasting the *madeleine* soaked in a cup of tea Marcel, the first-person narrator, feels an unaccountable and deeply physical sensation of joy, which is associated with a stream of memories from his childhood. Places, objects, and feelings emanate from the cup of tea to be vividly projected before Marcel as in a theatre. Marcel realizes he used to have the same cake when he was a child." "Baptism" in the Jordan functions as an object in this way, triggering the same kind of flow of memory for the biblical reader as the madeleine. The biblical reader, saturated in the tradition, knows almost experientially that they have been here before, with the host of characters they have read. The word "baptism," then, combined with this Jordan location, functions to unpack the genealogy of all the history that has happened in this place, as well as the emotion associated with each unfolding story. In a similar vein, Walter Brueggemann (*The Prophetic Imagination*, 2nd ed. [Minneapolis: Augsburg Fortress, 2001], 64) heralds the role of the prophet, which here applies to both John the Baptist (the prophet to the Israel of Jesus' day) and Mark himself (a prophet to his community by means of his Gospel): "What a commission it is to express a future that none think imaginable! Of course this cannot be

done by inventing new symbolism, for that is wishful thinking. Rather, it means to move back into the deepest memories of this community and activate those very symbols that have always been the basis for contradicting the regnant consciousness . . . And when the prophet returns with the community, to these deep symbols, they will discern that hope is not a late, tacked on hypothesis to serve a crisis but rather the primal dimension of every member in this community."

18. 2 Kgs 5:1–8.
19. 2 Kgs 5:10–14.
20. Long years prior, the ark of the covenant, also captured, refused to be a prisoner but rather elicited faith of gentiles, suggesting a particular posture in such circumstance. This little Israelite girl far gentler than the ark in Philistine territory (1 Sam 4:11, 5:1–6:18).
21. 2 Kgs 5:17.
22. Josh 3:3, 5.
23. Josh 3:9–11, 13.
24. Josh 3:15–16.
25. Mark uses σχιζομένους: rip, tear, rend. It is not the civilized opening of a door that can simply be closed again. Rather, tear the door off the hinges, rip open a hole in the sky, rescue without manners or reserve! The echo traces back to Isaiah 63:19. However, LXX uses "ἀνοίξῃς," "open," "unlock" the heavens, suggesting that Mark is using a Hebrew text. "Oh, that you would tear (קרע) the heavens and come down"—the violence of Mark's word choice absent in LXX is present there in the Hebrew. Hays (*Echoes*, 18) also draws specific attention to the desperation Mark conveys, calling Matthew's and Luke's LXX use of "ἀνοίξῃς" colorless: "'The gospel, according to Mark, is God's answer to Isaiah's intercessory cry: the tearing of the heavens and the descent of the Spirit upon Jesus signifies that God's eschatological work of deliverance is beginning. *God is coming to rule over Israel once again.*"
26. Mark 1:11.
27. Gen 12:1.
28. Gen 22:2, 18.
29. Gen 25:23, 29–34; Gen 27. Gary A. Anderson (*Christian Doctrine and the Old Testament* [Grand Rapids, MI: Baker, 2017], 80–81) shines sober light on election and chosenness: "The natural human response

to election is to assume that it represents a very good deal for the person so chosen . . . But there is another aspect to being chosen . . . election involves a *cost* . . . Election does not mean living a life of unending blessings; it means being chosen to give up one's all for God, even what one holds most dear." In Jacob's case, this means being parted from land and family, modeling what chosenness would look like forever more down the line.

30. "God" will represent the Hebrew Elohim throughout.
31. Gen 33:9–10.
32. Malachi's words, "Jacob I have loved, and Esau I have hated" (1:2–3), hover just under the surface. Mark relies on the Malachi passage to be elusive, a scent on the wind. It whispers by means of the other passages from Malachi already echoed in Mark's first chapter. But it remains deliberately shadowed by the Genesis passage, which Mark punctuates, making reconciliation and not division the last word for these brothers. This is especially important for Mark's Gospel, which desires to unify Jew and gentile as children of one god.
33. Mark 1:11.
34. General consensus seems to rest on Isaiah 42:1 as the best option for Mark's source for (ἐν σοὶ εὐδόκησα) "in you I am well pleased." Isaiah 42:1 is uncompelling if relying on LXX προσεδέξατο αὐτὸν ἡ ψυχή μου, "my soul has accepted him," especially as it doesn't actually share any word overlap with Mark. But the Hebrew parallel, בֹּו בְּחִירִ֖י רָצְתָ֣ה נַפְשִׁ֑י, "in him, my chosen, my soul is well pleased," is quite strong. Combined with the Jacob and Esau story, the undercurrent casts a very particular light, nuancing Mark's message.
35. There is a complex layering that happens as Mark builds his references. Mark doesn't specifically mention Noah's ark, but his mention of baptism in the Jordan evokes the ark (κιβωτὸν) of the covenant in Joshua. Forty days and the wild animals evoke the flood story from Genesis 6–9, despite James Edwards' claim (*The Gospel According to Mark*, Pillar New Testament Commentary [Grand Rapids, MI: Eerdmans, 2002], 40–41) that there is no exact parallel to Jesus being "with the wild animals" in the Bible. Noah's ark (κιβωτὸν) then comes into play. The two arks connect, and both arks connect back to Mark. All the stories mix and mingle.

36. Gen 6:5–6. While the LXX uses a term suggesting more the idea of the reflection of the heart (ἐνεθυμήθη), it is the Hebrew that carries more the punch of regret (וַיִּנָּחֶם). The NRSV actually translates this "was sorry;" "The LORD was sorry that he had made humankind."
37. Gen 6:7.
38. Gen 9:11.
39. Mark 1:10. Vincent Taylor (*The Gospel According to St. Mark* [New York: St. Martin's Press, 1966], 160–161) says, "The origin of the dove imagery is obscure . . . the best explanation is that the imagery is connected with the picture of the Spirit of God brooding or hovering creatively over the primaeval waters." It seems a rather constrained interpretation considering the other elements from the Genesis flood story (forty days, windows of heaven opened, and the wild animals) are all within close proximity to the appearance of the dove. Andrew T. Le Peau (*Mark through Old Testament Eyes* [Grand Rapids, MI: Kregel, 2017], 37), with his eye to intertextual interaction, does pick up on the allusion to Noah among a list of other potential references. Le Peau, however, while listing immediate possibilities of meaning, seems to be more interested in data, categorization, and creating an archive of potential Old Testament ties (hence the name of his book). His book functions as a reference work.
40. Mal 4:6.
41. Mark 1:11.
42. Francis Moloney (*The Gospel According to Mark* [Grand Rapids, MI: Baker, 2002], 39) ties the wild animals back to Adam and the garden: "In the Genesis story Satan's victory over Adam led to hostility and fear in creation. In the Markan story that situation is reversed. He is *with* the wild beasts. Prophetic tradition surrounding the new creation has been fulfilled." Moloney stretches all the way back to the prologue, demonstrating the tie to creation "provided by the ἀρχῇ." Werner H. Kelber (*Mark's Story of Jesus* [Philadelphia: Fortress, 1979], 19), while not distinctly tying to Genesis, still makes the claim that "by living in fellowship with the wild beasts while angels serve him, Jesus anticipates the realm of God."
43. Mark 1:12-13, 15; Book of Job; 1 Kings 17:4-6; Gen 7:1–4. Le Peau (*Mark through Old Testament Eyes*, 42) suggests, "Continuing the

exodus imagery, here Jesus calls his first disciples. Just as [in Exodus] Israel began as a redeemed community at the sea, likewise Mark portrays the new community beginning at the sea."

44. Richard S. Hess ("Chaldea [Place] Chaldeans," in *AYBD*, s.v., accordance ed., ed. David Noel Friedman [New Haven, CT: Yale University Press, 2008], 1:886) explains, "Because of the presence of marshlands, Chaldea, known as the Sealand, made an ideal center from which to wage a guerilla war against the rulers of the Neo-Assyrian empire." Judah would have been nothing in comparison to the powers the Chaldeans had successfully toppled. They were unfortunately an easy catch.
45. Habakkuk (1:14) describes the people (Judah) as being like the fish of the sea, a creeping thing with no ruler.
46. Hays also ties the fishing language in Mark to both Jeremiah 16:16–18 and Amos 4:1–2, a point of agreement. Though despite how much I admire his employment of his method, I could not disagree more with Hays' interpretive conclusions (*Echoes*, 24–25) regarding "fishers of men": "Against this background, Jesus' call of Simon and Andrew should be understood as a call to participate—like John the Baptist—in declaring the imminence of judgment . . . If in fact the mission of the disciples ultimately turns out also to include healing and caring for the abused flock (Mark 6:13, 6:37a; cf. 10:442–45), the transformation of their task from condemnation to mercy is made the more striking if we hear the overtones of judgment associated with the fishing metaphor in the opening call narrative." Whereas Hays sees distinct sections, I see Mark's overlapping of text—total fusion rather than echo. The ripping of the sky, the post-flood regret, the dove, the rescue language from Exile, the forty days in the wilderness with the wild animals are not separate textual ingredients but a combined, singular whole—like spices that have slowly built flavor over time. The good news announced from the beginning, that YHWH has come to rescue, overwhelms judgment. There is no 180-degree turn with the disciples. The disciples have been called to mercy from the beginning. The mention of the fisherman is part of Mark's irony, to reemploy the very thing that caused harm now to save. The rod of fisherman judgment has long ago been felt and now replaced with the hands of new fishermen to grant mercy. Taylor (*The Gospel According to St. Mark*, 169) finds this whole thing to be far more

straightforward: "The metaphor can quite naturally have been suggested by the daily occupation of the brothers and there is no need to trace it to a current logion."

47. Mark 1:1 and Gen 1:1.
48. Gen 1:28; 2:8; 3:8–9; 15:5–7.
49. Josh 1:3. Promises and inheritance seem like such a fairy tale, and it is, for Israel. The problem is that the land was occupied by another. Israel's Scriptures claim that divine mandate prioritized Israel as chosen, over and against the other nations, especially Canaan. Mark's claim is that the god of Israel's scope is now larger, occupying his role as god of the universe, including all, bringing all into inheritance. No longer zero sum, there is enough inheritance for all.
50. Mark 1:15; Ezek 7:2, 7; Tobit 14:5–6.
51. Anderson (*Christian Doctrine and the Old Testament*, 147) explains the salvific bond between Israel and the nations, especially as understood in Tobit: "As biblical scholars have come to emphasize, the universalism of the New Testament derives from the universalism already present in the eschatological promises of Israel's prophets. When redemption comes to the nation Israel, it will be of such magnitude that it will redound to the nations round about... The mission of the gentiles is a clear interest of Tobit, but it does not compromise in any way Israel's favored place in the eyes of God. Only when Israel is freed from captivity and restored to Jerusalem shall the nations come to recognize the sovereignty of Israel's God."
52. Mark 6:53.
53. 2 Kgs 15:29.
54. 2 Kings 15:29. Volkmarr Fritz ("Chinnereth [Place] Chinneroth," in *AYBD*, accordance ed., ed. David Noel Friedman [New Haven, CT: Yale University Press, 2008], 1:909) notes the early importance of Chinnereth due to its mention as the last of four cities in the upper Jordan Valley in the list of Thutmose III of thirty-four and then again in Papyrus Petersburg 1116A among ten other Canaanite cities. Chinnereth appears in Joshua 19:35 as one of the cities of Naphtali. Fritz also speaks of its renaming. Chinnereth was abandoned after the Assyrian conquest and replaced in Roman and Byzantine times as Gennesaret. Note 2 Kings 15:29.

55. Isa 8:23–9:1.
56. In general, only towns and villages are specified in the conquest narrative (Josh 13; 15; 21:12) with the surrounding fields included by implication. In 21:12, the towns and villages are given to the Levites, but the surrounding fields belong to Caleb; as it is an exception, fields are specified as belonging to a different owner.
57. Mark 6:54–56.
58. Zech 8:11–13.
59. Zech 8:20–23. The translation "let us surely go to be sick (לְחַלּוֹת)" is only possible in Hebrew, with חלה carrying both meanings, "to entreat" or "to be sick." The Greek "δεηθῆνα" means "entreat" but carries no nuance of sickness, suggesting once again Mark's reliance on a Hebrew text for this passage too. Moreover, Mark uses "ἅπτω" twice in the same verse, primary meaning "to ignite," secondary meaning "to touch or grasp." LXX Zechariah uses "ἐπιλαμβάνομαι," meaning "to take hold of or grasp." Similar meanings, different nuances, but notable that Mark doesn't mirror Zechariah's Greek.
60. Mark 6:56.
61. Zechariah himself notes such, saying, "But they refused to be attentive, and they stubbornly set their shoulder, and their ear they made heavy from hearing, and their hearts they set diamond hard from hearing, that the law and the words that the YHWH of Hosts sent by the hand of the former prophets" (7:11–12). Here it pairs with Numbers 15:39, "And it will be for you, *the fringe*, and you will see it and you will remember the commandments of YHWH and do them." There in Gennesaret, the descendants of those who had refused the law now cling to it.
62. Marcus (*Mark 1–8*, 438) connects this passage to the tumultuous sea passage (6:48) with Jesus "passing by" the many sick, though there is no verbal tie between the two passages. Adela Yarbro Collins (*Mark: A Commentary*, Hermeneia 62 [Minneapolis: Fortress, 2007], 337) connects this episode to the healing of the paralytic in 2:1–12. Robert A. Guelich (*Mark 1–8:26*, WBC 34A [Grand Rapids, MI: Zondervan, 1989], 357) suggests that this passage must be read in light of the other passages where supplicants touched Jesus for healing (3:10, 5:27–28): "The desire here to touch only the extremity of his clothing represents an intensification or progression not so much in Jesus' power to heal as

the faith of those seeking his help." Not Marcus, Collins, Guelich, nor Taylor connects this passage to Joshua or Zechariah. That the tassels on Jesus' garment were likely the tzitzit/fringes mentioned in Numbers 15:39 is common enough among commentators.

63. Hosea 11:1.
64. Mark 5:23.
65. Num 13:25–33; 14:6–10, 32.
66. Num 32:1–27.
67. Gen 31:44–50.
68. Num 32:39–41. One Greek rendering of Jair is Jairos.
69. Ben Geber was in charge not only of Ramoth Gilead, but he also held the villages of Jair, making an association between the Jair and Gilead as late as Solomon (1 Kgs 4:13).
70. 1 Kgs 17:1; 22:3, 19–23, 34, 37; 2 Kgs 15:29.
71. Raquel St. Clair (*Call and Consequences: A Womanist Reading of Mark* [Minneapolis: Fortress, 2008], 123) narrates the particular loneliness and isolation of the woman with the flow of blood from a womanist perspective: "The woman's experience exemplifies every facet of our womanist definition of agony. She is socially alienated because she and all that she touches are unclean (Lev 15:19–24). She is physically depleted, having grown worse rather than better under the care of her physicians (Mark 5:27). She is financially bankrupt. Finally, she has been separated from the community of faith for twelve years. According to Lev 15:25, she is unclean until seven days after the hemorrhage ceases. After her ailment is cured (with no help from the spiritual leadership), she can then come to the temple. The priest will then make an offering for her sin and atone for her uncleanness (Lev 15:29–30). Given Mark's description of her situation, one can reasonably assume that her illness and society's response to it have taken a mental and emotional toll on her." Shaye J. D. Cohen ("Menstruants and the Sacred in Judaism and Christianity," in *Women's History and Ancient History*, ed. Sarah B. Pomeroy [Chapel Hill: University of North Carolina Press, 1991], 273–299, esp. 278–279) has argued that there is no indication that any Jewish group of the Second Temple period would have isolated a menstruant from society regardless of what Leviticus said, and even there, Leviticus was not a blanket prohibition but a qualified one (a man may

not have sexual relations with a menstruant, and those seeking to keep purity must avoid her as well). He goes on to say, "For most Jews of the second temple period the locus of God's presence was the temple and the temple mount, and as long as those affected with impurity stayed away from the sacred precincts Jewish society did not care about their impurity." Cohen continues saying that for the woman in Mark, there is no mention that she was considered impure or suffered any degree of isolation. Cohen, however, seems to be relying on Mark to supply such details, even after he suggests that Judaism at the time likely could have at least prohibited this woman from "sacred precincts." One wonders if Mark had to supply such details if some sort of social isolation would have been assumed by Mark's readers. Matthew Thiessen ([*Jesus and the Forces of Death*, Grand Rapids, MI: Baker Academic, 2020], 200–207) discusses the various positions likely among first-century Jews, thus explaining a range of possibility for what would be allowed for her in general society. Thiessen settles with, "For over a decade, then, this woman has suffered a ritual impurity that, while not necessarily restricting her regular day-to-day movements, prevented her access to the Jerusalem temple and possibly even to the city of Jerusalem itself. Being impure, she could not enter into the court of women outside of God's temple. . . . [W]hat an unmitigated loss it was for this woman that she had not been able to go to the temple for twelve years and might never be able to go there again!"

72. Mark 5:24–26. The mystery of the twelve years has long perplexed and thus has been dismissed by many as unimportant, coincidence, or simply the device Mark uses to ensure that the two stories cast light upon each other. Regarding Mark's mention of the age of the young girl, Hooker (*The Gospel According to St. Mark*, 149–150), in line with Taylor (*The Gospel According to St. Mark*, 297), suggests that it was "perhaps an afterthought to explain she was old enough to walk." Collins (*Mark*, 286) concludes the same. Regarding the twelve years the hemorrhaging woman suffered, Collins (*Mark*, 280) plainly states, "It is unlikely that this number is symbolic. It signifies that the woman has suffered for a long time and that, therefore, the illness would be difficult to heal." There is no mention by any of these of an intertextual reference or any other reason that would tie the twelves together. That

they could have been unable to find a tie is reasonable, but to dismiss it outright as coincidence seems an underestimation of Mark's sophistication. Moloney (*The Gospel According to Mark*, 109–112) at least offers the refreshing response that even commentators that are willing to draw attention to the two twelves "do not make enough of the repetition." I agree with Moloney as he continues, "Our reading of the Gospel of Mark to this point would suggest that such details are not coincidental." Mark, with his economy, spends space on only that which is deliberate and important, especially when it comes to numbers. Moloney's explanation, though, is that Mark indicates the young girl is twelve specifically to indicate that she is a young woman, of marriageable age, and not a child. As such, Jesus is healing two women of unclean conditions (the unending flow of blood and death).

73. 1 Kgs 16:23–32.
74. The word used for "waters of testing or bitterness/ מֵי הַמָּרִים" in Numbers 5:18, 19, 23, 27 is from מרר, bitter, with the LXX rendering "τὸ ὕδωρ τοῦ ἐλεγμός / waters of reproach or reproof." Both Jeremiah 8:14–15 and 9:2–3, 15 use "מֵי־רְאשׁ / poisonous or bitter waters," with the LXX rendering ὕδωρ χολῆς /bitter, gall, poison, though notably not מרר. The words are a bit interchangeable as both Job 16:13 and 20:14 use χολή instead of ἐλεγμός for מרר. One notable point is that Lamentations 3:5, which is helpful in rendering meaning for the Jeremiah passages, only works when רְאשׁ is translated bitter, as poison does not fit the context: "He has built against me and surrounded with bitterness and hardship." As the more common rendering of רְאשׁ, however, is head, the LXX reads, "He built up against me and surrounded my head." It seems, then, Mark is doing a bit of double play as he alludes to the Jeremiah passages but understands those bitter waters to refer to the Sotah passage in Numbers by virtue of the woman's particular illness.
75. *Sotah* is the term for the ritual for woman suspected of adultery as well as the name of the tractate in the Talmud that handles this material.
76. This passage in Mark is similar to John 8:1–11 with the woman caught in the act of adultery. Sotah is in play there as well—Jesus arguably writing her charge (and perhaps the rest of their charges) in the dirt, the woman presented before him, and while no husband is present, the

religious leaders all collectively act as her wronged husband. But rather than even entertain their sham of justice, both Gospels make clear that what is needed is true justice and redemption.

77. Jer 8:18–22. Note how Mark doesn't just use one section of Jeremiah, but passage after passage, sits under the surface undergirding Mark's Gospel.
78. The old Black spiritual "There Is a Balm in Gilead" captures the pairing between sin and sickness that Mark and Jeremiah both employ: "There is a balm in Gilead, to make the wounded whole. There is a balm in Gilead, to cure the sin-sick soul." Mark's Jesus heals the woman with the flow of blood, who represents the broken sin-sick Israel. His healing of the one is the healing of the other.
79. 2 Kgs 2:13–14.
80. Mark 5:28–29.
81. Mark 5:30–31.
82. Phil 2:12; Mark 5:33.
83. Mark 5:33–34.
84. Despite Shaye Cohen's perspective that the Gospel doesn't portray this woman as impure or suffering any isolation, the narrative fusion at play, that this woman represents sinful Israel, suggests that Mark indeed meant to portray her as impure and suffering because of it. See note 71.
85. Mark 5:35–36; Num 14:9.
86. Mark 5:38; Jer 9:17–18, 21.
87. 2 Kgs 21:1–2; 2 Kgs 23:26.
88. 2 Kgs 24:3; Jer 9:12–14.
89. Mark 5:39–40. Psalm 13:1–3 speaks of sleep as death: "How long will my enemy be exalted over me? . . . How long will you hide your face from me . . . Consider and answer me YHWH my God. Light my eyes lest I sleep the death." Peter Craigie (*Ps 1–50*, 2nd ed., WBC 19 [Waco, TX: Word, 1983], 142) suggests that the enemy the psalmist refers to is death itself. It is particularly interesting here as the hiding of the face is related to sleeping the sleep of death. Jesus, in the presence of Peter, James, and John, will "wake her up" from death, and then later in Mark 9, they will see Jesus' face shine with radiance, no longer veiling who he is.
90. Mark 5:41–43. Hooker (*The Gospel According to St. Mark*, 151) explains that "the final command to give [Jairus' daughter] something to eat

underlines the reality of the child's restoration to life." More compelling, however, is that feeding this daughter of Israel, here, means that when Jesus suggests to the Syrophoenician woman in Mark 7 that the children (Jews) must be fed first, Mark has made sure the reader knows they have been—specifically, another little girl, healed/restored also on behalf of a distraught parent.

91. Many have considered the different reasons the woman healed from the issue of blood might be fearful and trembling. She could be humiliated over her long illness (Edwards, *The Gospel According to Mark*, 165) or because she took power without permission. It could simply be that she is in complete awe of such powerful healing after so much suffering (Guelich, *Mark 1–8:26*, 298). But once Manasseh and Omri cast light on the two women here as Judah and Israel in sin before exile, and the Jeremiah passages are summoned to inform, then this Jeremiah's passage regarding the gentile nations fits right into place.
92. One could argue that as Mark attributes to the woman healed from the flow of blood the *fear and trembling* Jeremiah ascribes to the gentile nations at Judah and Israel's restoration that this woman representing Israel is also the nations where Israel had been dispersed and intermarried at the hand of the Assyrians. For Israel to return is to bring the nations, those fearing and trembling, with her. See also note 16.
93. Hays (*Echoes*, 10–11) stresses the importance of understanding when "metalepsis" is at work—here meaning that when Mark echoes an Old Testament phrase/verse, he summons the entire passage and its context with it. Le Peau (*Mark through Old Testament Eyes*, 16) similarly says, "So often when alluding to an Old Testament passage, not only is the immediate passage in view but the whole context. When Jesus says, 'My God, my God, why have you forsaken me?' (Mk 15:34), not just Psalm 22:1, but the whole psalm is likely being invoked." But Mark does far more. He builds, he layers, he fuses multiple entire OT narratives into his prose with just a few words, and then he mixes, creating something wholly new, different from past or present, from OT or the simple surface reading of Mark. Quite a bit more complex than Hays' simple explanation of Auerbach's figural definition where two points, past and present, meet in the middle and become its own figure. Hays, however, is not at all simplistic. He demonstrates (*Echoes*, 26–27) how sometimes

more than one OT texts fuse, a prime example being Jesus' cleansing of the temple where Mark mixes together both Isaiah 56:7 and Jeremiah 7:11 to bolster his own temple indictment. But Hays assessment of Mark's fusion is far more tidy and contained than mine. I find Mark's fusion to be fast, furious, wild, entire, and mixing not just two or three but four, five, or even six OT texts, which still then requires Mark's surface text to ignite them into forming a complex narrative world, not just a figure. On the surface, Mark has intercalated two stories, the "Markan sandwich," as some like to say: Jairus' daughter and the woman with the flow of blood. Jairus evokes Jair, one to the claim of Gilead from the early days of Israel's conquest of Canaan. Interrupting the story of Jairus and his daughter on the brink of death is the woman with the flow of blood; she has suffered twelve years. Mark's economy makes any shared detail suspect; nothing is random, everything deliberate. Paired with Jairus' daughter being twelve years old, the two twelves must then have meaning, and they do. When the allusions are revealed, Omri, who reigned for twelve years in Israel, parallels the woman with the flow of blood; Manasseh, only twelve years old when he comes to the throne, parallels Jairus' twelve-year-old daughter; Israel, Judah, and two of their worst kings ever, leading their people astray. The twelves summon the kings. Jairus evokes Gilead. But talk of suffering daughters, Gilead, and worthless physicians summons Jeremiah. Once Jeremiah 8:18–22 is recognized, then all the surrounding text is in play as well, because Mark fuses entire narratives. It is not hard, then, to find Jeremiah 8:14, "He has given us bitter waters to drink," a clear reference to Sotah, especially in the context of Judah's infidelity in the Jeremiah passage, and Numbers 5:16–22 explains the punishment of which is the "discharge of the womb," confirming for those who might doubt that all of this has actually been strung together for purpose and makes its way back to Mark's surface text. With just a few words, an entirely new *narrative* has been fused from both Old Testament and Mark's surface story. The woman newly healed from the flow of blood, fearing and trembling, evokes more Jeremiah, this time a stretch away, ch. 33:6–9. But there Jeremiah also speaks of healing and restoration of Judah and Israel, the individual daughters in Mark's Gospel representative. Mark tells the story of fulfillment. It is the end of the Exile. Mark's "figure" is an evocative story that explains how Israel and Judah arrived at their sad state of affairs so long ago and how the promises of Jeremiah have met their fulfillment of restoration here in the person of Jesus. Moreover, Mark seizes on Jeremiah's understanding that salvation of Judah and Israel means salvation for the gentiles by simply describing the woman freed from her illness of flowing blood as *fearing and trembling*.

CHAPTER 2: YHWH'S MAN

1. Mark 1:1. Much ink has been spilled over this phrase. That "son of God" is missing from certain manuscripts and may not be original is inconsequential. Mark has either stated explicitly or heavily alluded to Jesus as the son of God enough times (1:11, 3:11, 5:7, 9:7, 15:39) that the term eventually being commandeered and brought to the forefront is not surprising. Mark makes clear that Jesus is the long-awaited messiah. See n. 2 in chap. 1 for the earlier discussion on this.
2. Exod 28:41, 30:30, 40:13–15; 1 Sam 9:16, 10:1; See note 1 Sam 16:13; 1 Kgs 19:16; Isa 45:1.
3. Juel (*Messianic Exegesis*, 10–11) captures the nuances of the term *messiah* in the first century: "The Messiah, is, to be sure, one of the eschatological deliverers in Jewish tradition . . . The noun, with the definite article, refers to a royal figure, usually called the King-Messiah or Messiah-King . . . The matter is more complicated when the question turns to pre-Christian tradition. The absolute 'the Messiah' never appears in the OT . . . Usage in the NT presumes a stage in the development of messianic language beyond that of Qumran . . . For the NT, as for the later rabbis, 'the Messiah' refers to the expected king from the line of David."
4. 1 Kgs 17:17–22; 2 Kgs 4:32–35.
5. Mark 5:39.
6. 6:14–16. I disagree with Collins (*Mark*, 304), who says, "The evangelist portrays [Herod], as superstitious, fearing vengeance for his execution of John." It seems more likely that Herod might be happy—happy that Herodias' meddling failed and John was alive. Egotistical as the Herods are remembered in history, it seems that he would assume providence to have somehow bent to his desires.

7. Mark 1:2–3.
8. With his attention to narrative aspects of Mark's Gospel, Moloney (*The Gospel According to Mark*, 126, including fn. 47) surprises with the rigidity of his statement: "Mark has made some glaring errors of fact . . . It was incorrect to call Herod Antipas a 'king,' and Philip was not married to Herodias but to her daughter Salome." Guelich (*Mark 1–8:26*, 331) explains the potential confusion surrounding this group of Herods: "'Herodias, the wife of Philip his brother' identifies Herod's wife. . . . But who is 'Philip his brother'? Many have assumed this refers erroneously to Philip the Tetrarch, half-brother to Herod and son of Herod the Great's fifth marriage (Cleopatra of Jerusalem), who had actually married Salome, Herodias' daughter (Josephus, *Ant* 18.5.4). According to Josephus (*Ant* 18.5.4), Herodias originally had married another Herod, a son of Herod the Great's third marriage (Mariamne II) . . . Yet it is more likely that 'Philip' was a second name for another Herod and does not mean Philip the Tetrarch."
9. Mark 5:16–17. John's announcement recalls Elijah meeting Ahab just as he, too, takes possession of that which is not his to take, Naboth's vineyard (1 Kgs 21:17–18). Marcus (*Mark 1–8*, 400) similarly notes, "John thus appears as an Elijah-like figure . . . willing to risk the wrath of a king in order to press the Law's imperious claims." Hooker (*The Gospel According to St. Mark*, 160) reminds us as well that Ahab's marriage to Jezebel was considered a great sin by the writers of 1 Kgs (16:31).
10. 1 Kgs 21:20.
11. Mark 6:22–23.
12. Mark 6:24–25. Alan Culpepper's playful narrative analysis of Mark's wordplay ("Mark 6:17–29 in Its Narrative Context: Kingdoms in Conflict," in *Mark as Story: Retrospect and Prospect*, ed. Kelly R. Iverson and Christopher Skinner [Atlanta: SBL, 2011], 158) highlights the irony potent in this passage: "She asks not for half of Herod's kingdom but half of his prisoner: 'the head of John the Baptizer.' The daughter herself adds the macabre request, 'on a platter,' which further links the death of John to the banquet scene. Ironically, whereas Jesus will offer his disciples his body and blood (Mark 14:22–24), Herodias' daughter offers her mother John the Baptist's head."
13. Judg 11:1, 2, 5, 8.

14. Judg 11:28–31.
15. Even the book of Hebrews remembers Jephthah.
16. 1 Sam 25:21–22, 32–35.
17. Mark's irony is at its best right here. Summoning the Jephthah text by means of the dancing daughter, Mark highlights child sacrifice (Judges 11:33–39). But as Trent Butler (*Judges*, WBC 8 [Nashville: Thomas Nelson, 2009], 289) stresses, "Surely, the narrator has not pictured God accepting the sacrifice in any way, especially not in some causal fashion . . . The narrator shows Jephthah's unfaithfulness to God, not God's demand for faithfulness to a terror-filled vow." K. L. Younger (*Judges, Ruth*, NIV Application Commentary [Grand Rapids, MI: Zondervan], 2020, Hoopla ebook, 138) addresses the irony in Judges, saying, "Jephthah delivers the Israelites from the Ammonites, who along with their neighbors sacrifice their children to their gods; then he sacrifices his daughter to Yahweh, who does not accept human sacrifice!" But this is trickier than it seems. *Yehidah* / יְחִידָה / μονογενής evokes Genesis 22 and the binding of Isaac—binding as he was never sacrificed because YHWH intervened. The absence of similar intervention especially in a story where YHWH has been immediately active is puzzling at best. One could blame it on the characterization of the period of the judges, "There was no king in Israel and all the people did what was right in their own eyes" (Judg 17:6), but that doesn't account for the behavior of YHWH. Butler (*Judges*, 288) continues, "Surely Trible goes too far in saying that because the divine Spirit came on Jephthah, this "clearly establishes divine sanction for the events that follow." I think Butler has misunderstood and thus misquoted Trible, whose statement applies specifically to events before Jephthah's terrible vow. Phylis Trible (*Texts of Terror* [Minneapolis: Fortress, 1984, PDF version], 106) actually says in full, "'Then the spirit of Yahweh came upon Jephthah' (11:29). The formulaic speech clearly establishes divine sanction for the events that follow and predicts their successful resolution. But Jephthah himself does not evince the assurance that the spirit of Yahweh ought to give. Rather than acting with conviction and courage, he responds with doubt and demand. At the very center (11:30–31) of the battle episode, he disrupts the narration (11:29, 32–33) to make yet another bargain. So serious are his words that the storyteller designates

them a vow. 'Now Jephthah vowed a vow to Yahweh' (11:30a)." I, however, will go where Trible did not. In a passage where John the Baptist has already died without God's intervention, and he prepares the way for Jesus, already described as the beloved son, Mark has buried under the surface of the text this story where the beloved child dies under the forbidden practice of human sacrifice, and YHWH does not intervene but lets her die. As such, Mark seems to suggest that YHWH not only has tolerated child sacrifice but has engaged in the practice as well.

18. Esther 2:5.
19. Esther 1:11–14, 2:4.
20. Esther 2:17; 4:14.
21. Esther 5:1–3, 7:3–10.
22. Mark 6:26.
23. Esther Rabbah 4:9, supplying details, explains that King Ahasuerus executed Queen Vashti and had her head brought in on a platter. Marcus (*Mark 1–8*, 402–403), noting the same, considers, "There are also some significant differences between Esther and Mark, the most important being that Herod and Herodias' daughter are negative characters whereas King Ahasuerus and Esther are positive, but the contrast may be deliberately ironic: whereas Esther saved God's people through her ability to please men, Herodias' daughter uses the same talent to bring about the death of God's prophet."
24. Marcus (*Mark 1–8*, 399–400) is only one among many who have noted the discrepancy between Mark's account and Josephus': "Mark presents Herod as positively inclined toward John; he is only manipulated into killing him by the scheming of Herodias and the enthralling dance of her daughter. Josephus, however, says that Herod arrested and executed John because he feared he would start a revolution . . . Mark's is gossipy and sensational, like a contemporary soap opera or the outpourings of the tabloid press, whereas the atmosphere of cold political calculation in Josephus is intrinsically more credible." Marcus attributes Mark's telling as corresponding to an early Christian apologetic that portrays rulers as favorably inclined toward Christian heroes. Collins (*Mark*, 307) makes the more compelling argument when she says, "This passage seeks to exonerate Antipas for the execution of John and to place the blame on Herodias . . . Josephus does not report Herodias' involvement

in Antipas' decision to execute John, even though he is otherwise quite critical of her and reports her role in Antipas' quest for kingship. The shift of responsibility evident in Mark is due in part to the legendary assimilation of Herodias to Jezebel and John to Elijah."

25. 1 Kgs 19:2–8, 13, 19; 2 Kgs 2:11.
26. 2 Kgs 6:31.
27. But neither was Elisha taken up to heaven like Elijah, though he did roughly twice as many miracles. Instead, Elisha dies of illness, a strangely anticlimactic end. It is, however, not the final word. The last miracle recorded of the Elijah-Elisha ministry is a powerful one. As the remains of Elisha lie at peace in his grave, on the edge of the field of battle, an unknown man was tossed into Elisha's grave with him. When the dead man touched the bones of Elisha, he was jolted back to life and stood on his feet (2 Kgs 13:20–21). Resurrection through the death of Elisha.
28. "King Herod" is a title Mark would know that this Herod, Herod Antipas, never held. Guelich (*Mark 1–8:26*, 329), Marcus (*Mark 1–8*, 392), and Collins (*Mark*, 303), all suggest that the unofficial title "king" might simply reflect popular usage. While that may be so, it seems that Mark uses the title both with a bit of mockery and to solidify the parallel with Ahab.
29. Mark uses John the Baptist to do for his Gospel what the infancy narratives do for Matthew and Luke—prove through historical memory, not just declare, the identity of Jesus as the long-awaited messianic "king."
30. Who are "they"? Joel Marcus (*Mark 8–16*, The Anchor Bible [New Haven, CT: Yale University Press, 2009], 598) suggests they are the man's relatives or friends. In the previous pericope, however, the dialogue is between Jesus and the disciples, and so the verbs take the form *he* (3ms) and *they* (3mp), unless it is direct address from *him* to *them* with *you* (2mpl). This comes over seamlessly to 8:22, which begins, "They came to Bethsaida; they brought a blind man." NRSV and ESV both supply "*some people* brought to him a blind man," providing an explicit subject to the 3mpl verb. The motivation of the translators here seems to be to make sense of the fact that "they" (the disciples) just arrived, and so someone else must be bringing. But the subject has never

changed. The disciples who were the "they" in the past verses are still performing all the actions; they have just arrived, and they are responsible for the bringing. The Fourth Gospel (1:44) identifies Bethsaida as Philip, Andrew, and Peter's hometown. It is possible that this was simply common knowledge that Mark assumes.

31. Mark 8:23.
32. 2 Kgs 15:29.
33. The textual history of Tobit is complicated. I use the longer Greek recension of Codex Sinaiticus unless otherwise noted. Marcus (*Mark 8–16*, 594) also notes the tie to Tobit (S).
34. Tobit 1:1–11, 17–18.
35. The repeated washing necessary because of his constant contact with the dead.
36. The alternative, shorter text of Tobit does not have Tobit washing a second time but simply returning home after burying the dead, and he sleeps outside because he is unclean from his interaction with the dead. I think Mark is dependent on the longer text and that the repeated washing influences Mark's description of the Pharisees' repeated washing in Mark 7, in the dispute with Jesus in Gennesaret (Naphtali).
37. Mark 2:9–10. Tobit's tragedy is tied directly to his charity. Had he not honored the dead on Pentecost, he would not be suffering now. Contrast to the Pharisees, who think Jesus should wait and not heal on the Sabbath (Mark 3:2, 6).
38. Tob 3:6; 4:20.
39. Tob 3:17.
40. Tob 5:5.
41. Tob 11:10, 16.
42. Sinaiticus has ἐνεφύσησεν (he blew/breathed), whereas Vaticanus and Alexandrinus have προσέπασεν (he sprinkled).
43. Tob 11:11–13. There is more than just the immediate healing that has correlation between the two stories. Similar to Tobit's son Tobias venturing out of Nineveh, Peter, Andrew, and Philip left Bethsaida. They eventually followed Jesus, one with the power to heal, and they, too, found their inheritance, their lives, so to speak. They return with Jesus, who heals the friend they left behind, and like Tobit, the healing is a

restoration (8:25; ἀπεκατέστη), the return to wholeness of one who was not always afflicted.

44. Mark 8:23–24. Mary Healy (*The Gospel of Mark*, Catholic Commentary on Sacred Scripture, ed. Peter S. Williamson and Mary Healy [Grand Rapids, MI: Baker Academic, 2008], 158) notes, "The fact that he knows what trees look like indicates that he was not born blind but lost his sight due to illness or injury . . . The gradualness of his recovery symbolizes the slow and difficult process of opening the disciples' eyes to an understanding of Jesus and his mission."
45. Judges 6:2–6. Judges 6:5 uses the phrase "thick as locusts" to describe the enemies of Israel coming and taking their produce. The word for locust used in the LXX, ἀκρὶς is the same word used to describe the locusts John the Baptizer eats in Mark 1:6.
46. Judg 6:11–14.
47. Angel of Elohim here instead of Angel of YHWH.
48. The NRSV translates this as "And the angel of the LORD vanished from his sight." But this implies a more magical quality than the literal Hebrew. The angel of YHWH walks on, and one minute he is visible, and then next minute, he is out of sight.
49. The consuming of the drenched offering followed by the replacement of the altar of Baal with an altar to the LORD reminds one of Elijah and the prophets of Baal in 1 Kings 18.
50. Judg 6:19–21, 25–27; 7:8. It is notable that Naphtali is specifically named as being among those going to battle with Gideon (Judg 7:23), tying both to Tobit 1:1, Jesus' healing and reinheriting Israel at Gennesaret and the dispute with the Pharisees over washing hands (Mark 6:53–7:23).
51. 1 Sam 8:7.
52. Judg 2:11–19.
53. Judg 8:22–23.
54. Judg 8:33.
55. Judg 6:14–15; 9:1–2.
56. Judg 6:19–20; 9:5–6.
57. Robert G. Boling (*Judges*, AB [New Haven, CT: Doubleday, 1974], 173) notes, "The verb *hlk*, 'to walk,' preceded by its infinitive absolute used adverbially evokes an image of persistence."

58. R. S. Sugirtharajah ("Men, Trees, Walking: A Conjectural Solution to Mark 8:24," *ExpTim*, 103, no. 6 [March 1992]: 172–174) also sees the tie between Mark 8 and the parable in Judges 9. He reads the Judges parable to be communicating the utter uselessness of the monarchy. He understands Mark to be appropriating that interpretation as well, thus communicating that Jesus will not be the expected king, but his kingship will exercise humility and rejection.
59. Judg 9:16–21.
60. The correlation in Mark is no less apparent. As Mark has already established that Jesus is both the god of Israel and the rightful king, and he has made clear that the Pharisees and Herodians in league with each other are dangerous (3:6; 8:15), his use of this story is particularly poignant.
61. Once again, it is likely once again that Mark is reliant on a Hebrew text as נוּעַ can mean both "shake/tremble" and "roam around." Isaiah 7:2 and Judges 9:9, 11, 13, all use נוּעַ, a connection that Mark seems to enjoy, while LXX uses ἄρχειν ("to rule over") for the Judges passages and both ἐξέστη ("were amazed/confused") and σαλευθῆλ ("made to shake/move to and fro"), respectively, for Isaiah 7:2.
62. 1 Sam 8:20.
63. Isa 7:4.
64. 2 Kings 16:7–8. 2 Chronicles 28:20–21 also gives a similar account, but there, Assyria does what it wants and simply dominates Judah.
65. Not only did Judah deny Israel help, but they also gave Assyria a base of operations to oppress Israel from the south now as well as the north. Moreover, as Assyria was always going to destroy the northern kingdom, they did Judah no favors. Judah was never free of Assyria again, becoming a vassal to them until Assyria finally fell to Babylon. The bramble after all never provided good shade and only really ever offered threats of destruction by fire. Unfortunately, even in all their fear and a God that offered them comforting words and protection, Judah could not find their way to trust him.
66. Judg 2:16–19; 6:4–5; Deut 28.
67. "He handed them over to plunderers who plundered them" (Judges 2:14).
68. This bit of intertextuality is unique in its form, even in Mark. With one phrase, "walking trees," Mark is able to evoke a specific repetitive

history that goes from Judges all the way to the Exile. Like a rock skipping across the water, Mark's echo hits the continuum of the tradition at very specific places. The temptation is to figure out which one passage Mark might be relying on to bolster his surface passage (if any) as it seems unlikely that Mark could be relying on every reference at once. But I suggest that he is, that he has found a marker that repeats throughout the history of Israel, evoking particular posture and circumstance. Innovative, Le Peau (*Mark through Old Testament Eyes*, 152) explains that the walking trees show up in Mark just before Jesus explains that folks will have to "deny themselves and take up their cross (8:34)": "People carrying crosses could, from a distance or with deficient eyesight, look like trees walking."

69. Mark's narrative fusion operates here with unique range, creating a complex figure resting just under the surface of Mark. Jesus' two-part healing involving spit, evokes Tobit. The blind man's simple mention of walking trees goes back to Jotham's parable in Judges. The entirety of that parable, the bramble, the fire, the treachery, the desire for rule to the point of submitting to thugs, all becomes part of Mark's story. The clever coincidence that Mark happens to trip on two Jothams involved with walking trees makes this allusion all the richer. That Mark could summon the particular history that strings together events from before the monarchy in the chaotic time of the Judges all the way to the Exile under Assyria and Babylon with just the walking trees allusion is nothing short of serendipity (see previous note). But Mark places this healing, with all its allusion and the narrative figure it creates, immediately after warning the disciples to beware of the leaven of the Pharisees and Herod. Thus, the surface texts mix together themselves, and then mix with the multiple echoes Mark summons, giving new life to the story of the bramble, the rightful king, the petty thugs desiring power, and the foolish rulers who pair with them in the present. Jesus' warning to the newly healed blind man to avoid going back into the village is able to find its echo because of the tie to Tobit at the beginning; Tobit tells his son not to go back to Nineveh because of coming destruction. Like Jotham, he should run. The bramble's fire has found its climax in the persecution of Jesus, the warning embedded in Mark's narrative. Those governing, the Pharisees and the Herodians,

are dangerous and should be avoided. "Beware!" Mark's Jesus says. Again, neither the echoes nor Mark's surface text have near the depth on their own, but the fused-together narratives say something rich with complexity and completely new.

70. Mark 6:29.
71. Exod 33:20.
72. Gen 1:2–3; 7:4,11; 8:1–3; Exod 7:17–21; 14:21; Josh 3:13–16.
73. Mark 4:38–41.
74. They believed Jonah's claims (1:9–10) that they were encountering YHWH, God of the Heavens. Collins (*Mark*, 260) understands Mark's subtle mode of communication when she says, "The narrative thus portrays Jesus behaving not like a devout human person but like God, who caused the sea to cease from its raging in the Jonah story. Thus, Jesus is portrayed not so much as a human being who has trust in God's power to save, but as a divine being. The amazement of the disciples is intelligible in light of the cultural context and parallel texts: they have God manifest in the boat with them!" Joel Edmund Anderson ("Jonah in Mark and Matthew: Creation, Covenant, Christ, and the Kingdom of God," *BTB* 42, no. 4 [2012]: 172–186, especially 177) similarly comes so very close to suggesting that Mark's Jesus is YHWH but stops just short: "Jesus is not just a prophet. He has the very power of God himself . . . Whereas Jonah reveals to the sailors the power of YHWH, Jesus reveals that he himself has the power of YHWH."
75. Exod 12:42; Mark 6:47.
76. Jon 1:13; Mark 6:48.
77. Mark 6:48; Exod 14:24; That fourth watch is also the morning watch.
78. Exod 34:29–35.
79. Quentin Quesnell (*The Mind of Mark*, Analecta Bible 38 [Rome: Pontifical Biblical Institute, 1969], 60–61) notes, "This pericope has been construed as misplaced resurrection appearance; as a doublet of 4,35–41, as a combination of such a doublet with a divine epiphany," but Quesnell is unconvinced. He concludes, "In this particular instance of the appearance on the water, form-criticism has not yet come to a convincing and certain conclusion as to the nature of this pericope."
80. Mark 6:49. This is not doubled in LXX Job 9:5. The word παλαιῶν carries both meanings, "making obsolete" and "wearing out." I am doubling to stress both meanings.

81. LXX Job 9:11. Richard Hays (*Reading Backwards* [Waco, TX: Baylor University Press, 2014], 25) compels when he says, "This metaphor accords deeply with Mark's emphasis on the elusiveness of the divine presence in Jesus. Thus, the story of Jesus' epiphanic walking on the sea, read against the background of Job 9, can be perceived as *the signature image of Markan Christology* (emphasis mine)." I agree with Hays, going perhaps even further than he intended; I think that the primary lens by which Mark's Jesus should be understood is Job. Chapter 9 is but one place where Mark relies upon Job; there are more. The crossing into the divine realm already treads into the unknown, a place of rumor, ecstatic vision, and prophetic insight. But Job, Job is wholly other—a world where the atmosphere, rules, and the deity himself is utterly foreign. YHWH breaks YHWH's own rules there, rules that have long governed and functioned in proper and cultured society. The world of Job is the Wild West, an untamed landscape for an untamed god. Mark diverts into that world multiple times. And thus, the "image of Markan Christology" that Mark projects is a type of cowboy Christology, one that seems rather reckless with the Old Testament passages he appropriates, compelling both Matthew and Luke to reign him in for more polite company.
82. Mark 6:48.
83. LXX Exod 33:22; 1 Kgs 19:11.
84. Mark 6:49–50.
85. These are late watches in the night.
86. Job 4:12.
87. Exod 19:19.
88. 1 Kgs 19:11–12.
89. Exod 33:19; 1 Kgs 19:11; Job 9:11; Mark 6:49.
90. 1 Kgs 19:18.
91. Mark 6:50; LXX Exod 14:13; LXX Exod 3:14.
92. Relying primarily on the letters of Paul, Larry Hurtado (*One God, One Lord*, 3rd ed. [London: Bloomsbury T&T Clark, 2015], 105) has built the case that the veneration of Jesus as the god of Israel happened at the earliest stages of the Christian movement: "The binitarian shape of early Christian devotion did not result from a clumsy crossbreeding of Jewish monotheism and pagan polytheism under the influence of gentile Christians too ill-informed about the Jewish heritage to

preserve its character. Rather, in its crucial first stages, we have a significantly new but essentially internal development within the Jewish monotheistic tradition." Hurtado goes on to say (112), "The evidence indicates that the heavenly Christ was regularly invoked and appealed to in prayer and that this practice began among Jewish Christians in an Aramaic-speaking setting, probably the first stratum of the Christian movement . . . as is true of the dominant place of Christ in hymns . . . and the practice of prayers addressed to the risen Christ." As such, though Mark's style is subtle and submerged, his high Christological claims should not be seen as an aberration or something out of character even for the early church. Hurtado has demonstrated Mark's claims to be norm and not oddity.

93. Jacob sees God "face to face" and lives as well (Gen 32:31). Marcus' bar is set exceptionally high when he says (*Mark 1–8*, 431), "Mark never explicitly says that Jesus is divine, he comes very close to doing so here, and this high evaluation of Jesus is consonant with indicators elsewhere in the Gospel (cf. e.g. 4:35–41; 14:61–62)." Marcus is not content to let Mark's subtle and weighty intertextual allusions make his claims for him; he seems to want Mark to say the words "Jesus is YHWH." Similarly, I disagree with David Rhoads, Joanna Dewey, and Donald Mitchie (*Mark as Story* [Minneapolis: Fortress, 1999], 107) when they portray Jesus to be the exemplary disciple of YHWH: "In the story, Jesus has extraordinary trust in God. He leaves his work and his family, depending on others to provide food and houses as he travels about. Jesus is the prime example in the story of how everything becomes possible for one who has faith, because he remains dependent on God, for whom all is possible . . . The narrator portrays Jesus' faith as total submission to God's rule not only in terms of trust but also in terms of obedience." Jesus is able to do what the disciples cannot, not simply because he has more faith but because of who he is. In Mark's Gospel, he is no mere human disciple; he is Israel's god. He is YHWH.

94. "Who do others say that I am? And they answered him saying, 'John the Baptist, and others Elijah, and others one of the prophets'" (Mark 8:27–28).

95. Mark 8:29–30.

96. Mark 8:31–32. Mark just finished drawing upon passage after passage of subtext to subtly hint to what Jesus now explicitly says.
97. Mark 3:6.
98. Whether the context is the different factions in the book of Judges or the different religious or political leaders in the time of Jesus, the debates are internal to Judaism. There is no room for anti-Jewish sentiment here. Mark has written a thoroughly Jewish Gospel, with Jesus operating well within the tradition. Internal groups are at intense odds with each other. The portrayal of the Jewish religious leaders should not be taken as opportunity to foster hostility to Judaism or Jewish people. Mark portrays a messiah, YHWH himself, whose mission it was to come and die. Those in power may kill Jesus but, like John's Gospel (10:18), only because he is a willing participant.
99. It is notable that Mark only uses the term "Satan" in his Gospel, and nowhere does he use "devil." His utilization of Job and Zechariah makes this wholly unsurprising.
100. Mark 8:32–33.
101. Job 1:8.
102. Job 2:13.
103. Job 9 is but one place.
104. Job 42:7, 10.
105. Job 1:9.
106. Zech 3:2.
107. Jer 5:14. Mark's juxtaposition seams these otherwise disconnected stories together.
108. Zech 3:4–5. It is the Hebrew וִיהוֹשֻׁעַ that captures the white, which will be relevant later for Mark during the transfiguration. LXX has ποδήρη, meaning "foot-length robe."
109. Zech 3:8. The parallel between Jesus in Mark's Gospel and Joshua (Jesus) in Zechariah is encouraged not only by their names but by both having to endure Satan.
110. Zech 3:8.
111. Jer 23:5, 33:15. It is this branch that corresponds to Mark's Jesus, and not Joshua the high priest in his filthy rags (בְּגָדִים), despite their initial obvious similarities. The same word, בגד, is used in both Jeremiah 5:14

and Zechariah 3:4. Its primary meaning is "to deal treacherously," while a secondary meaning is "clothes."

112. Zech 3:8–9. There is even a stone present in Zechariah, one with names inscribed on it.
113. See pages 38–41 on the Jotham cycle and compare to Zech 3:10.
114. Both the life of Jeremiah and the Servant Songs of Isaiah would attest to this.
115. Mark 8:29.
116. Mark 8:34. The second half of the clause, "them/themselves," is singular. Note the parallel with Elijah's call of Elisha in 1 Kings 19:19–21: Elisha's words (ἀκολουθήσω ὀπίσω σου) mirror Jesus' call, "If anyone wants to follow after me."
117. Josh 5:13–15.
118. St. Clair describes the "mixed bag" regarding Black women's identification with Jesus' suffering on the cross. On the one hand (*Call and Consequences*, 5), "Because African American women carry a profound legacy of suffering, I maintain that it is important that we acknowledge Jesus' suffering as well as our own. Our suffering includes bodies that were raped, beaten, and broken. It includes minds imprisoned and impoverished through 'mis-education' and the lack of education. Our suffering includes spirits tortured by the calumnies of inferiority, inadequacy, and worthlessness, lies that said we were created more in the image of a gorilla than in the image of God. Because of this history, I contend that African American women want suffering—past and present—acknowledged so as not to be repeated." On the other hand (*Call and Consequences*, 19), "The relationship between African American women's perception of Jesus and their perception of themselves is a critical issue since Jesus as the divine cosufferer is one of their dominant understandings of Jesus. By espousing an understanding that makes suffering a sole or necessary point of identification with Jesus, African American women cast themselves into the role of perpetual sufferers. Should they escape from the context of their tridimensional suffering, they would risk disconnecting themselves from a dominant cultural understanding of Jesus. Rather than ignore the biblical testimony of Jesus' suffering, I would assert that African American women would benefit by following the lead of womanist theologians in

broadening their understanding of and identification with Jesus so that their primary connection to Jesus is not based on suffering." St. Clair (*Call and Consequences*, 167) continues with summary clarification: "Mark's Gospel reveals that Jesus suffered as a result of his ministry that challenged the status quo, not because his suffering was the will of God." This is very important for the womanist point of view, lest there be any legitimization of their suffering as Black women, not as ministers, because of language of "taking up one's cross."

119. Lev 16:29–30.
120. Lev 16:32–34.
121. Lev 23:29. While LXX captures the destruction of the soul who does not participate by using ἐξολεθρευθήσεται, which means to "eliminate by destruction" or "utterly root out" (BDAG), it still uses ταπεινωθήσεται for "afflict."
122. Mark 8:35.
123. Mark 8:37.
124. Matt 4:8–9. Mark does not have such a conversation, but his allusion here, especially paired with Jesus' calling Peter "Satan," suggests he imagines one.
125. Perhaps Matthew (4:10) and Luke (4:5–7) derive their expanded dialogue of the temptation narrative from Mark's allusion in 8:37.
126. Mark 8:37.
127. Job 2:4.
128. Exod 20:19.
129. Deut 18:15–19.
130. Deut 34:10. Even as Mark takes the baton, the promise still hangs. Fashioning his story to be a continuation of Israel's story, but more, he ties the "my words" on Jesus' lips to the "my words" of God that would be put on the new prophet's lips. Mark understands Jesus to be the fulfillment of God's promise to Israel in Deuteronomy 18. As such, YHWH alone will take to account the one who does not heed his words. In combination with his earlier passages, Mark now completes a three-part identity for Jesus; he is now designated the long-awaited prophet (not just stepping in time and playing the role of the various prophets of old), along with having already been marked as priest and king.
131. Exod 33:11.

132. Mark 8:38.
133. Mark 14:66–72.
134. Judg 6:13.
135. Mark 1:17.
136. Mark 8:29.
137. 1 Sam 13:8.
138. "On the seventh day . . . " (Exod 24:16, 18).
139. Abraham's three companions would follow him to the place that YHWH showed them (Gen 22:3); YHWH had said to Israel wandering in the wilderness generations later, "I am sending a messenger before you . . . to bring you *to the place which I have established* (Exod 23:20)"; "In any year Sukkot was explicitly celebrated *wherever* the LORD commanded them" (Deut 16:15).
140. Mark 5:37.
141. Mark 9:3.
142. Zech 3:2–3.
143. Yet another instance where Mark is relying on a Hebrew Text. מַחֲלָצוֹת is pure white, especially fine white garments, and is often translated "festival dress." The LXX's "ποδήρη" is rendered "foot length robe" (HALOT & BDAG).
144. Zech 3:9.
145. Despite the fact that Deuteronomy 34:5 explicitly mentions Moses' death and his burial by God himself, the legend behind Moses never actually officially "dying" lived on until the time of Mark. Josephus (*Antiquities*, 4: 325–326) describes a cloud overshadowing Moses when he went to give his last embrace to Eliezar the priest and Joshua on the mountain called Abarim, which overlooked Canaan. Under the cloud, Moses simply disappeared, but death was what was recorded in the biblical text lest Moses appear overly pious. In any case, the cloud that took Moses seems able to bring him back to this very mountain. Mark seems to know this tradition.
146. Exod 33:18.
147. Zech 4:2–3.
148. Exod 25:31–40.
149. Zech 4:12.
150. Zech 4:14.
151. Exod 6:21.

152. For Moses, see Ex 6:16–20. Elijah's history is a bit less secure, yet rumor and supposition still play into suggested meaning in the story. See Bava Metzia 114b:2 for reference to Elijah as priest. While dated hundreds of years after Mark, it is possible the tradition still loomed as early as Mark's day.
153. Zech 7:14.
154. Zech 14:9; Deut 6:4.
155. Zech 14:16.
156. Mark 9:5.
157. Mark 9:7.
158. Gen 32:26.
159. Gen 22.
160. Gen 24.
161. Gen 25:23.
162. Gen 27:19, 33.
163. Gen 27:13.
164. Sanh 89b.
165. Gen Rab 56:8.
166. Mark 9:7.
167. Marinus de Jonge ("Christ," in *AYBD*, accordance ed., ed. David Noel Friedman [New Haven, CT: Yale University Press, 2008], 1: 917) notes, "In 1:1 the evangelist characterizes the story he is going to tell as 'the gospel of Jesus Christ.' Important manuscripts add 'the Son of God,' bringing out an essential feature of Markan christology: *Jesus, who is called the Christ, and who often refers to himself as 'the Son of Man,' is God's Son*. Demons recognize him as such (3:1; 5:7), as does the Roman officer present at the crucifixion (15:39). Jesus accepts this designation during his trial before the Sanhedrin (14:61, cf. 8:38; 12:6–8; 13:32), and most significantly God himself is introduced in the story twice with a solemn declaration: 'you are/this is my beloved son' (1:11; 9:7)." *Son of God*, especially with the affirmation from the voice booming from heaven, is in itself a powerful claim. But through his many allusions, Mark makes clear that YHWH's son is of YHWH's "stock" and, thus, YHWH incarnate.
168. Readers should not be surprised that Mark fuses whole narratives from multiple places to craft one or two lines of his Gospel. What I am tracking here in Mark, Umberto Eco labels a "creative abduction" (an explanation that requires a certain aesthetic) as opposed to an

"under-coded" abduction (selecting the most probable hypothesis from among many suggested ones). Umberto Eco's insights ("Horns, Hooves, and Insteps: Some Hypotheses on Three Types of Abduction," in *The Sign of Three: Dupin, Holmes, Peirce*, ed. Umberto Eco and Thomas A. Sebeok [Bloomington: Indiana University Press, 1983], 198–220) help explain the reluctance in the interpretive tradition of Mark to dare such a bold hypothesis. The line walked is very close to meta-abduction; like Sherlock Holmes, the payoff is grand if correct.

CHAPTER 3: YHWH REPENTS

1. Naḥum, נחם, occurs in both Numbers 23:19 and 1 Samuel 15:29, meaning "repent," though it can also mean "regret" or even "comfort." The word "ish" is notable in Numbers 23:19 (לֹא אִישׁ אֵל), which is distinctly "man" as opposed to "adam" ("human"), though LXX uses ἄνθρωπος. Naḥum, נחם, shows up with YHWH as subject in Genesis 6:6, also meaning "repent/regret," and then multiple other times (Exod 34:12; Judg 2:18; 1: Sam 15:11, 35; 2 Sam 24:16; Jer 18:8, 26:3, 13, 19; Amos 7:3, 6; Joel 2:13–14; Jon 3:9–10, 4:2; 1 Chron 21:15), demonstrating that YHWH does in fact repent and change his mind. It seems that Mark seizes on this well-established precedent to usher in the end of the exile. YHWH repents, and thus the exile is over.
2. Gen 1:3.
3. Gen 6:6–7.
4. This is a distinctly Hebrew reading of Gen 6:6. LXX reads, "God carefully *considered* (ἐνεθυμήθη)" rather than *regret/repent*.
5. Gen 7:19, 21; 8:21.
6. The baptism of repentance by Jesus is utterly perplexing outside of the light cast by Noah. Jesus' baptism is not just symbolic; his actions are real. Jesus repents. However, instead of a reflective regret in isolation from the people that results in their destruction or the hints of regret after they are all destroyed, Jesus participates in public repentance in communion with the people, one that saves them from destruction.
7. Matthew, who borrows his baptism scene from Mark, addresses the awkwardness of such an act by having John and Jesus discuss its appropriateness, indicating that Jesus' baptism is as baffling for Matthew as

anyone else. Matthew 3:13–15: "Then Jesus came from Galilee to the Jordan to John, to be baptized by him. John would have prevented him, saying, 'I need to be baptized by you, and do you come to me?' But Jesus answered him, 'Let it be so now, for thus it is fitting for us to fulfill all righteousness.' Then he consented." Marcus (*Mark 1–8*, 164) notes as well, "Early Christians indeed were rather embarrassed by John's baptism of Jesus, both because of the possible implication of Jesus' sinfulness (cf. 1:4) and because of his apparent subordination to John the Baptist."

8. Under Joshua (Josh 3:16), Elijah (2 Kgs 2:8), and Elisha (2 Kgs 2:14).
9. Mark 1:17.
10. Mark 6:12, 30–31. The intimacy expressed in this passage is almost uncomfortable. I cannot help but wonder over the smoke screen effect of the term "apostle." It is the only time "apostle" is used in Mark's Gospel (3:14 is disputed), and as such, it catches all the attention. Guelich (*Mark 1–8:26*, 338) notes, "Contextually, it picks up the ἀποστέλλειν of 6:7 and designates those sent as the 'sent ones' or 'missionaries.'" Guelich does not rush his discussion on *apostle*, but then he moves straight to "an uninhabited place," bypassing completely "Come away." Collins (*Mark*, 316–318) and Marcus (*Mark 1–8*, 405) do the same. The tie to Hosea does not play into any of their commentaries. But as such, Mark's potential pun is also missed. The use of "apostle" here is a bit odd, especially since it is a one-time use and not repeated later. But the particular passage in Hosea is about Exile and return (a common Markan theme). Thus, the sentence on the surface reads, "Those sent ones now return," and then Jesus says, "Come away by yourselves to a desolate place," triggering the Hosea passage, which, on grand scale, says the same, casting particular contextual light on the surface text.
11. Hos 1:2.
12. There is a distinct difference in tone between the MT and the LXX of Hosea 2:16 (2:14 in most English renderings). MT says, "Thus, Behold, I am *alluring* her and *bringing* her to the wilderness and I will speak over her heart." The LXX is harsher: "For this, Behold I am *deceiving* her and I will *station* her in the wilderness and I will speak over her heart." Where the MT uses מְפַתֶּיהָ (Hos 2:16), which in this form (*piel*)

conveys the notion of to lure, persuade, allure, the LXX (Hos 2:16) uses πλανῶ, which conveys to deceive or lead astray, casting a shadow on the idea of a love story. Similarly, MT uses וְהֹלַכְתִּיהָ for "I am bringing her," whereas LXX uses τάξω, meaning more "I will station, order," implying command versus love, less intimate. Furthermore, in 2:17, MT says, "From there I will give her her vineyards and make the Valley of Achor a door of hope. There she shall *answer* (וְעָנְתָה) as in the days of her youth." LXX, however, translates וְעָנְתָה as *affliction* (choosing the secondary meaning instead of the first meaning, *answer*), thus "And I will give her her possessions from there and the Valley of Achor will open up her understanding and she will be humiliated (ταπεινωθήσεται) there as in the days of her infancy." Mark is prioritizing a Hebrew text or a text that follows more closely the MT in this instance over Greek.

13. Jos 2:11; 6:20–21.
14. Jos 6:18; 7:1.
15. Josh 7:3–5.
16. Josh 7:6.
17. Jos 7:7–12.
18. Jos 7:19, 21, 25–26.
19. Mark 6:31–33.
20. Hosea 2:20.
21. Mark 6:34; Hosea 2:23.
22. Num 27:17.
23. 1 Kgs 22:17.
24. 1 Kgs 22:17.
25. On the one hand, Mark does not lump all Jewish leadership together under the name οἱ Ἰουδαῖοι, ("the Jews"), avoiding the problem of Jesus versus the Jews (as in John's Gospel) with no distinction as to subgroups or the populace as a whole. On the other hand, scribes, Pharisees, Sadducees, chief priests, etc. are distinctly Jewish groups, and from the beginning of the Gospel, Jesus has been in conflict with all of them. As such, it is possible for the reader of Mark to understand Mark's Jesus to be anti-Jewish and possibly then slide into anti-Jewish attitudes and sentiment themselves. Mark's Jesus' antagonism is not just limited to Jewish leadership; rather, it seems to be with all, his impatience with

all. Jesus' disciples don't understand any more than the Jewish leadership, and though Jesus heals, he also called the Syrophoenician woman a dog. He is an equal-opportunity insulter. Mark's Jesus has not just come to save but to retune and revise everyone's understanding of Israel's god. Mark's claim is that Jesus is YHWH. Moreover, Jesus is YHWH come as a Jewish man, recruiting first Jewish disciples. He has come for his own, which not only includes the Jews but begins with them, the Jewish leadership too. But throughout history, the New Testament has been used to legitimate oppression and persecution of the Jews. Not only do I think that the Gospel writers never intended such, but let me condemn in the strongest language the adoption of anti-Judaism or anti-Semitism of any kind, especially finding its backing in the biblical text or here in these pages.

26. Mark 2:16–18, 3:20, 6:31.
27. Moshe Greenberg (*Ezekiel 21–37*, AB [New Haven, CT: Yale University Press, 1974], 695) notes, regarding this passage in Ezekiel, "For the exiled community—the real audience—the message is that this discredited leadership will be replaced by God." Mark writes of fulfillment. YHWH has come in Jesus to shepherd his sheep.
28. Mark 6:35–37.
29. Mark 6:36. All these renderings convey.
30. Mark 6:37. With Mark's economy, his mention of two hundred denarii must have meaning. Collins (*Mark*, 324) notes that their question demonstrates they remain "on the mundane level and shows even more clearly than their initial proposal that they do not expect a miracle." Guelich (*Mark 1–8:26*, 341) and Marcus (*Mark 1–8*, 407) explain the value of the denarii as one day's wages. The two hundred denarii remain a mystery until tied to Achan's stolen silver, and until then, most commentary lacks the potency of the narrative fusion that Mark intends. The denarii is not simply about the disciples' lack of faith or buying rather than multiplying bread; it is about YHWH come, making right past wrongs, and the old histories bearing weight on the present and creating something new and magical in the mix.
31. Mark 6:38–39.
32. 2 Kings 4:42. With Elisha already established under the surface of Mark, the connection between Elisha's miraculous feeding (multiplying

bread to feed a large crowd) with Jesus' feeding of the five thousand borders on the obvious. Mark has already established Jesus as one greater than Elisha in part by means of greater versions of similar miracles (the raising of the Shunnamite's son and the resurrection with Elisha's bones).

33. 2 Kgs 4:43; Mark 6:37.
34. Exod 18:21–22.
35. LXX adds καὶ γνώσονται ὅτι ἐγώ εἰμι κύριος ("and they will know that I am the Lord") to the end of v. 15.
36. Psa 23:2–4.
37. Mark 6:21, 26, 28.
38. Marcus (*Mark 1–8*, 403) notes, too, "The verb used for the true king's commanding the crowds to sit down, *epetaxen*, is exactly the same one that is used in [the] passage for the false king's commanding his henchman to execute John (6:27, 39)."
39. Hosea 3:1; Ezek 34:23–24.
40. Rhoads, Dewey, and Mitchie (*Mark as Story*, 109) claim, "In Mark, Jesus is not 'the son of David,' for it is not the 'rule of our father David,' that Jesus inaugurates, but 'the rule of God'—in which people in family-like relationships are to serve each other and not to lord over anyone. These relationships are non-patriarchal—that is, they are without fathers." I appreciate much their desire to remove from Mark's good news any hint of traditional domination or oppression. But they have thrown the baby out with the bath water. *Son of David* is the sign of the messiah that Mark chooses for verification to argue fulfillment of Scripture. Moreover, Jesus is the beloved *son.* There are indeed fathers present; YHWH is portrayed as father, and it is patriarchal. It does not have to be either/or; rather, Jesus does inaugurate the "rule of God"—it just also happens that Mark claims him to be the son of David, long ago promised and waited for.
41. Num 11:4, 6, 9.
42. Num 11:11, 18–20, 33.
43. While the bread is clearly reminiscent of manna in the wilderness, from where the fish comes is less certain. Marcus (*Mark 1–8*, 418–419) notes, "Bread and fish were the staples of most Galileans, but these foods probably also have a symbolic significance. Bread was a symbol of the

Torah and miraculously produced bread, the manna, was associated with Israel's wilderness wanderings; fish, moreover, could be linked with the wilderness trek on the basis of Num 11:22b ('Shall all the fish of the sea be gathered together for them, to suffice them?')." While Marcus does not tie it specifically to the Israelites *asking* for fish, he does tie to the same overall event, to Moses' inability to comprehend how YHWH could provide meat for so many people in the wilderness, though he does ascribe to it a "minor" role (407). Guelich (*Mark 1–8:26*, 343), too, suggests a "lesser" role to the fish. Le Peau (*Mark through Old Testament Eyes*, 124) notes with a bit of wordplay, "Jesus helps the disciples fish for people with literal fish."

44. Mark 6:41. I disagree with both Guelich (*Mark 1–8:26*, 342) and Taylor (*The Gospel According to St. Mark*, 324), who say that Jesus looking up to heaven is an act of prayer. Taylor specifically mentions the Jewish prayer over bread. Jesus is not so much "praying" as fulfilling Hosea by looking up to the heavens, beginning the chain of events that will result in grain from the earth. Mark's Jesus is YHWH.
45. The rest of the Hosea 2:21–23 passage mentions wine and oil as well. Moreover, Hosea talks of restoration: "I will sow her for myself in the land. And I will have mercy on No Mercy, and I will say to Not My People, my people." The gestures of Jesus that mirror Hosea are gestures to mark the restoration from the Exile.
46. Mark 6:42–44.
47. Josh 8:1–2, 19, 24–25.
48. Mark knows these numbers. It is no mere coincidence that he mentions *five thousand men* (ἄνδρες) in particular and not simply *five thousand people*. Many have puzzled over this, even Matthew (14:21), who adds, "women and children" to Mark's specific mention of men. Marcus (*Mark 1–8*, 414) suggests that it is likely Mark is echoing the OT passages by only counting the men. It is notable the one verse, Joshua 8:12b, that mentions the five thousand men in MT is missing from LXX Vaticanus, suggesting once again Mark's reliance on Hebrew. Michaël N. van der Meer (*Formation and Reformulation: The Redaction of the Book of Joshua in Light of the Oldest Textual Witness*, VTSup 102 [Leiden: Brill, 2004], 417–429) discusses the complicated nature of LXX Joshua's relationship to the MT, especially in chapter 8, and the

different theories of the missing verses. One solution embraced by certain scholars is that the shorter Greek version preserves a more original Hebrew than the MT, which is evidence of an expanded version of Joshua. If so, then it seems that this expansion occurred early enough for Mark to have relied on it.

49. Hos 2:18.
50. Psa 78:8.
51. Psa 78:29. Once again, Mark picks and chooses, drawing Psalm 78 in with the words "They all ate and were filled." If that were the last verse of the psalm, one might think it ended well. Mark pulls just that one line. He knows the rest will be found; he knows it will advise, but he also knows that the story has been rewritten—in fact, *he* has rewritten it.
52. Jos 8:25–29. It is only two chapters later (Jos 10:1–27) where similar practice is imposed on the five kings (five loaves) that banded together to wage war against Gibeon. The five kings hid in a cave, were found and killed by Israel, were then hung on trees, taken down, and "buried" in the cave that hid them. It seems that Mark may have this instance in mind too.
53. Once again, the figure that Mark creates is a composite narrative, formed by the words imbedded in his Gospel, deliberately seeded to echo and summon the tales of old from the tradition. Like winds blowing together from the farthest corners, Mark pulls together Hosea 2, Joshua 7–8, Ezekiel 34, Psalm 78, and Numbers 11. The figure he creates is wholly dependent upon what Mark does to the surface text of his Gospel. The mixture of the OT passages is a mishmash situated underneath. Joshua, the Psalm, and Numbers evoke the episodes in the past where Israel failed and YHWH's anger lashed out. Hosea, tied by the Valley of Achor, stands upon Joshua but mixes with Ezekiel to offer hope—a promising future where YHWH will collect his people back, redeeming them from punishment, personally shepherding the people. Ezekiel goes even further, involving the Davidic king. The way Mark arranges his texts together directs their meaning. Mark's Jesus, sitting five thousand men down, showing them compassion, and feeding them fish, forms the figure. The figure is a new world, formed by the new narrative fused together from the five OT texts *and* Mark, that says

YHWH has come, he has fulfilled, he has replaced the specific angry past of quail in the wilderness and the Valley of Achor with a loving present and future by remaking the events of long ago.

54. Mark 15:24, 42, 46; 16:4.
55. Mark 9:7; Mark 1:11.
56. According to Targum Pseudo Jonathan (32:1, 19, 24), it was not that Israel simply turned away. Satan himself incited Israel to abandon their god. Satan entered into their midst, in a moment of vulnerability, while Moses and Joshua were all occupied elsewhere, and he was able to turn them back to their pride—that pride that comes before a fall. Hathor and the Apis bull were known objects of worship in Egypt; the Canaanites also worshipped a bull. The bull was not an uncommon deity in many of the neighboring cultures for long periods of time. It seems like Mark knows of the common tradition that is reflected in Targum Pseudo Jonathan as Mark, too, understands Satan to be at work with the golden calf episode.
57. The punishments/provocations came in near exact order with Israel as with the woman suspected of adultery in Numbers 5. When Moses came down, Israel had been *let loose* by Aaron, running wild like the accused woman's hair (פָּרֻעַ in both Exodus 32:25 and Numbers 5:18). The woman suspected of adultery by her husband would be subject to a near-identical test as Moses grinding their sin to dust and forcing Israel to drink it. Her suspected sin was also written in *the dust* of the ground and then mixed *into water* for her *to drink*. Unlike the woman under suspicion, though, who drinks for her innocence or guilt to be determined, there is no question here of Israel's guilt; she is guilty. See Exodus 32:19–25 and Numbers 5:11–31.
58. Exod 32:26–29. In the corresponding passage in Targum Pseudo Jonathan (32:20, 28), a mark developed on each person who gave a golden earring to make the calf, everyone who was involved in the idolatry. As such, the slaughter of the Levites was not just random, whomever they could get to by slashing their swords one traverse across the camp and back. Rather, they slaughtered everyone with the mark. Moreover, the mark became visible upon drinking the water that Moses forced them to drink, with the dust of the golden calf in it. Like the woman caught in adultery, this drink, too, exposed those who were guilty.

59. Exod 34:6–7.
60. Tzvetan Todorov (*The Fantastic*, trans. Richard Howard [Ithaca, NY: Cornell University Press, 1975], 25) explains the uncertainty of "the fantastic": "In a world which is indeed our world, the one we know, a world without devils, sylphides, or vampires, there occurs an event which cannot be explained by the laws of this same familiar world. The person who experiences the event must opt for one of two possible solutions: either he is the victim of an illusion of the senses, of a product of imagination—and the laws of the world then remain what they are; or else the event has indeed taken place, it is an integral part of reality—but then this reality is controlled by laws unknown to us . . . the fantastic occupies the duration of this uncertainty. Once we choose one answer or the other, we leave the fantastic for a neighboring genre, the uncanny or the marvelous." The danger in both Mark and the tradition is that people would choose the safety of the uncanny instead of the truth of the marvelous. Mark's entire world teeters on this fulcrum as his project is to demonstrate that the marvelous world of the kingdom of god has invaded our reality as we know it.
61. 1 Kgs 8:10–11, 57, 60.
62. 1 Kgs 9:3, 6–7.
63. Roberto Calasso (*The Book of All Books*, trans. Tim Parks [New York: Farrar, Straus and Giroux, 2021], 59) catches the awesome and awful nuance of this exchange between YHWH and Solomon: "Solomon boldly asked for something unheard of, and in a voice that might have sounded like it was giving an order: 'You will listen in the heavens, which are your dwelling, and will act in everything according to the stranger's invocations, so that all the peoples of the earth might know your Name.' It was as if Solomon were daring to tell Yahweh how he should behave with 'the foreigner'—and even the 'stranger' . . . Yahweh was not taken aback by such boldness, which he had preordained. And his response was equally blunt . . . He reassured Solomon that he would support Israel if it obeyed his laws. But 'if you turn away from me' . . . Israel will become an object of satire and sarcasm among all peoples. Or so it runs in Édouard Dhorme's cautious translation. The Hebrew word is mashal, 'stories,' 'similes.' But also 'wisecracks,' 'jokes.' The chosen people risked becoming the butt of jokes 'among all peoples.'"

64. Heightened adherence to religious prescriptions would be an obvious response to the tragedy and turmoil of exile and suffering if failure of the former was thought to be the immediate cause of the latter, which it was.
65. Mark 9:4–7.
66. Mark 9:14; Exod 32:1; Mark 2:5–12.
67. Mark 1:22; 2:4.
68. Mark 2:16; 3:22; 8:31.
69. Exod 34:30–31; Aaron and the Israelites were afraid, but then came near.
70. Mark 9:15–17.
71. Exod 4:22–23; 12:29; 14:27–28.
72. Exod 4:11.
73. Mark 9:18.
74. Job 15:20 MT (מִתְחוֹלֵל/writhe or tremble); LXX has different wordings with different meanings (anxious/φροντίδι).
75. Job 15:22, 25. "Marked for the sword" especially reminds one of Ps Jon's rendition of the Levite's slaughter.
76. Job 16:8–9.
77. Mark 9:18; Job 15:20, 25–26; 16:7–9; 42:7.
78. Mark 6:7, 13; 9:18, 28–29; 2 Kgs 4:29–37.
79. Num 14:6–11; Mark 9:19.
80. Deut 32:10, 12, 15, 19–20.
81. Mark 9:21. Collins (*Mark*, 438) notes that the question Jesus asks—"How long has he been like this?"—appears to be somewhat anticlimactic and thus has provided a basis for the argument that the story is not a unity. But the question allows for the answer "from childhood," which allows for Mark to bring in Hosea. This problem with idolatry, the lack of faith in YHWH, has plagued Israel since childhood, since Sinai, since the beginning. The surface dialogue is what Mark uses to summon all the rest, an integral part of Mark's world-building technique.
82. Hosea 11:1–2.
83. Isa 44:18–28.
84. Jer 2:5.
85. Hab 2:18.

86. Deut 32:16–17.
87. For demons, recall Deuteronomy 32:16–17; Satan see Targum Ps. Jonathan 32:1, 19, 24.
88. Mark 9:22; Exod 32:20; Isa 43:1–3.
89. Mark has already referenced the interaction between the Gibeonites and Joshua before; it underlies 8:1–10. It comes back up again here. In fact, this episode picks up exactly where Mark left off the last time. These particular stories remain like currents under the surface.
90. Josh 10:6 וְהוֹשִׁיעָה לָּנוּ וְעָזְרֵנוּ; LXX Josh 10:6 ἐξελοῦ ἡμᾶς καὶ βοήθησον ἡμῖν·; Mark 9:22 βοήθησον ἡμῖν σπλαγχνισθεὶς ἐφ' ἡμᾶς.
91. Josh 10:6–11.
92. Mark 9:22–24; Ps Jon Exod 32:22. The similarity between this father's statements and Aaron's in Pseudo Jonathan Exodus 32:22, along with the multiple mentions of Satan's involvement in the golden calf episode (both found only in Ps Jon), accentuates even more the parallel between the two stories and suggests that Mark was either aware of an early version of Pseudo Jonathan Exodus or they both likely knew a similar earlier tradition.
93. To the third generation.
94. Mark 9:25–27.
95. Isa 42:5–6, 8. With this complex bit of weaving, Mark 9:25–27, Exodus 32, and now Isaiah 42:5–6, Mark gives his own commentary on the golden calf episode. YHWH does not give his praise to another, hence, his reaction at Sinai to the idolatry. Ye, Jesus is the mercy of YHWH described in both Exodus 34 and Isaiah 42, no longer destroying but grasping Israel by the hand and saving.
96. Marcus (*Mark 8–16*, 602–603) describes Caesarea Phillipi, the last named place mentioned in 8:27 before Jesus is transfigured on the mountain and then comes down to this moment, as a predominately gentile town. That said, relying on Josephus, Marcus also notes that much of the Jewish population was massacred during the Great Revolt, both providing an appropriate backdrop to the question of Jesus' identity as messiah and making evident that despite the gentile nature of the town, it had a significant Jewish population, hence this father and his son.
97. Relying on Yochanan Muffs, "Who Will Stand in the Breach," Anderson (*Christian Doctrine and the Old Testament*, 28) notes, "Moses

is not simply an exemplary human being standing before God. *He, in fact, represents part of God to God.* He assumes a part of the divine personality . . . Who God is in this story is represented by a combination of what both God and Moses say. 'God allows the prophet to represent in his prayer His own attribute of mercy.' Moses is also strongly tied to the people Israel . . . when Moses sees the great favor he has won in God's eyes, he is not in any way content. For Moses, favor becomes a valuable commodity only when it is deployed to Israel's benefit." Anderson makes the argument that even in the case of Moses, "God's identity is revealed by the interaction of prophet and Lord." How much more, then, with Jesus, who, by design, represents Israel, prophet, and YHWH in the same person? The comedy of the statement "If you want something done right, come down and do it yourself" could not be better applied to a situation. Jesus occupies all parties and all parts of the conversation in one, a one-man show changing his respective hats to match his role and dialogue.

98. Achan, Uzzah, poisoned quail, David's census, the Exile, and other hard moments stand out in memory.
99. I am intrigued by detailed explanation given by Jeffrey B. Gibson ("The Rebuke of the Disciples in Mark 8:14–21," *JSNT* 27 [1986]: 31–47, especially 35–36), who says, "According to Mark, Jesus' rebuke arises because the disciples have shown themselves to be opposed to the extension of Israel's inheritance of salvation to those not of Israel . . . the particular verb used in the description of the disciples' action (ἐπιλανθάνομαι), this 'forgetting' is not inadvertence, not an unintentional lapse of memory or attention, but willful neglect . . . When [the disciples] perception of the import of this journey dawns upon them, they then recall that it was from the extra loaves which they had with them on previous journeys that Jesus had fed the crowds (cf. 8.19, 20). In light of this, their refusal to take no more than one loaf is an action designed to make certain that Jesus will have no extra loaves at his disposal when he arrives on 'the other side' . . . The reason for the disciples' 'forgetting' to take extra loaves is, therefore, to deny those not of Israel the 'bread.'" Gibson's theory is just this side of compelling, though. In that feeding of the five thousand Jewish men, Jesus made sure the people were fed even though the disciples had not had rest and

there was not enough bread for them all. It seems easy to assume that Jesus would not hesitate to take the disciples one loaf and use it to feed a crowd, most especially if the disciples were stingy over it. He would not even have to deny them—his propensity for leftovers would not leave the disciples wanting. Moreover, by the time they get to that gentile crowd, they have seven loaves of bread with them.

100. Mark 8:14–15.
101. Mark 2:23–36.
102. 1 Sam 8:5.
103. 1 Sam 9:17; 1 Sam 10:1.
104. 1 Sam 9:2.
105. 1 Sam 15:15, 22.
106. 1 Sam 15:26–28; 16:13.
107. 1 Sam 24:6.
108. 1 Sam 21:1–6.
109. Mark 2:27.
110. Gen 1:26; 2:2.
111. Abraham Joshua Heschel (*The Sabbath* [New York: Farrar, Straus, and Giroux, 2005], 14) calls to attention how the Aristotelian approach to Sabbath, which would say, "We need relaxation because we cannot work continuously. Relaxation is not an end then. It is for the sake of activity, for the sake of gaining strength for new efforts," is inconsistent with the biblical mind. Heschel resists this entirely, embracing the opposite: "The Sabbath is a day for the sake of life . . . The Sabbath is not for the sake of weekdays; weekdays are for the sake of the Sabbath."
112. See also Isa 56–58.
113. 1 Sam 21:7; 22:9–11, 16, 18–19.

    The story Mark's Jesus tells is more complicated, more allusive, more subversive than it seems at first glance. The one-to-one mapping linking Jesus and his companions with David and his men also allows for a parallel between those who are hostile. As such, the Pharisees are compared to Saul, the failed king whose misguided righteousness began by misunderstanding piety. Moreover, this backstory explains Mark's perplexing yet deliberate and incorrect mention of Abiathar as high priest during this event. Mark, of course, would know that it was Ahimelech, and not Abiathar, his son, who was high priest; the story of David and the shewbread repeats Ahimelech's name three times in the first two verses (1 Sam 21: 1–2), and Abiathar is not mentioned at all in that pericope. By mentioning Abiathar, Mark ensures that his reader will have to go find Abiathar in the larger tale and thus read wider than just about the bread; they would also uncover the murder of the priests at Nob as Abiathar is the only priest to escape Saul's command and Doeg's sword. The naming of Abiathar forces the entire larger tale to the surface, reminding us of Saul's not often remembered evil deed. Saul did not just disobey the God of Israel; before it was all over, he became a murderer of the holy ones of God, shedding their blood by the hand of a gentile. Mark recalls this tragedy to say that before it's all over, these Pharisees will do the same. Both Taylor (*The Gospel According to St. Mark*, 217) and Edwards (*The Gospel According to Mark*, 94–95) comment on the problem of Abimelech and Abiathar. Taylor suggests it goes back to a primitive error, while Edwards suggests that the event described is associated with Abiathar rather than Abimelech in popular memory. Mark's superior knowledge of both Hebrew and Greek Scriptures suggests, however, that he was not writing carelessly or in ignorance.

114. Mark 3:4.
115. The "watch" stands out here in the Hebrew but not the LXX's pay attention (πρόσεχε), indicating once again that Mark is reliant on a Hebrew text.
116. The attitude of these Pharisees is particular to them and not representative of Judaism, even in the first century. Jesus does not supersede Judaism in his actions against these Pharisees but pulls from biblical tradition. Heschel (*The Sabbath*, 17) notes well, "This is what the ancient rabbis felt: the Sabbath demands all of man's attention, the service and single-minded devotion of total love . . . The glorification of the day, the insistence upon strict observance, did not however, lead the rabbis to a deification of the law. 'The Sabbath is given unto you, not you unto the Sabbath.' The ancient rabbis knew that excessive piety may endanger the fulfilment of the essence of the law. 'There is nothing more important, according to the Torah, than to preserve human life . . . Even when there is the slightest possibility that at life may be at stake one may disregard every prohibition of the law.' One

must sacrifice mitzvot *for the sake of man* rather than sacrifice man '*for the sake of mitzvot*.'" See also Mekilta de-Rabbi Yishmael 31:13.

117. Mark 7:3 details how the Pharisees are known by the way their wash their hands with their fists (ἐὰν μὴ πυγμῇ νίψωνται τὰς χεῖρας). There is a certain irony at play that defines the closed hand as a disability that needs healing.
118. Herod the Tetrarch never held the title of king, though Mark mockingly calls him the king to highlight the parallel between Herod and Ahab during the flashback story of Herod's killing of John the Baptist in Mark 6.
119. Mark 3:6.
120. Macrobius, *Saturnalia*, Book 2:11; Genesis 1:1.
121. Mark has employed the story of Saul and Doeg with such exactitude, so detailed in its likeness and so sharp in its critique, that to have simply called the enemies of Jesus false pietists and murderers would have been mild in comparison. Instead, he has so deftly cast them in these ancient villainous roles that once they are seen as such, it is nearly impossible to see their animosity toward Jesus as anything other than lesser men plotting to secure their own power against both YHWH's and Israel's interests.
122. For Matthew, the leaven of the religious leaders is their teaching (16:12), a teaching that has them focus on the wrong things, leading them astray. For Luke, leaven is hypocrisy; the Pharisees demand a standard of living that they themselves do not live (12:1). Matthew and Luke are both right as they interpret Mark but only in part. What they describe and clarify are but symptoms, aspects of the Pharisee's misappropriated interaction with leaven, but the problem Mark highlights is greater.
123. Lev 7:12; 23:17.
124. Lev 2:11; Exod 13:3.
125. Psa 103:3–4.
126. Mark 2:24; 3:2.
127. Mark 6:49–52; 8:17–18.
128. Mark 8:18.
129. Exod 13:3.
130. Exod 20:8.
131. Gen 8:1, 21; 9:11–17; 18:17; Gen 30:22; 1 Sam 1:19.

CHAPTER 4: YHWH, GOD OF ISRAEL

1. Marcus' (*Mark 1–8*, 168) expresses with great mythological style how "the Spirit, which Jesus has just received now challenges Satan by hurling Jesus out into the wilderness, where the two will inevitably clash; for the wilderness, in addition to being the site of God's past and future redemption, is also the abode of evil spirits in the OT and later Jewish and Christian traditions . . . It is as though the Spirit, having finally found a human instrument through whom it can accomplish its ends, is now spoiling for a fight with the Adversary." I prefer to nuance it differently, but it makes all the difference. Jesus is not just a human instrument, anointed by the Spirit for this task; Jesus is the god of Israel, YHWH, who has come to earth for this task—but spoiling for a fight he was.
2. Mark 1:21–28.
3. Mark 1:32–34 ; 3:7–8.
4. Mark 3:9–10; 4:1, 35–36, 38.
5. "Rebukes" (ἐπετίμησεν) and "be silent" (πεφίμωσο) are both used in Mark 1:25.
6. Mark 4:37–41.
7. 1 Kgs 18:19, 21.
8. "While Nineveh, the capital of the Assyrian empire, no longer existed by the likely time of Jonah's composition; however it is remembered as the power that entirely destroyed the northern kingdom . . . To send a Hebrew prophet to Nineveh would be rather like sending a Jewish speaker to deliver moral exhortation to the Germans in Berlin in 1936." Robert Alter, *The Hebrew Bible*, Vol. 2: Prophets Nevi'im (New York: W. W. Norton, 2019), 1289.
9. Gen 8:21; Jonah 1:1–3.
10. Gen 1:2; Jonah 1:4; Gen 3:13.
11. Jon 1:4–12.
12. Jon 1:14–15.
13. Jon 1:16.
14. Jon 1:40-41.
15. Jon 1:17; 3:1–3.
16. Regarding Jesus' calming of the sea, Kelly R. Iverson (*Gentiles in the Gospel of Mark*, LNTS 339 [London: T & T Clark, 2007], 21) picks up

on its oddness: "The command for 'silence' seems peculiar for an inanimate object like the sea. Nonetheless, it provides a narrative echo that recalls the exorcism of the possessed man at the beginning of Mark's Gospel (cf. φιμόω, 1:25; 4:39). Like the possessed man, the sea is possessed by demonic powers. In OT literature, the sea is frequently portrayed as a chaotic and unruly power that can only be subjugated by God." But while Iverson comes close, his understanding of the sea being demonic is generic, not specific. This sea is mustered to storm by Legion. As such, Jesus' command is not to an inanimate object but once again to a very specific demonic presence.

17. Mark 5:1–2.
18. (λεγιὼν . . . ὅτι πολλοί ἐσμεν); 1 Kings 18:28.
19. Gen 2:18.
20. Both Mark 5:5 (κατακόπτων ἑαυτὸν) and 1 Kings 18:28 (κατετέμνοντο . . . ἕως ἐκχύσεως αἵματος ἐπ' αὐτούς) use κατακόπτω.
21. Mark 5:5 (κράζων) uses κράζω, while 1 Kings 18:28 (Ἐπικαλεῖσθε) uses ἐπικαλέω. That said, the Hebrew of 1 Kings 18:28, וַיִּקְרְאוּ בְּקוֹל גָּדוֹל (he called out in a great voice), fits nicely with the Markan passage, especially with Mark 5:7, κράξας φωνῇ μεγάλῃ (he cried out in a great voice).
22. 1 Kgs 18:40.
23. Rhoads, Dewey, and Richie (*Mark as Story*, 64–65) explain that in Mark's Gospel, the cosmic setting is changing as a result of Jesus' arrival: "This world is inhabited by God and angels, Satan and demons, unclean and clean animals as well as humans . . . In Mark's story world, this creation is awry. Humans were created to have dominion over the rest of creation, but the actual situation in the story is the reverse of this: Humans are possessed by demons, wracked by illness, and threatened by storms at sea . . . The world is the house of the strong one, Satan's territory, an atmosphere hostile to human need and antagonistic to God's rule . . . Yet, the beginning of this story proclaims that the whole cosmic setting is changing. Into the midst of this bounded world gone awry, God opens the heavens and sends the spirit upon Jesus, who announces that 'the rule of God has arrived.' Here in particular this cosmic setting begins the task of reframing 'enemies.' It is not the gentile. This story gives glimpse into one gentile's very oppressed life. In the same way the two Jewish women elicit sympathy, despite Israel and

Judah's sin, so to the same here with the representative gentile. He is portrayed as a nightmare, scary, and yet Jesus sees the man in need of deliverance not destruction, and intervenes to rescue him."

24. Mark 5:6–7.
25. Mark 5:9–13. A nice touch for a Jewish messiah. Whereas Rhoads, Dewey, and Richie saw the cosmic setting, Hays (*Echoes*, 93) notices the comic setting: "When Jesus demands to know the name of the unclean spirit that is possessing and destroying his human host, the spirit replies, 'My name is *Legion*, because we are many' (Mark 5:9). No first-century reader would need to be reminded that the Legions stationed throughout the Mediterranean world and ready to respond to rebellion and revolt belonged to Rome. When Jesus then powerfully dispatches the demons into a herd of unclean pigs who plunge to their death in the sea, Mark hardly needs to explain the joke. It's a kind of political cartoon, in which the Roman army is driven out by Israel's true king, sent back into the sea from which their invading ships had come."
26. Mark 5:18–20.
27. Mark 6:55–56.
28. Mark 7:1–4.
29. Mark 7:5; Exod 19:6, 30:17.
30. Mark 7:6-8; Isa 29:13.
31. Mark 7:9–13.
32. LXX Exod 20:12 and Deut 5:16: "Honor your father and mother, *so that you will be long in the good land which the Lord your God is giving you.*"
33. LXX of this passage is harsher: "For this, behold, I will again remove this people, and I will remove them and destroy the wisdom of the wise and understanding of the intelligent, I will hide" (Isa 29:14). Considering the gentle way Jesus invites the crowds to learn his new teaching on this matter rather than sending them away, it is evident that Mark is using a Hebrew text.
34. 7:14.
35. Mark 7:18–19.
36. Mark 7:18–23.
37. Acts 10:17–29. Mark seems to know the Acts 10 tradition. See also Jason Staples, "'Rise, Kill, and Eat': Gentiles as Animals in Early Jewish Apocalyptic Literature and Acts 10," *JSNT* 42, no. 1 (2019): 3–17.

38. 1 Kgs 17:8; Mark 7:24.
39. Mark 5:20; 7:24–25.
40. Jon 1:5, 15; Mark 4:5, 15.
41. Mark 7:26. Le Peau (*Mark through Old Testament Eyes*, 136–139) catches the wind of allusion but does not quite narrow in on the details. Le Peau puts this episode into the genre (my word) of the "gentile woman who takes initiative to get help from a male prophet for her sick child, and the prophet brings healing," noting in particular the widow of Zarephath (1 Kgs 17:8–24) and the Shunammite woman (2 Kgs 4:18–37). Similarly, he understands the parallel between Elijah and the widow of Zarephath as "testing." Both women are tested by the prophet. The Syrophoenician is tested by his harsh words to her, the widow with giving the last of her bread. Le Peau doesn't, however, note the detail in parallel between the crumbs of the bread but, rather, understands the Syrophonician's response, her positive reframing of Jesus' offensive dog comment, "as passing the test." My disagreement with Le Peau on this passage begins in earnest when he says, "The fact that Jesus so quickly and readily made a one-hundred-and-eighty-degree turn from apparent insult to fully granting her request suggests he was not fixed in a racist frame of mind but had another purpose." It peaks as Le Peau continues in a section called "Going Deeper into Accepting Jesus as He is: Mark 7:24–30": "For some, no explanation of context or culture can justify Jesus using a racial slur. Even if we imagine a twinkle in his eye and half jest in his voice, they believe such language is unacceptable." Yes, I am in the camp of those "some." Mark can give details of Jairus' daughter being twelve years old (5:42), he can give narrator glosses such as "for the Pharisees and all the Jews do not eat unless thoroughly washing their hands (7:3)," but he leaves out the details of Jesus' winking or eye twinkling? No, this is wishful thinking on Le Peau's part. "Embracing Jesus as he is" might well be to recognize that as a Jewish man, in a context of gentile oppression, he carried with him some racist attitudes, which made him less than kind in certain moments. But what he models is important, the ability to be moved, both in opinion and compassion, and to change his mind and heal, despite initial resistance. Finally, I find Le Peau's gloss to the reader in the context of this passage dangerous: "We will not necessarily be able to understand everything

Jesus did . . . but we should be careful not to fall into a pattern of judging God and judging Jesus. As we legitimately struggle with such issues, our attitude should ultimately be one of allowing Jesus to weigh and evaluate us, rather than the other way around." C. S. Lewis understood well how such ideas can lead to oppression. Early on in the *Lion, the Witch, and the Wardrobe*, Aslan is described as "not a tame lion." By the end of the series in *The Last Battle*, evil has adopted that phrase to allow for all forms of religious oppression while at the same time suppressing legitimate questioning of such. Neither the god of Israel nor Jesus are portrayed to be so weak and small that they cannot stand up to human scrutiny.

42. Jonah 3:4. The Hebrew word (הפך) for destroy/overturn used here also means to turn or be transformed (alluding to repentance). Thus the pun being, 40 days and Nineveh will be overturned, or repent.

43. Mark 7:27. Gerd Theissen (*The Gospels in Context*, trans. Linda Maloney [Minneapolis: Augsburg Fortress, 1991], 78–79) offers a theory of historicity that "behind Jesus' cynical words there lies a bitterness grounded in real relationships." It comes at the end of his explanation that "the economically stronger Tyrians probably often took bread out of the mouths of the Jewish rural population, when they used their superior financial means to buy up the grain supply in the countryside. It is possible that there was a common saying that the condemned in this situation: should one take food away from one's own children and give it to the dogs (i.e., the pagans)? In that case, what is special about the story in Mk 7:24ff. is that, from the start, the power relationships are different. A representative of the Hellenized class, which normally gave the tone to everything, comes begging the help of an itinerant preacher and exorcist from the Jewish hinterland. She begs help from a member of a group that otherwise always gets the short end of things." It is not hard to imagine that Mark could mix the real historical present and mingle it with stories from the tradition to make theological claims, namely that Jesus, who is a Jewish man with Jewish sensibilities, could still change his mind and be persuaded to help one against whom he himself holds a grudge.

44. The notion that the human person Jesus could harbor nationalistic grudge is distasteful to many. I lean, though, on Abraham Joshua

Heschel (*The Prophets* [New York: Perennial, 2001], xxii) and his description of the prophet as parallel: "The prophet is a person, not a microphone. He is endowed with mission, with the power of a word not his own that accounts for his greatness—but also with temperament, concern, character, and individuality. As there was no resisting the impact of divine inspiration, so at times there was no resisting the vortex of his own temperament. The word of god reverberated in the voice of a man." How much more with Jesus? Anyone who wishes to affirm the full humanity of Jesus must reckon with the same as Heschel explains regarding the prophet. Jesus was not kind to the Syrophoenician woman; his words offensive. Efforts to make them pedagogical and a type of disguised kindness naïve at best. Old memory, old offenses, old grudges affect the human. Yet, as Jesus does, so must the disciples, the church of Mark's day, and all who would come after. They too must set aside their grudges, change their mind, and offer compassion, just as it was modeled for them. "The servant no greater than the master."

45. Gen 25:29–34; 1 Kgs 21:1–4.
46. 1 Kgs 21:8–16.
47. I am grateful to T. A. Burkill ("The Historical Development of the Story of the Syrophoenician Woman [Mark vii: 24–31]," *NovT* 9 [1967]: 161–177, especially 172–173), who, despite the sea of opinions that try to whitewash the harshness of Jesus' response here, leans in and finally says what long needed to be said: "We may safely assume that any intelligent Hellenistic woman, addressed in such terms by a barbarian, would have immediately reacted by slapping the man's face. And, as in English, so in other languages, to call a woman 'a little bitch' is no less abusive than to call her 'a bitch' without qualification." Marcus (*Mark 1–8*, 468), while not as inflammatory as Burkill, still acknowledges, "Despite the offensiveness of the saying, the most straightforward reading of it on the historical level is a literal one: Jesus was initially inclined to refuse the woman's request, and his subsequent decision to heal her represented a change of mind." Marcus continues with playful incredulity by citing Vincent Taylor, who hypothesizes that Jesus was talking to himself and not the woman; F. V. Filson (*A Commentary on the Gospel according to St. Matthew*, BNTC [London: A. & C. Black, 1960], 180), who suggests that Jesus' facial expression or tone of voice

tipped the woman off that his refusal was not final; and I. Hassler ("The Incident of the Syrophoenician Woman [Matt XV, 21–28; Mark VII, 24–30]," *ExTim* 45 [1934]: 459–461), who speculates that Jesus may have winked.

48. Mark 7:28.
49. Lawrence E. Stager ("Why Were Hundreds of Dogs Buried at Ashkelon?" *BAR* 17, no. 3 [1991]: 27–42), reporting archaeological excavation, determines that the Phoenicians considered the dog to be a sacred animal, possibly even thinking of them as healers, and buried them in cemeteries when they died.
50. 1 Kgs 17:1.
51. While the Greek words are different, it is inconsequential considering Mark's propensity to rely on Hebrew texts in other parts of the Gospel.
52. 1 Kings 17:8–16.
53. 1 Kgs 17:18–19.
54. "The story of the Syrophoenician woman is disturbing to me, as a person treated as an 'outsider', seeing how Jesus attributes secondary-ness to someone in the story," remarks Surekha Nelavala in her article "The Smart Syrophoenician Woman: A Dalit Feminist Reading of Mark 7:24–31" (*ExTim* 118, no. 2 [2006]: 64–69). She continues, capturing the importance of the move from resistance to concession by the one in power, saying, "The liberation process is incomplete without the reconciliation of the oppressor. Although the Syrophoenician woman's claim is a powerful initiation, Jesus' readiness for reconciliation actually leads to the implementation of justice . . . in my experience, without the oppressor's readiness to change, the voice of the oppressed is in vain." Jesus fully occupies the role of the stronger party, relenting to the one who is powerless except her voice to make claim. The implications of this for Mark's church are powerful.
55. Marcus (*Mark 1–8*, 470) highlights Mark's narrative skill when he explains, "Jesus responds to the woman's audacious stroke with a reply beginning, 'Because you have said this, go . . .' (7:29a). This is another fine example of the rhetorical art of the narrative, for these words could momentarily be construed as a final rebuff, as though Jesus were punishing the woman's impudence by dismissing her. But the tension is

quickly resolved by Jesus' concluding statement that 'the demon has gone out of your daughter' (7:29b)."

56. Mark 7:29–30.
57. Mark 7:31.
58. Zech 9:1–4.
59. Tyre would return to her trade—prostitute of the nations—but all her wages would be dedicated to the LORD, preserving his faithful ones (Isa 23:13–17).
60. Exod 4:11; Mark 7:32.
61. Isa 43:8–9.
62. Psa 135:15–18.
63. Frank Gonzalez-Crussi, "The Bizarre Cultural History of Saliva," accessed June 21, 2024, https://thereader.mitpress.mit.edu/the-bizarre-cultural-history-of-saliva-as-powerful-therapeutic/.
64. Gen 22:16.
65. Isa 6:5, 8.
66. Isa 6:9–10.
67. Isa 6:11.
68. Mark 7:32.
69. Ezek 21:11–12. It seems that the Hebrew of Ezekiel is more appropriate here because of the complexity of Mark's using Ezekiel combined with Isaiah, but it is worth noting that Mark uses the same verb as is used in the LXX.
70. "They" is emphasized with the separate pronoun הֵ֫מָּה and not just contained in the verb form.
71. Throughout this Gospel, Mark has had some places where he overlaps with LXX and others that are clearly reliant on a Hebrew text. In this case, this section, it appears he is using both. It is the Hebrew תִּפָּתַ֫חְנָה, which translates nicely to "unstopped," that seems to match the Markan ἠνοίγησαν, meaning "opened" or "to have an obstruction removed," rather than the LXX's ἀκούσονται, meaning "hearing" or "obeying." On the contrary, μογιλάλων, rendered here as "stammerer," is the same word, μογιλάλον, Mark uses and is a better match than Hebrew אִלֵּ֫ם, meaning simply "dumb" or "speechless."
72. Isa 35:10. This is Mark's punchline, his point of emphasis, but how to denote the *absence* of the sigh out of the blue? The absence of the sigh

is only made manifest by the sigh itself, one that is being undone. As Jesus stands mirroring Ezekiel the prophet, sighing before the open heavens, opening this deaf man's ears and mouth, and changing his life, Mark highlights that there is no more reason to sigh, fulfilling Isaiah. God himself has come to save and to put an end to the sighing that came with the devastation of the Exile, the sighing predicted by Ezekiel.

73. Lev 8:12.
74. Lev 8:18–19; See Lev 8 for a comprehensive description of the ritual for consecration of the priests.
75. Lev 14.
76. Lev 21:17–20.
77. Isa 66:18–21.
78. Mark 7:37.
79. Mark 8:1. *In those days*, the Nephillim were on the earth (Gen 6:4). *In those days*, there was no king in Israel (Judg 17:6, 18:1, 19:1, 21:25). *In those days*, the word of the LORD was rare (1 Sam 3:1). Throughout the history of Israel, many of *those days* were perilous, leaderless, godless.
80. Mark's second feeding not an accidental doublet by any means. Carey Newman's (*Mango Tree* [Wyncote, PA: Friendship Press, 2023], 29) excursus on the paragraph pertains nicely to Mark's two feedings: "The addition of a second transforms *a* into *the*. Indefinite converted to definite through predicate. The first no longer signs as an indeterminant only; the second re-assigns it to a new, paired vocation. The pairing disambiguates the mystery surrounding transmission: the first now reaches for the second, and the second countenances the first. Two, placed together, side by side, defined. The writing of the second presumes the first, and the first finds itself in the second's reflection."
81. "Compassion" (ἐσπλαγχνίσθη/σπλαγχνίζομαι) is same word used in this passage.
82. Mark 6:34.
83. Mark 8:1–3.
84. Jon 1:17, 3:3–5, 4:2.
85. Exod 32:10.
86. Exod 32:13; 32.
87. Exod 32:14—וַיִּנָּחֶם יְהוָה עַל־הָרָעָה אֲשֶׁר דִּבֶּר לַעֲשׂוֹת לְעַמּוֹ.

88. Anderson (*Christian Doctrine and the Old Testament*, 33–34) explains the particular novelty of the divine-prophetic interaction in Jonah: "What is striking here is that we see what happens when our appointed Mosaic prophet does not rise to the accepted standard of his office. It is not the case that all bets are off and God's rage will now burst forth unchecked." The question of whether god's wrath would get the better if god's agent proved fallible is answered here: "In the story of Jonah, we see the bottom line: if we have to choose between a narrative that will preserve human free choice but compromise God's mercy and a narrative that will compromise human choice in order to effect God's mercy, the direction God will take is clear." I think there is more here. The conversation regarding sin/offense against YHWH and forgiveness functions as a type of necessary logos in itself. The offense against YHWH must be vocalized, the desired wrath imagined and declared as real possibility, and then the intervention that interferes with the planned wrath, reminding of past promises, resulting in divine forgiveness and relationship restoration. Jesus, like YHWH before Jonah, plays the role of mercy, compelling this group of Jews (the disciples) chosen by YHWH for ministry to have compassion, and when they refuse, he has mercy anyway, inviting them to a change of heart.
89. Exod 33:5–6; Jon 3:5–6.
90. Mark 8:4.
91. Mark 8:2; Jon 4:11.
92. Mark 8:5.
93. 1 Sam 4:1–2. LXX 1 Samuel 4:1 specifically says "in those days/ἐν ταῖς ἡμέραις ἐκείναις," while the Hebrew text does not. Alternatively, the Hebrew of 1 Samuel 4:2 has what seems to be an inconsequential כְּ not captured in LXX. It suggests once again that Mark was working with both a Greek and a Hebrew text as he deliberately captures the about with ὡς.
94. 1 Sam 4:4, 8.
95. 1 Samuel 4:10. Both LXX (σκήνωμα) and MT (לְאֹהָלָיו) use the term "tent." The MT especially can be rendered "tent" or "home"; Mark is drawing on the MT with his "if I send them fasting to their home (οἶκον)."
96. 1 Sam 5:2–7, 12.

97. 1 Sam 6:1–3, 5–6, 19.
98. Anderson (*Christian Doctrine and the Old Testament*, 4–7) captures the unique and misunderstood nature of the ark of the covenant, noting, "But this deeply 'incarnational' character of the tabernacle carries a particular danger along with it . . . In response to their grave misdeed, the people [of Beth Shemesh] cry out: 'Who is able to stand before the LORD, this holy God? (1 Sam 6:20)' . . . The men of Beth Shemesh do the rational thing: they forward this dangerous cargo to the inhabitants of Kiriath-jearim." Anderson contrasts this to David with enlightening analysis: "Here is a man who possesses a divine promise regarding the eternal character of his kingdom (2 Sam 7), but even with this promissory note in hand, when he is driven from the city of Jerusalem by his upstart son, Absalom, he refuses to use the ark as a guarantee of safe return . . . The king said to Zadok, 'Carry the ark of God back into the city. If I find favor in the eyes of the LORD, he will bring me back and let me see both it and the place where it stays. But if he says, 'I take no pleasure in you,' here I am, let him do to me what seems good to him' (2 Sam 15:25–26)."
99. Mark 8:3.
100. Josh 9:2.
101. Josh 9:5, 6, 10.
102. Josh 9:14–16, 24.
103. Josh 9:23, 26–27.
104. The Philistines were at war with Israel and found themselves at war with Israel's god. The Ninevites were under divine judgment for their wicked deeds, the stench of their evil rising to the heavens much the same as the corruption of Noah's day. The Gibeonites stood condemned simply for being the current inhabitants of the land now promised to Israel. All three peoples were under the threat of danger, death, and destruction, and all three used their own ingenuity and boldness to negotiate with the god of Israel for their lives. In all three cases, the gentiles survived and somehow merited grace from a god they did not know but who knew them and had compassion on them.
105. Mark 6:40; Exod 18:21; Mark 8:6.
106. Its meaning more about equality than making amends for past wrongs, as it was with Israel.

107. Mark 8:6–8.
108. 1 Sam 4:2; Mark 8:9.
109. 1 Sam 6:1; Mark 8:8.
110. The potency of Jonah as *the* preferred opinion from Israel's tradition regarding gentile interaction explodes full force onto the surface of Mark's Gospel here in this feeding. Ruth, Rahab, and even Esther, married to King Ahasuerus, are all exceptions to the rule of separation and generally palatable as such. A gentile, here or there, coming in as a convert to Judaism or a powerful political marriage serving the larger cause of the Jews is an acceptable anomaly in the grand scheme of salvation history. But the book of Jonah advocates for the compassion and redemption of 120,000 gentiles all at once—and enemies of Israel at that. Its scope of grace is well beyond the fences, and Mark openly casts his lot with Jonah.

CHAPTER 5: YHWH, GOD OF THE NATIONS

1. In general, scriptural references have their own line-by-line index so as not to litter the notes as there are so many. Exception is made in this section, however, in order to highlight the presence of certain words in certain passages and because of the important parallel language between Job and Psalm 78.
2. Mark 8:10.
3. Mark 7:1.
4. Mark 8:11.
5. Testing/*πειράζοντες* in Mark 8:11 and tested/*ε'πείρασαν* in Ps 78:18; Ps 78:19–20.
6. Mark 7:19.
7. Mark 8:12. *ἀναστενάξας τῷ πνεύματι*/groaned deeply in his spirit.
8. LXX Job 30:25 does not capture *spirit* the way MT does, suggesting again Mark's dependence on the Hebrew as well, perhaps a mix of the two. Instead of "was my soul not grieved for the poor (עָגְמָה נַפְשִׁי)," LXX says, "And I groaned, seeing a man in distress" (*ἐστέναξα δὲ ἰδὼν ἄνδρα ἐν ἀνάγκαις*).
9. Mark 8:12.
10. *ἡ γενεὰ αὕτη*—this generation in Mark 8:12; LXX Gen 7:1; *ἡ γενεὰ αὕτη*.

11. Gen 1:14–18; Psa 19:4–6.
12. τοῦτο τὸ σημεῖον τῆς διαθήκης—this is the sign of the covenant; πάσης ψυχῆς ζώσῃ—every living being; εἰς γενεὰς αἰωνίους—to unending generations.
13. LXX Gen 9:12–13.
14. ἐν τῇ νεφέλῃ; cf. σημεῖον ἀπὸ τοῦ οὐρανοῦ in Mark.
15. Mark 8:12. Though Mark's Greek says "ἀμὴν λέγω ὑμῖν, ***εἰ*** δοθήσεται τῇ γενεᾷ ταύτῃ σημεῖον," which translates as "Truly I say to you, *if* a sign is given," most, including NRSV and ESV, alter the translation to say "no sign will be given," matching Matt 16:4, "σημεῖον οὐ δοθήσεται αὐτῇ."
16. Dalu Menosh (דָּלוּ מֵאֱנוֹשׁ): The Hebrew phrase, the last words of Job 28:4. The *sh* would easily become a *th* in Greek, and vowels are always in flux.
17. Job 28:3–4. There is no mention of Dalmanutha in any text outside of Mark. As such, many have posited other locations that it could be. The most common suggestion is that Dalmanutha might be another name for Magdala that Mark knew. Collins (*Mark*, 841, fn.34) notes that Andreas Bedenbender argued that "Dalmanutha" is a symbolic name meaning roughly "Doubts-city," created by Mark.
18. Sanh. 109A (Jacob Neusner, ed. *The Babylonian Talmud: A Translation and Commentary* [Peabody, MA: Hendrickson, 2005]), commenting on the men of Sodom and the punishment allotted to them because of their arrogance and overindulgence of god's blessing, says, "What does it say? 'They open shafts in a valley from where men live. They are forgotten by travelers. They hang afar from men, they swing to and fro (Job. 28:4). In the thought of one who is at ease there is contempt for misfortune; it is ready for those whose feet slip. The tents of robbers are at peace, and those who provoke God are secure, who bring their god in their hand' (Job. 12:5–6)." If Mark understands the punitive associations with this place in Job, Jesus' mission to Dalmanutha is all the more grace-filled. NRSV, ESV, and Marvin H. Pope (*Job*, AB [New Haven, CT: Yale University Press, 1974]) smooth out the translation, supplying subjects, plurals, and departing from the literal to try to make sense of difficult and gapped Hebrew. Pope (200–201) reads this passage to be a full description of mining, "foreigners build shafts" (who

Pope reads as foreign slaves) and "they hang" (because they are lowered on ropes). The same story read in very different ways by means of minor alterations.

19. Pathway (נָתִיב); Job 28:6–7, 9–11.
20. Abaddon (אֲבַדּוֹן); Death (מָוֶת); Deep (תְּהוֹם); Sea (יָם); Job 28:14; 22.
21. Job 38:4, 8, 11; paths (נָתִיב/נְתִיבוֹת); Job 38:19–20.
22. darkness of death (צַלְמָוֶת); Job 38:16–17, 19–20.
23. Job 42:3, 6. Carl Jung (*Answers to Job*, trans. R. F. C. Hull [Princeton, NJ: Princeton University Press, 2010], 7) captures the same duality in YHWH that Anderson (*Christian Doctrine and the Old Testament*, 33–34) does regarding Jonah. Jung says, "This is perhaps the greatest thing about Job . . . he does not doubt the unity of God. He clearly sees that God is at odds with himself—so totally at odds that he, Job, is quite certain of finding in God a helper and an 'advocate' against God . . . In a human being who renders us evil we cannot expect at the same time to find a helper. But Yahweh is not a human being: he is both a persecutor and a helper in one, and the one aspect is as real as the other. Yahweh is not split but is an antinomy—a totality of inner opposites—and this is the indispensable condition for his tremendous dynamism, his omniscience and omnipotence . . . Yahweh is also man's advocate *against himself* when man puts forth his complaint."
24. Job 38:25; Psa 78:26.
25. Psa 78:23.
26. Job 28:10,26; Psa 78:20.
27. Psa 78:39.
28. There is a significant linguistic overlap between Job 28 and Psalm 78. Mark notes this and pairs these together in his work. The juxtaposition of Job 28 and Psalm 78 creates the back-and-forth of the god of the cosmos taking care of Israel's intimate needs.
29. Psa 78:32, 38, 49, 53.
30. Job 38:16–17.
31. Mark 8:31, 34; 9:31; 10:33.
32. Mark 10:29–30; 5:37, 41–42; 9:2–3.
33. Mark 10:35–36; 6:22–23. Collins (*Mark*, 495) notes the parallel as well, but I disagree with her conclusion that "the similarity of the two

statements suggests that James and John are speaking in an equally thoughtless and extravagant manner."

34. Mark 10:37–38. Mark, like John, understands glorification to be the cross.
35. Num 13:30–33.
36. Mark 10:39–40.
37. Typical interpretation suggests that James and John, opportunists, attempt to go to the head of the line, to be honored, above the rest, and that appears to be so but inverted. They run to the head of the line to be persecuted so that they can be honored afterward. Rather than trying to usurp the treasured positions out from under the other disciples, which they are in fact doing, they inadvertently put pressure on the others to be persecuted, too, to be crucified too! Jesus' lecture is not to James and John and not to all of them to address James and John's "wrongness." No, it is for the rest of the disciples' reaction to James and John's right conclusions. They are the only two who have it right!
38. Mark 10:41–45.
39. Gen 37:2–11, 28; 41:40–41, 57; 45:5; Mark 10:45.
40. Mark 10:46; Josh 6:23, 25.
41. Interestingly, Rhoads, Dewey, and Mitchie (*Mark as Story*, 71) note this same "family dynamic": "The conflicts between Jesus and the disciples occur in these private settings. Jesus has very few conflicts with the disciples in public, for in public the disciples are aligned with Jesus in his conflicts with the authorities. In private settings, the conflicts between Jesus and the disciples bring no threat to public honor, either for Jesus or the disciples . . . Therefore for the readers, it is clear that the disciples are 'with' Jesus even when they are in opposition to him." A similar dynamic occurs in Numbers. Despite poisoned quail, serpents, and terrible inner turmoil between Israel and their god, when Balaam is summoned to curse Israel, nobody would know there had been any in-house strife. YHWH defends, protects, and owns Israel. Culturally, this strikes me as a very Eastern sensibility. As a woman from the East, we don't air our family grievances for outsiders to see, no matter how bad they are; we smile and, though fires may be burning on the inside of the house, nobody from the outside would ever, ever even catch a whiff of the smoke.

42. Num 22:5–6, 12.
43. Num 22:22–31, 41; 23:1.
44. Mark 10:46–52; Tobit 11:14–15.
45. Num 24:17.
46. Moloney (*The Gospel According to Mark*, 209) not only notes the tie to Solomon but that by the first century, Solomon had developed the reputation as a healer.
47. 1 Kgs 1:33, 38; 1 Chron 22:8; 1 Kgs 11.
48. Mark 11:2, 7; Gen 49:10–11.
49. See also Nehemiah 13:4.
50. Mark 11:17.
51. 1 Kgs 8:41–43.
52. I agree with Hays (*Reading Backwards*, 7) as he says, "By citing this passage, Mark portrays Jesus' protest action as an indictment of Temple authorities for turning the Temple into a bazaar, cluttering the outer 'court of the Gentiles' and making in unsuitable as a place of worship for the Gentile 'others' who might want to gather there to pray. By driving out the merchants, Mark's Jesus clears the way figuratively, for the restored worship of the kingdom of god, in which all nations will participate along with the returning exiles of Israel. *Thus, Jesus' action looks forward to the eschatological redemption of Jerusalem (emphasis mine).*" But I wish he had gone further. I do not think Jesus' action looks for the future; Jesus' action in Mark is about the now—the kingdom of god has come. *Has come*! It is like Jesus' response to Martha in John 11:24–25, when she says, "I know [Lazarus] will rise again in the resurrection in the last day." Jesus there has none of that. No last day; it is now! "I am the resurrection and the life." Mark is the same. First Jesus clears out the temple with prophetic words undergirding all he does, and then at the crucifixion, the episode of which begins here with Jesus' entry into Jerusalem, the temple veil will tear, and the first one (theoretically) to see inside will be the gentile. Mark's mixing, mingling, and reaching back to OT Scripture is about the end of the exile and the end of all exile, the god of Israel's kingdom near, and gentile inclusion. The particular passages Mark draws on here are specifically about these things.
53. Mark matches LXX Jer 7:11 with ληστῶν, which captures all three meanings. Mark 15:27 also uses ληστής to describe those crucified on Jesus' right and left side, likely insurrectionists.

54. Mark 12:38–44.
55. Mark 13:2.
56. Jer 8:10–13.
57. Mark 11:21. Jonah's vine also withered (4:7), the vine that had grown up to give this angry prophet shade, angry over the god of Israel's mercy to the gentiles.
58. Hays (*Echoes*, 76) also draws on this passage as one more instance building the case for Mark's subtle way of suggesting that Jesus is the god of Israel: "It is *God* who is represented as seeking unsuccessfully to gather grapes and figs. What, then, are we to think when Mark tells the ominous and obviously symbolic story of *Jesus'* fruitless search for figs on the fig tree . . . What does this suggest about the identity of the one who searches for the fruit? This is yet another case in which Jesus steps, at least functionally, into a role given exclusively to the LORD God in the Old Testament." Mark's Jesus in some ways operates like a one-man show, slipping in and out of roles, featured from past episodes in the tradition of Israel. He was Jonah, Joshua the commander of Israel's armies, the Davidic king, Joshua the high priest, Israel as a whole, and throughout Mark, he is also YHWH. Anderson (*Christian Doctrine and the Old Testament*, 28) also notes, "Moses is not simply an exemplary human being standing before God. *He, in fact, represents part of God to God.*" This practice of multiple parties, multiple roles, all displaying a part of YHWH, is not isolated, then, to Jesus but has been seen in the tradition before. It reinforces the YHWH-ness of Jesus despite initially looking like it would undermine it.
59. Isa 5:4, 5, 7.
60. Hays (*Echoes*, 43) explains the hope of resurrection hinted in the intertextual allusions to Isaac and Joseph: "Mark causes the story of the sacrifice of Isaac to echo in the background of Jesus' parable, with the effect that the murder of the vineyard owner's son is not necessarily only a grim ending to the tale—death is not necessarily the final word . . . Joseph was thrown into a pit by his brothers but later rose to rule over all the land of Egypt and to provide saving aid for his family in a time of famine. This figurative 'resurrection' of Joseph also foreshadows Jesus' fate."
61. Gen 37:20.
62. Mark 10:37, 39; 14:29–31.

63. Mark 14:32–41.
64. Gen 15:2–6, 9.
65. Gen 15:12, 17–18.
66. 1 Sam 2:22–25.
67. 1 Sam 1:15–17, 28; 3:4–8.
68. Jon 4:8–11.
69. Anderson (*Christian Doctrine and the Old Testament*, 84) also notes the connection between the pit and death, citing Psalm 30:8–9, "To you, O LORD, I cried, and to the LORD I made supplication: 'What profit is there in my death, *if I go down to the Pit?* Will the dust praise you? Will it tell of your faithfulness?'"
70. Mark 14:41–42, 45.
71. The psalm comes full circle—there at the opening of Mark, now here at the end.
72. Gen 50:20.
73. Anderson (*Christian Doctrine and the Old Testament*, 91) directly addresses the problem of Joseph's suffering and, thus, Jesus' suffering too: "Had the brothers of Joseph not slain' their brother, would they have survived the famine? And what of the rest of humanity? Their fate as well seems to have depended on what occurred between the brothers: '*All the world* came to Joseph in Egypt to buy grain, because the famine became severe throughout the world' (Gen 41:57)." I agree wholeheartedly with Anderson's thoughtful and reflective sentiment when he says, "I have often thought that the story of Joseph should be read on one's knees."
74. Mark 14:50. Anderson (*Christian Doctrine and the Old Testament*, 89–90) catches some of the "bleakness" of Mark's Gospel. His perspective, though not new, is made weightier through the Joseph analogy, which saturates the Markan narrative as well: "Like the brothers of Joseph, we reject the Elect One of Israel . . . And strikingly *the culpability* of the brothers or the disciples that allows them to experience and ponder the miracle of forgiveness. As Robert Jenson so aptly puts it: 'To the question "Who crucified Jesus?" only the church is able to say, "We did." The [human] race in general must, in justice, say, "we were not there," and just so go its way.'" Resounding with truth, this perspective rejects any type of historical or theological anti-Judaism.

Moreover, it forces the beneficiaries of grace to bear the weight of culpability as well, as one is inseparable from the other.

75. Mark 14:53–62.
76. Mark 14:62; Dan 7:13; Psa 110:1.
77. The climax of Jesus' self-revelation in these verses makes it the perfect place to engage William Wrede and his seminal messianic secret theory. There he argues that the constant concern of Mark's Jesus to keep secret his messianic identity was crafted by the Gospel writer for apologetic purposes. While I agree with Wrede that Mark has been heavily involved in crafting his Gospel, I disagree with the stakes of it. Wrede (*Messianic Secret*, 9–10) begins by focusing his attention on the miracles described in Mark's Gospel, deeming them impossible, and, as such, uses the inclusion of them to question all: "No critical theologian believes his report on the baptism of Jesus, the raising of Jairus' daughter, the miraculous feedings, the walking of Jesus on the water, the transfiguration, or the conversation of the angel with the women at the tomb, in the sense in which he records them . . . we are certainly warned forcefully by the Gospel itself against a too ready confidence and from the start are challenged to check its contents rigorously." Wrede (*Messianic Secret*, 22) continues, "Just as much by what he does not say as by a series of definite statements, Mark shows he was unaware of the view of history ascribed to him." Wrede couldn't be more wrong in his reading. Mark knows his history; it is mixed and mingled and undergirds every single pericope that he has carefully structured in his work, most especially the miracles Wrede mentions by name. Mark is saturated in biblical tradition. Wrede, however, is afflicted by precisely the same concerns he has accused his counterparts—an overzealous concern regarding the details of historicity. As such, Wrede, too, has missed Mark's real agenda. Mark's Gospel is not an apology; it is a call to action combined with the seaming together of an old history with the events of his day to argue that YHWH still has a plan, and it includes all people. Moloney (*The Gospel According to Mark*, 111) addresses the oddity of Jesus commanding silence after raising Jairus' daughter from the dead, theologically contextualizing the entire "Markan secret": "Mark's secrecy theme continues. It is crucial that Jesus not be understood as Messiah or Savior on the basis of his wonderful miracles. It is

not as a wonder-worker that Jesus will respond to the design of God, but as a crucified and risen Christ and Son of God."

78. Mark 14:63.
79. Mark 14:65–72; 15:1, 10, 13, 15, 18–20, 24.
80. Brueggemann (*The Prophetic Imagination*, 94–95) casts the light of the prophetic on the crucifixion in the most compelling fashion: "The crucifixion of Jesus is not to be understood simply in good liberal fashion as the sacrifice of a noble man, or should we too quickly assign a cultic, priestly theory of atonement to the event. Rather we might see in the crucifixion of Jesus the ultimate act of prophetic criticism in which Jesus announces the end of a world of death . . . and takes death into his own person. Therefore we say that the ultimate criticism is that God embraces the death that God's people must die. . . . The contrast is stark and total: this *passionate* man set in the midst of *numbed* Jerusalem. And only the *passion* can finally penetrate the *numbness*."
81. Mark 15:27, 33.
82. Throughout her book *Call and Consequence*, St. Claire wrestles with the question of divine will regarding Jesus' suffering and death. The question is most important from a womanist perspective because of the impact it has on the acceptance or resistance to the imposed suffering of Black women. She concludes (167) by saying, "Jesus' presence among us empowers us to fight on because our existential contexts of suffering due to racist, classist, and sexist oppression are not divinely preordained. We should not passively accept domestic violence and domestic jobs; dropouts and drive-bys; the corporate glass ceiling and election vote stealing; high incarceration but low graduation rates; inadequate healthcare and inferior housing; stereotypes that depict us as caricatures rather than complete persons. These are not crosses for us to bear. They are challenges that we must overcome. And the call, the challenge, is not suffering with Jesus; it is ministering like Jesus."
83. Mark 15:34.
84. In Ps. 22: 7 (LXX Ps. 21:8), Hebrew יַלְעִגוּ translates as *mock/deride*, ἐξεμυκτήρισάν as *deride/ridicule*. Juel (*Messianic Exegesis*, 95) notices how Mark plays with the wording, altering Hebrew/Greek to ἐβλασφήμουν, meaning more directly "all who pass by me blaspheme me." Donald Juel (*The Gospel of Mark*, IBT [Nashville: Abingdon,

1999], 100–101) goes on to discuss how midrash on the Psalms connects Psalm 22 to Esther. An unusual phrase, *ayeleth ha-Shachar, hind of the dawn*, that comes up in the preface "provides a possibility for imaginative interpretations . . . In the ancient world, the morning star was personified as Ishtar. It is likely that reading *ayeleth ha-Shachar* as 'morning star,' the name Esther was suggested to imaginative interpreters because of its similarity to the name of the goddess Ishtar." Though Juel doesn't address this, it is all the more relevant here as Psalm 22, with such connections, is placed right at the spot in Mark's narrative where not only does a god die, but like Ishtar, he will resurrect. Moreover, it is not the first time Esther appears in Mark. Jairus evokes Esther in 5:22, as does Herod's banquet in 6:21–22.

85. Psa 22:27–28.
86. Psa 22:30–31.
87. Mark 15:37–38.
88. Many have noted the tie between the heavens tearing open in Mark 1:10 and the veil of the curtain being ripped the moment Jesus dies. Juel (*The Gospel of Mark*, 62–63) asks the question, "What does it mean that the curtain is torn? It may mean that God is no longer one to be feared, that we have 'access' to God. The Gospel story could then be construed as an account of how that access has been opened, with an implied invitation to enter." But Juel continues, recounting the response of one of his students, "'That isn't what it means,' [the student] said vehemently. 'It means that the protection is gone and now God is among us, on the loose.' The imagery may as well suggest the removal of protection . . . What would it mean if God were to remove the barriers and intrude into the 'safe space' in which humans live? The story might then be imagined not as an invitation to come to God but as an account of how God has come into the world, with Jesus as the means by which God 'intrudes.'" This pairs nicely with the invitation of Jesus to come and die in light of Yom Kippur in ch. 2. To be in YHWH's presence is to risk death, but friendship with this god is worth such cost. Rhoads, Dewey, and Mitchie (*Mark as Story*, 79) similarly note, "God now crosses boundaries. Instead of remaining in the temple, God breaks out to become available everywhere (signified by the tearing of the curtain)."

89. Mark 15:39. Whose god? What god? As if some understanding between Jew and gentile were common. But the god that flooded was Lord of the whole earth. Le Peau (*Mark through Old Testament Eyes*, 290–291) notes both "the hope and vindication [of Psalm 22] that the nations will turn to God" and the pairing of the torn temple veil and the centurion's acclamation at Jesus' death: "As soon as the curtain is torn, opening God's presence to everyone, we have a Gentile see that he is now in the presence of the Son of God."
90. Mark 15:46; Josh 8:29.
91. Mark 16:2; Gen 1:3–4.
92. Mark 16:1; 14:3, 8.
93. Mark 14:51–52; Gen 39:12, 20.
94. Once restored and reconciled with his brothers, Joseph bestowed on them tunics.
95. Gen 37:24; 41:14, 40–42; Mark 16:5.
96. It is likely the Gospel ends here, the empty tomb. Still, I read the significance of this differently than Hays (*Echoes*, 33), who says, "Of all the Evangelists, Mark is the most reticent about claims of fulfillment and the most sensitive to the 'not yet' side of the eschatological dialectic. Surely that is one of the reasons for his remarkable decision not to narrate any resurrection appearances of Jesus." The decision actually does not seem so remarkable for the first Gospel with no exact model before it. Rather, the inclusion of a post-resurrection scene seems more remarkable. Mark plays with faerie, with mystery, with "the fantastic," the empty tomb far more allusive, far more powerful, than the reappearance of the dead. It hints to realms rather than normals. Even in Luke and John, part of what makes the post-resurrection appearances so marvelous and unsettling are the supernatural aspects: the disappearing at the breaking of the bread (Luke 24:30–31) and the appearing within locked rooms (John 20:19, 26). The stone rolled away and the strange young man in white sitting in Jesus' place at the tomb all provide this mystical function, keeping the reader in the realm of Todorov's "fantastic," the place of unsettling unsure uncertainty. (See chap. 3, n. 62, on Todorov.)
97. Mark 16:6–7.
98. Without seeming to notice the verbal connections between the Joseph story and Mark, Anderson (*Christian Doctrine and the Old Testament*,

85) still notes the thematic connections which he ties to Luke 24:11: "Consider well the situation of the father. He sent Joseph out to find the brothers, and only a bloodied robe returned . . . The loss of Joseph is a type of death; his return, as ruler of Egypt, a type of resurrection glory. Like the apostles, Jacob is dumbfounded."

99. Gen 45:5, 12–13, 24.
100. Mark 16:7–8.
101. Mark 16:7; Gen 45:28.
102. Mark 16:9–11; Gen 45:26.
103. Mark 16:15. I could not disagree more with Burton Mack's final assessment of Mark's Gospel in *Myth of Innocence* (Minneapolis: Fortress, 1991, 386) as being one of exclusion rather than inclusion: "The Markan legacy is a myth of innocence that separates those who belong to the righteous kingdom within from those without. The boundaries, however, are not at all static. The borders shift as conflicts arise both within and without. Separation occurs when the mission to convert the other is thwarted . . . If all else fails, both martyrdom and the destruction of the wicked can be imagined as the means for vindicating the cause and trusting in the power of God to resurrect a new creation from the ashes . . . Fair exchange can hardly be imagined, much less delight in a multicolored world, if the borders are defined by a Markan rationale." Mack's presumptions so color his assessment of the text that it makes it impossible for him to see any other possibility. Mack transforms the very act of divine nonviolence into an act of violence, the act of sacrifice into dominance. Thus, the myth created is not Mark's but Mack's. Mark's story is precisely the opposite of Mack's claims. Still, I tread carefully with full awareness of Jason Staples' critique of modern Western biblical scholars (*Paul and the Resurrection of Israel*, 5). Though Staples' focus is on Paul and Pauline studies in particular, the warning is no less valid here: "It is hardly mere coincidence that a group of Western scholars from the late twentieth century discovered that Paul's gospel was really about inclusiveness and opposition to racism. 'Inclusiveness' is, after all, arguably the highest virtue in postmodern Western culture. The New Perspective has therefore exchanged an antithesis more at home in the sixteenth century (merit/grace) for one better suited to the twenty-first century (racism/inclusiveness). By interpreting Paul's message

as the gospel of inclusiveness, Paul's interpreters have once again looked down the deep well of history and seen their own faces reflected back at them." Staples' warning heeded, I press forward. That inclusion remains a contemporary virtue does not preclude Mark from having such concerns in the first century, especially with postexilic concerns over mixing with the gentiles. The issue is not forced on history but alive and well in both times. Mark is so concerned about inclusion that his opening lines feature the God of Israel repenting amid the shadow of Noah's destructive flood, where only a handful were elected for salvation. The Gospel closes with this same god taking upon himself death and destruction after preaching a message of inclusion (Mark 7) and then calling for this good news to be preached to all creation. Mark highlights throughout his Gospel the long-asserted eminence of YHWH as god of the universe, desiring Jew, gentile, and "all creation" for himself.

CONCLUSION

1. Exod 33:15–16.

WORKS CITED

Alter, Robert. *The Hebrew Bible*. Vol. 2, Prophets Nevi'im. New York: W. W. Norton, 2019.

Anderson, Gary A. *Christian Doctrine and the Old Testament*. Grand Rapids, MI: Baker, 2017.

Anderson, Joel Edmund. "Jonah in Mark and Matthew: Creation, Covenant, Christ, and thc Kingdom of God." *BTB* 42, no. 4 (2012): 172–186.

Boling, Robert G. *Judges*. AB. New Haven, CT: Yale University Press, 1974.

Brueggemann, Walter. *The Prophetic Imagination*. 2nd ed. Minneapolis: Augsburg Fortress, 2001.

Burkill, T. A. "The Historical Development of the Story of the Syrophoenician Woman [Mark vii: 24–31]." *NovT* 9, no. 3 (1967): 161–177.

Butler, Trent. *Judges*. WBC 8. Nashville: Thomas Nelson, 2009.

Calasso, Roberto. *The Book of All Books*. Translated by Tim Parks. New York: Farrar, Straus and Giroux, 2021.

Cohen, Shaye J. D. "Menstruants and the Sacred in Judaism and Christianity." In *Women's History and Ancient History*, edited by Sarah B. Pomeroy, 273–299. Chapel Hill: University of North Carolina Press, 1991.

Collins, Adela Yarbro. *Mark: A Commentary*, Hermeneia 62. Minneapolis: Fortress, 2007.

Craigie, Peter. *Psalms 1–50*. 2nd ed. WBC 19. Waco, TX: Word, 1983.

Culpepper, Alan. "Mark 6:17–29 in Its Narrative Context: Kingdoms in Conflict." In *Mark as Story: Retrospect and Prospect*, edited by Kelly R. Iverson and Christopher Skinner, 145–164. Atlanta: SBL, 2011.

de Jonge, Marinus. "Christ." In *AYBD*, accordance ed., edited by David Noel Friedman, 1: 917. New Haven, CT: Yale University Press, 2008.

Eco, Umberto. "Horns, Hooves, and Insteps: Some Hypotheses on Three Types of Abduction." In *The Sign of Three: Dupin, Holmes, Peirce*, edited by Umberto Eco and Thomas A. Sebeok, 198–220. Bloomington: Indiana University Press, 1983.

Edwards, James. *The Gospel According to Mark.* Pillar New Testament Commentary. Grand Rapids, MI: Eerdmans, 2002.

Filson, F. V. *A Commentary on the Gospel according to St. Matthew.* BNTC. London: A. & C. Black, 1960.

Fritz, Volkmarr. "Chinnereth (Place) Chinneroth." In *AYBD*, accordance ed., edited by David Noel Friedman, 1:909. New Haven, CT: Yale University Press, 2008.

Gervasi, Paolo. "Fetishizing Memories. Emotional Objects in Literature." Paper presented at the Emotional Objects: From Lost Amulets to Found Photos event at the Human Being Festival 2017. Queen Mary University. London, November 20, 2017. https://blogs.history.qmul.ac.uk/litcaricature/?s=fetishizing+&submit=Search.

Gibson, Jeffrey B. "The Rebuke of the Disciples in Mark 8:14–21." *JSNT* 27 (1986): 31–47.

Gospel, Mark. *Myth of Innocence*, 386. Minneapolis: Fortress, 1991.

Greenberg, Moshe. *Ezekiel 21–37.* AB. New Haven, CT: Yale University Press, 1974.

Grossman, Maxine. "Exile." In *The Oxford Dictionary of the Jewish Religion*, edited by Adele Berlin. Oxford: Oxford University Press, 2011, https://www.oxfordreference.com/view/10.1093/acref/9780199730049.001.0001/acref-9780199730049-e-1032.

Guelich, Robert A. *Mark 1–8:26.* WBC 34A. Grand Rapids, MI: Zondervan, 1989.

Hassler, I. "The Incident of the Syrophoenician Woman [Matt XV, 21–28; Mark VII, 24–30]." *ExpTim* 45 (1934): 459–461.

Hays, Richard B. *Echoes of Scripture in the Gospel.* Waco, TX: Baylor University Press, 2016.

———. *Reading Backwards.* Waco, TX: Baylor University Press, 2014.

Healy, Mary. *The Gospel of Mark.* Catholic Commentary on Sacred Scripture. Edited by Peter S. Williamson and Mary Healy. Grand Rapids, MI: Baker Academic, 2008.

Heschel, Abraham Joshua. *The Prophets.* New York: Perennial, 2001.

———. *The Sabbath.* New York: Farrar, Straus, and Giroux, 2005.

Hess, Richard S. "Chaldea (Place) Chaldeans." In *AYBD*, s.v., accordance ed., edited by David Noel Friedman, 1:886. New Haven, CT: Yale University Press, 2008.

Hooker, Morna. *The Gospel According to St. Mark*. BNTC 2. Peabody, MA: Hendrickson, 1991.

Hurowitz, Victor. "Critical Notes: אכל in Malachi 3:11—Caterpillar." *JBL* 121, no. 2 (2002): 327–330.

Hurtado, Larry. *One God, One Lord*. 3rd ed. London: Bloomsbury T&T Clark, 2015.

Iverson, Kelly R. *Gentiles in the Gospel of Mark*. LNTS 339. London: T&T Clark, 2007.

Jacobs, Louis, ed. "Exile." In *A Concise Companion to the Jewish Religion*. Oxford: Oxford University Press, 1999, https://www.oxfordreference.com/view/10.1093/acref/9780192800886.001.0001/acref-9780192800886-e-205

Juel, Donald. *The Gospel of Mark*. IBT. Nashville: Abingdon, 1999.

———. *Messianic Exegesis*. Philadelphia: Fortress, 1988.

Jung, Carl. *Answers to Job*. Translated by R. F. C. Hull. Princeton, NJ: Princeton University Press, 2010.

Kelber, Werner H. *Mark's Story of Jesus*. Philadelphia: Fortress, 1979.

Kessler, Kay. "Setting as Character." In *Encyclopedia of Romance Fiction*, edited by Kristen Ramsdell, 323–327. Santa Barbara, CA: Greenwood, 2018.

Le Peau, Andrew T. *Mark through Old Testament Eyes*. Grand Rapids, MI: Kregel, 2017.

Marcus, Joel. *Mark 1–8*. The Anchor Yale Bible. New Haven, CT: Yale University Press, 1974.

———. *Mark 8–16*. The Anchor Bible. New Haven, CT: Yale University Press, 2009.

Moloney, Francis. *The Gospel According to Mark*. Grand Rapids, MI: Baker, 2002.

Nelavala, Surekha. "The Smart Syrophoenician Woman: A Dalit Feminist Reading of Mark 7:24–31." *ExpTim* 118, no. 2 (2006): 64–69.

Newman, Carey C. *Mango Tree*. Wyncote, PA: Friendship Press, 2023.

Neusner, Jacob, ed. *The Babylonian Talmud: A Translation and Commentary*. Peabody, MA: Hendrickson, 2005.

Pitre, Brandt. *Jesus, the Tribulation, and the End of the Exile*. Tübingen: Mohr Siebeck, 2005.

Pope, Marvin H. *Job*, AB. New Haven, CT: Yale University Press, 1974.

Quesnell, Quentin. *The Mind of Mark*, Analecta Bible 38. Rome: Pontifical Biblical Institute, 1969.

Rhoads, David, Joanna Dewey, and Donald Mitchie. *Mark as Story.* Minneapolis: Fortress, 1999.

Stager, Lawrence E. "Why Were Hundreds of Dogs Buried at Ashkelon?" *BAR* 17, no. 3 (1991): 27–42.

Staples, Jason. *Paul and the Resurrection of Israel: Jews, Former Gentiles, Israelites.* Cambridge: Cambridge University Press, 2023.

Staples, Jason. "'Rise, Kill, and Eat': Gentiles as Animals in Early Jewish Apocalyptic Literature and Acts 10." *JSNT* 42, no. 1 (2019): 3–17.

St. Clair, Raquel. *Call and Consequences: A Womanist Reading of Mark.* Minneapolis: Fortress, 2008.

Sugirtharajah, R. S. "Men, Trees, Walking: A Conjectural Solution to Mark 8:24." *ExpTim* 103, no. 6 (March 1992): 172–174.

Taylor, Vincent. *The Gospel According to St. Mark.* New York: St. Martin's Press, 1966.

Theissen, Gerd. *The Gospels in Context.* Translated by Linda Maloney. Minneapolis: Augsburg Fortress, 1991.

Thiessen, Matthew. *Jesus and the Forces of Death*, 200–207. Grand Rapids, MI: Baker Academic, 2020.

Todorov, Tzvetan. *The Fantastic.* Translated by Richard Howard. Ithaca, NY: Cornell University Press, 1975.

Trible, Phylis. *Texts of Terror.* Minneapolis: Fortress, 1984. PDF version.

van der Meer, Michaël N. *Formation and Reformulation: The Redaction of the Book of Joshua in Light of the Oldest Textual Witness*, VTSup 102, 417–429. Leiden: Brill, 2004.

Walsh, Michael. "How the *Phantom of the Opera* Led Me to a Long-Lost Musical Treasure in Paris." *Smithsonian Magazine*, March 2008.

Witherington, Ben, III. *The Gospel of Mark.* Grand Rapids, MI: Eerdmans, 2001.

Wrede, William. *Messianic Secret.* Translated by J. C. G. Greig. Cambridge: James Clark, 1971.

Wright, N. T. *The New Testament and the People of God.* Minneapolis: Fortress, 1992.

Younger, K. L. *Judges, Ruth.* NIV Application Commentary. Grand Rapids, MI: Zondervan, 2020. Hoopla ebook.

INDEX OF ANCIENT SOURCES

INDEX OF MODERN AUTHORS